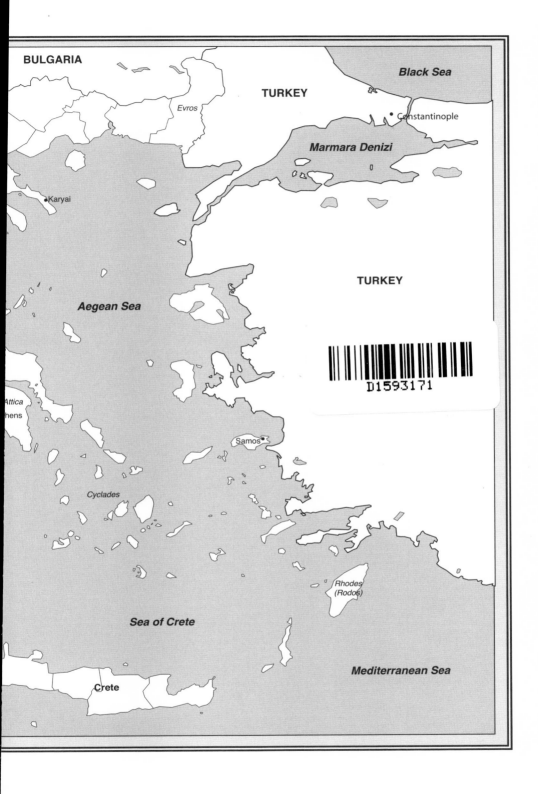

BULGARIA

TURKEY

Evros

Black Sea

Constantinople

Marmara Denizi

Karyai

TURKEY

Aegean Sea

Attica
hens

Samos

Cyclades

D1593171

Rhodes
(Rodos)

Sea of Crete

Mediterranean Sea

Crete

A Weft of Memory

A Greek Mother's Recollection
of Folksongs and Poems

Theodoriana in winter.

A Weft of Memory

A Greek Mother's Recollection
of Folksongs and Poems

by
Vasiliki Scotes

Transcribed, Translated
and Annotated
by
Thomas J. Scotes

Published by Aristide D. Caratzas
New York & Athens

A Weft of Memory
A Greek Mother's Recollection of Folksongs and Poems

Aristide D. Caratzas, Publisher • Melissa International Ltd.
P.O. Box 344H Scarsdale, NY 10583 USA
Web Site: www.caratzas.com
Email: contact@caratzas.com

ISBN [13] 978-0-89241-190-0
ISBN [10] 0-89241-190-2

Table of Contents

viii

List of Illustrations

Cover Illustration: Women from Theodoriana bringing goods to the village through the snow, *courtesy of Photis E. Meletzis.*

Introduction

A ll of the songs and poems in this collection with two exceptions were dictated to me by my mother from memory over approximately a three year period from her mid ninety-seventh year and into the beginning of her hundredth year. The two exceptions are the Christmas and New Year's Carols, whose initial verses my mother had taught me as a child and whose additional verses I learned later. The great majority of the works in the collection are folksongs with a small component of poems learned in school. There are also several songs and poems composed by my mother's father or by my mother, five of which in her ninety-ninth year.

My mother, Vasiliki Papachristou, brought the songs and poems with her when she came to the United States as a young bride in 1931 from a remote mountain village in the northwestern Greek province of Epirus. Some of them I had heard and learned as a young child growing up in Harrisburg, Pennsylvania where my parents finally settled. Most of them, however, I heard for the first time in the summer of 2004 as we sat together and my mother reminisced about her childhood in "the village."

What follows is a brief account about that childhood and about the life, traditions and history out of which this collection emerged. My original intent was to translate the songs and poems in the collection for the family and particularly for my mother's grand- and great-grand children. As the songs and poems poured out of her, however, I realized that this was a trove of memories, which might be shared not only with the family but with others of Greek heritage born in the English-speaking diaspora as well as with all those who are interested in and are lovers of folklore from countries and cultures around the world.

Theodoriana, the village of both my mother and father, is located in the heart of the Pindus range at an altitude of 3,148.8 ft (960 m.). The region has since the Middle Ages been called the Tzoumerka, a word of Slavic origin meaning place of the hellebore (a plant which flowers widely on the mountainsides in the spring and was a source of poison in ancient times; the villagers use it when they have a toothache). The village is surrounded on all sides by rugged mountains, the highest of which is Kostilata, whose peak is called Pyramida and reaches a height of 7,849 ft (2,393 m.).

On the lower slopes of Kostilata, Theodoriana sits in the midst of what appears at a distance to be an ancient theatre encircled by a wall of mountains. In the winter it can be difficult and sometimes impossible to reach the village because of heavy snowfalls. In my mother's time the village might be cut off from the outside world for weeks as the passes were often blocked; mules and horses were still transporting goods well into the sixties. Today automobiles, trucks and busses still have to travel over two poor roads to get up to the village from the nearest main highways to the south and to the west.

In July, 1956 when my sister and I first visited the village we disembarked from a rickety truck-cum-bus at a nearby small town on the main road and clambered onto mules for the last ten miles of an upward magical climb through fir and pine trees towering over ferns and wild flowers. As we finally approached the village on foot, you could hear the sound of running water and the tinkling of sheep and goat bells everywhere.

The villagers of Theodoriana cite the isolation and difficulty of access, because of the need for safety, as the reasons for the location of the village in this high remote valley of the Pindus. This was certainly true during the long and often oppressive Ottoman-Turkish occupation. Whatever the reasons, when looking up from the main road at the bulwark-like face of the Pindus, one would never know that a rather sizeable village nestles somewhere up there in an alpine embrace.

The fact is that there are no firm historical records to indicate why or when the village was established. The name Theodoriana may be an echo of the name Theodoria, one of the seventy Epirote cities and towns destroyed by the Romans in 167 B.C. Theodoriana can mean the lands and area belonging to Theodoria; its exact location has not been identified in the area that was known to the ancients as Athamania after Athamas, father of Helle (for whom the Hellespont is named) and of Phrixos of the Golden Fleece. The Tzoumerka were called at that time the Athamanian Mountains.

The villagers say the village was named for a Queen Theodora, who reigned sometime during the Byzantine period. This might refer to Theodora Petralipha (1225-1270), wife of Michael II Doukas, who was the ruler of the Despotate of Epirus in the mid-1200's and who might have owned the rich pastures on the uplands of Kostilata in the name of his wife. The latter was remembered for her piety and good works and is known to this day as St. Theodora of Arta, the capital of Epirus during that period. These days Arta is the administrative center of the prefecture where Theodoriana is located.

Some villagers also claim that the village was established by refugees from Souli, a group of isolated mountain settlements about forty miles north of Theodoriana. The Souliotes were a fierce and proud Greek people, whom Lord Byron admired and praised in his writings. They were defeated by Ali Pasha, the notorious Turco-Albanian ruler of Ioannina, in 1803, after years of bitter fighting. We know from other records that the village existed long before that dire event. Several surviving Souliote families, however, did seek refuge in the village at that time including that of Markos Botsaris, who went on to play a heroic role in the Greek war of independence.

The earliest mention of Theodoriana is in a document signed in 1690 between Venice, which then ruled the Peloponnese, and a group of seventy-three towns and villages in Epirus including Theodoriana. For an annual payment of 1500 reals (a Spanish gold coin which at that time could buy approximately fifty pounds of meat, presumably mutton and goat) the Most Serene Republic promised to defend Theodoriana and the other signatories against the Turks, who had put an end to the Eastern Roman (Byzantine) Empire with their capture of Constantinople in 1453. Theodoriana was required to pay fourteen reals of the total annual amount and ranked eleventh on the list of the places being protected, an indication of its position as a relatively prosperous village of sheep herders.

The following years saw the final consolidation of Ottoman-Turkish rule over all of Greece (*Tourkokratia* in Greek). The Pindus Range and especially the Tzoumerka region, however, soon became a place of refuge for the enslaved Greeks. Because of its rugged inaccessibility and relative poverty, the Turks allowed the region a fair amount of autonomy with its own local leaders and institutions. Several large villages including Theodoriana were designated *kephalochoria* or chief villages. The local leaders were expected to collect the taxes themselves from these villages and the surrounding areas and deliver them to the Turkish authorities on the plains. The income arising from taxes on the inhabitants of the Tzoumerka was allotted to the estate of the mother of the sultan (the *valide sultan*); this gave them some protection from the more rapacious Turkish beys or landowners, who occupied the more productive areas below the mountains. The Ottoman Turks at first called all their subjects *reaya*, cattle or flocks to be milked. In time, however, the term was applied principally to the second class non-Muslim subjects of the sultan. Thus, those Christians who lived under the direct rule of the Turks on the plains were often far worse off than the mountaineers of the Tzoumerka. The Turks left the latter pretty much alone to run their paltry (in the eyes of the Turkish authorities) affairs during most of the four hundred years or so that the Greeks were enslaved.

From the outset the Ottoman Empire also often utilized local strongmen to control and to keep order in many of the outlying and remoter areas like the Tzoumerka. Muslim and Christian depending on the district, these men in the Greek-speaking regions of the empire were called *armatoloi* (singular *armatolos*, man-at-arms in Greek). As the empire began to falter and weaken during the late seventeenth and subsequent eighteenth century, they acquired considerable power in several parts of Greece including the Tzoumerka. Initially appointed to keep order and assure the collection of taxes, the *armatoloi* eventually became, in effect, independent and often hereditary strongmen willing to cow and to take advantage of both Christians and Muslims whenever the opportunity might present itself.

The Turks then began to appoint fellow Muslims and particularly Muslim Albanians to replace the Christian *armatoloi*. This angered many of the latter, driving them to take up arms against the Turkish authorities to protect their pre-rogatives and positions. In the eyes of the Turks these renegades were considered bandits. In the eyes of the oppressed Greeks they soon began to acquire the aura of the patriot. Although the Greeks had always maintained a strong linguistic, cultural and religious sense of their identity, they and the *armatoloi* were also beginning to be influenced by the stirrings of modern nationalism coming from Europe. These ideas were introduced to Greece through the activities of Greek merchants and professionals traveling and being educated there. This growing sense of nationalism further enhanced the feeling of oppression among the Greeks.

For most of the eighteenth century and during the first two decades of the nineteenth century, therefore, there was almost constant fighting between the Greek *armatoloi* and the Muslim Albanian minions of the Ottoman Empire. Skirmishes, ambushes, assassinations, raids, captive-taking and even major battles took place. Sometimes belligerents changed sides; other times rivals became friends and allies. It was a difficult, unpredictable and threatening time.

As law and order broke down, highways and travel became unsafe; robbers and thieves were everywhere. They were called *klephtes* in Greek (a modern variant of the word *kleptes*, thieves). These men, many of whom were Christian, made the life of both Muslims and Christians unsafe and dangerous. Soon, however, in the almost chaotic conditions of the period it became difficult to distinguish at times who were *klephtes* and who were *armatoloi*, particularly from the weakening position of the Turks. Eventually, the struggle became much more of a religious and nationalist encounter between Christian and Muslim, between Greek and Turco-Albanian. Thus, by the time of the start of the Greek War of Independence in 1821 the pejorative epithet of *klephtes* had become the proud title of the Greek fighters for freedom.

Many of the songs and poems in this collection are called *klephtika* and date back to that period. In many ways they resemble the Scottish border ballads, which came out of a similar era of brigandage and ethnic conflict. They keep alive the names and exploits of many of the hero *klephtes* and *palikaria* (in English, klephts and palikars, as Byron and other philhellenes called them), who were active during those years, often combining the roles of Roland, Robin Hood and Jesse James.

The Tzoumerka throughout this period was the scene of and much affected by armed encounters and battles between *armatoloi/klephtes* and Turco-Albanians at various times in its mountains, valleys and passes. While Muslims never permanently occupied or lived in my mother's village at any point during the Ottoman rule, Turco-Albanian troops did pass through on several occasions burning and pillaging. As the villagers tell it, only once did a Turk try to settle in the village, but he was promptly killed out of fear that if one Turk succeeded in staying, others would follow.

Although the Turks suffered one of their first major defeats in August 1821 at the battle of the Stavros Pass near the village and the people of the Tzoumerka fought gallantly during the War of Independence from 1821 until 1828, they did not gain their freedom from the Turks at that time. It was only in 1881 after many hardships and further struggles that liberation from the Turkish yoke was finally realized. The memory of those struggles for freedom is also recorded in many of the songs and poems of the collection.

The next major event to inspire the local folk muse was the battle to gain control over the rich, high pastures of Kostilata, the mountain which dominates the village. With the departure of the Turks in 1881, many of their properties were acquired by wealthy Greeks. The Kostilata pastures, which over the years had been given by the Turkish authorities to Turkish landowners on the plains, were one such property. When the new Greek owners tried to take possession and extract rents from the shepherds, the village rose up in anger. More exactly, the village women rose up and drove off the hirelings of the aspiring owners with sickles, axes and whatever else they could get their hands on, while the men folk shot off their guns menacingly in the background. Having gotten rid of the Turks from lands that they believed were always theirs, they were not going to accept new Greek overlords from the lowlands.

After two years of legal disputes and even of plotting to assassinate the new owner, in 1883 an agreement was reached between him and a newly established cooperative (one of the first in modern Greece). The latter consisted of 131 heads of family (including my maternal great-grand father and my paternal grandfather) and other individuals. For a price of 57,000 drachmas the people of Theodoriana finally gained undisputed ownership of their beloved pastures.

Every year on the 15th of August commemorating the major feast day of the Dormition of the Holy Virgin, the villagers also celebrate their great victory and acquisition in a joyous *panegyri* or festival. The highlight of this *panegyri* is a stately dance around the huge plane tree in the village square accompanied by musicians singing a song now famous throughout all of Greece, "High up on Kostilata." Along with the traditional verses of the song, the dancers also make up their own verses. These are remembered and incorporated in the folk memory and are also in this collection along with the famous song itself.

I mentioned earlier that my mother left her native village in 1931 at the age of twenty-three. Thus, she escaped the trials and hardships of the German occupation of Greece from 1941 to 1944, during which the village was bombed twice, temporarily occupied and partially burnt by the invaders. This was because its seeming inaccessibility had made the village the center of a major resistance movement and a base for a British sabotage team. One of my mother's younger sisters was among the bombing victims and one of her younger brothers later died of typhoid. The village suffered greatly during the Second World War and also during the Civil War that followed, being occupied by one side and then the other. In 1964, the village was greatly damaged by an earthquake and major landslide. In many ways this was the final blow to the traditional lifestyle of the village, which stretched back unchanged for centuries. Many of the villagers accepted a government offer to resettle on a tract of land on the plains near Arta. Others moved elsewhere in Greece.

Henceforth, the village would not be permanently occupied all year round as in the past. When my mother was a child, some two to three hundred villagers (mostly the old, the school-aged and some women) would remain at home during the winter months. The remaining thousand or so would leave to seek winter pastures for their flocks on the plains or to seek other work there. Thus, there was no break in the social or economic rhythms of life in the village. With this final dispersal of families and friends in 1964, that is what now happened.

Up to 1940 and the beginning of the Second World War, life in the village took its primary cue from the rhythms of sheep and goat herding. This way of life was, of course, a manifestation of a deeper set of rhythms, those of the changing seasons and resulted in an annual ritual of transhumant pastoralism. In the winter, before the snows blocked the passes and covered the village the flocks would be taken down to plains to the winter pastures, the *cheimadia*. In the spring, they would be brought back up again to the rich pastures of Kostilata.

The fall trek usually started on or about October 26 (the Feast Day of St. Dimitrios). It took almost two weeks of walking before reaching the various pastures on the plains, which were rented year after year in the same places around Arta or in the region of Aitolo-Akarnania farther to the south and east of the Tzoumerka.

These pastures and lowlands would become the temporary homes of at least three quarters of the villagers. Living in primitive cane huts they and their families would take care of their livestock and sell the products of their labor like milk, cheese, meat, wool and skins. If they had no flocks (only about a third of the 300 or so households did and only a few flocks consisted of more than 100 sheep or goats), they would engage in other seasonal work like orange and olive picking, tobacco planting and road building. Some had special skills like cheese making and basket weaving but most were unskilled and uneducated. All in all life was hard.

Wintering on the plains, the folk of Theodoriana could not wait for spring to come so they could return to their beloved village with its cold running streams and springs, its wild flowers and brooding fir trees, its snow-capped mountains and lush green pastures and above all their own sturdy stone houses and well-maintained terraced fields of wheat and corn. Down on the plains they might appear to be poor, primitive and uncultured, itinerant workers and shepherds. Up in the mountains they were free and proud, masters of their beautiful valley and of a rich patrimony of songs and traditions, which sustained their hard existence.

On April 21 (the Feast Day of St. George), therefore, they would begin the spring trek back up to the highlands. Loading their belongings on horses and mules they would again embark on two weeks of weary walking with their flocks and families. Both the winter and spring treks may have appeared colorful and perhaps even romantic to a city or foreign onlooker. To the participants, however, they were grueling undertakings often in the cold and rain without adequate shelter or food, an uncertain time of separation, sickness and possible death.

Because life was so demanding and harsh, the need to go off to seek one's fortune was recognized and accepted, albeit with great reluctance and heartache. As a province, Epirus was particularly afflicted by the need to escape poverty and lack of opportunity. In countries far from their homeland like Wallachia (present-day Rumania), Egypt, and Russia Epirotes became famous for their work ethic, frugality, probity and shrewdness, something much akin to the spirit of the Scots and in many instances for the same reasons and with the same results. Epirotes are known among Greeks as good businessmen, scholars and major philanthropists.

Theodoriana shared in this aspect of Epirote life and its children began leaving, especially after independence came. Most of them settled down in and around Arta. Some went off to larger cities like Patras, Athens, Piraeus and a few left for America. The big push for emigration, however, did not come until after the Second World War when many went off to Germany and Australia.

No matter when they left because of need, the strong desire to return was always there. My father, Dimitrios or Jimmy as he was known in America, was a typical example. A boy of twelve, he left his village and father, returning thirty years later after the latter was long dead to find himself scarcely remembered. These deeply held sentiments expressed themselves in a group of songs of absence and separation relating the sorrows of living on foreign shores and the dream of coming back home to family and hearth. Songs describing *xenitia* and the plight of the *xenitimenos* (words impossible to translate directly except by circumlocutions like "strange and foreign places where one is alone without family, friendless and forlorn;" "a stranger lost and wandering among indifferent foreigners") are found in this collection.

Along with these plaints of separation is a similar type of song, the songs for the dead, keening laments or *moirologia*. These are sung at funerals as well as at other occasions. Often interchangeable with the songs of absence and separation, both types of songs are marked by dramatic and often frightening imagery and a stark sense of the vicissitudes of life. Some of these, too, can be found in the collection.

My mother's gathering of songs could be characterized as a kind of time capsule because it hearkens back to an era when the village traditions and lifestyle were much as they had been for centuries and only just beginning to be affected by the outside world.

My mother's family, Papachristos of the Kyrtsias lineage, was one of the oldest and most prominent in the village. Although her father and his father were not priests (as their name would indicate), their line had priests and monks in it going back for several hundred years. Her paternal grandfather's father and his father before him were priests; her grandfather's brother and first cousin were priests. One ancestor had gone to Mt. Athos and became a monk. Another forebear, Anthimos Argyropoulos-Kyrtsias, was also a monk and was active in the period before the Greek War of Independence as a member of the Philiki Etaireia or the Friendly Society. This was the secret organization, which prepared the way for that struggle. In 1819 he initiated Theodoros Kolokotronis, a klepht captain from the Peloponnese, into that society on the island of Zakynthos. The latter went on to become the leader of the Greeks during the War of Independence. Father Anthimos also initiated Dionysios Solomos, the poet and author of the Greek national anthem.

My mother's paternal grandfather's grandfather, a nephew of Anthimos the monk, was, as mentioned, also a priest (Papa Dimitrios Kyrtsias) and was active during those years in the struggle against the Turks. His house was often the meeting place for the klepht captains active in the area. In fact his wife was the sister of one of the klepht leaders of the time, Giannakis Koutelidas, who was later assassinated by the Turks in that very house on October 22, 1838. In addition he hosted St. Kosmas the Aitolian, the famous and dedicated preacher-monk who visited and blessed the village in 1777 and 1779 and was later martyred by Kurt Pasha, a local Turco-Albanian war lord, on August 24, 1779. Father Kosmas was instrumental in setting up the first grammar school in the village during his first visit in 1777. He went on to erect a huge wooden cross at the southern pass leading on to the village at an altitude of 4100 ft. (1250 m.) and there he preached to the people of the surrounding villages. The place has since then been called Stavros or the Cross and was the scene of a major battle against the Turks in August, 1821.

Anthimos with the support of Papa Dimitrios was also involved in establishing in the village a small monastery to house the school, dedicated to the Virgin. This was part of the effort at that troubled time to strengthen the faith and increase the awareness of their fellow villagers. Later in America, my mother's first cousin, James Christon (Dimitrios Papachristos), became a priest; he carried the name of his grandfather's grandfather, Papa Dimitrios Kyrtsias, and was one of the first American-born priests of the Greek Church in the New World.

My mother's father, Christos, was a cheese maker by trade but also known in the village for his singing voice, for his playing of the flute and *tzamara* (a clarinet-type of instrument) and for his composition of songs. He was in great demand at weddings and other festive occasions but never for pay and only for his friends.

My mother's mother, Lamprini Plevris, was of Sarakatsan stock, clannish Greek-speaking nomadic shepherds, who for centuries wandered the highlands of the Balkans and even western Asia Minor. With the emergence of the modern Greek state, however, they began to settle down more permanently in the liberated areas pursuing a transhumant mode of living in more prescribed areas, while affiliating themselves, as appropriate and convenient, with selected sedentary fellow Greek families. My father's mother, Eleni Tsirkas, was also of the same group, but he never knew her as she died shortly after his birth.

My father came from a family called Skoutelas (he shortened his name to Scotes, or Σκότης in Greek, while working in England as an able-bodied seaman and formally adopted the shorter version in both languages when he acquired American citizenship in 1922 after serving on American freighters during the First World War). His family, too, was a large and respected group in the village with several branches. They were hard-working, honest folk and many were skilled basket weavers. They were known in the village for their high spirits and love of singing and for this reason called the "crickets" in good-natured jesting. The family today can count among its ranks two successful writers as well as members of other professions and trades. My paternal grandfather's grandfather, Athanasios, fought in the Greek War of independence. My paternal grandfather, also Athanasios, had studied to be a priest but was never ordained.

I was christened with their name, following the Greek custom of naming the eldest son after the father's father. In the United States during the early 1900's and the arrival of the first significant numbers of Greek immigrants the name was arbitrarily rendered as Tom, supposedly because Athanasios or its diminutive Thanasis was too difficult to pronounce or write for the immigration officials at Castle Garden, the entry point for immigrants at New York before Ellis Island. This was also the case with other names unusual to the American ear: Dimitrios became Jimmy; Charalampos, Harry; Stavros, Steve; Panagiotis, Pete; and Vasiliki, Bessie or Vicky, among many more.

The men folk on both immediate sides of my family were literate and for the village relatively well off with flocks and livestock as well as significant landholdings. The dowry tradition, however, in time impacted adversely on these holdings as both families had many daughters and sisters to provide for.

My mother's paternal grandfather, Dimitrios, was much interested in the introduction of new crops and plants to the village and brought from Volos improved types of walnut and cherry trees as well as better-producing bee hives. One of the many walnut trees he planted became over the years the source of the largest walnuts ever seen in the village. These provided good eating and cooking but also the boys with the means to play a popular local children's pastime similar to the game of marbles.

He was also something of a reformer in his thinking. In Greek churches at that time, it was still the custom for women and children to sit upstairs in a rear balcony screened so that the men might not see and perhaps ogle them during the liturgy. My mother's grandfather thought the custom was backward and Turkish-inspired, although in fact it dated to Byzantine times. In any case, what finally precipitated his anger and subsequent action was that the women above would often perch their children on the ledge of the screen. Directly below was the main entry of the church. Here the vestrymen, of whom he was the chief, would stand behind a counter. This counter held the candles to be purchased as the worshippers first came in. What would happen was that the babies would often urinate down on the heads of the vestrymen. After trying innumerable times to get the women to stop perching their children on the ledge, he demolished the screen with his cane one afternoon when no one else was around. He then ordered that henceforth the women and children would stand downstairs in the main part of the church alongside the men, although still in a separate section.

Before 1881 and the liberation of the village from the Turks, he was also the village representative responsible in accordance with the traditional Turkish tax system for reporting the amount of taxes to be paid, as he was one of the few in the village who knew Turkish. Once he was captured by Greek bandits, who thought he was rich because of his position, and held for a ransom of sixty gold British sovereigns and gold watches for each of the three or four outlaws. If the ransom was not paid, the family was threatened that the bandits would cut off his head, a real probability in those lawless days. The amount was huge for the time and place. It was raised with the help of many of the villagers, who liked and admired him because he would dissimulate and lie on their behalf to the Turks in order to minimize the amount of taxes due. The family never got over the financial blow and my great-grandfather never completed the construction of the new house that he had been building.

My paternal grandfather, Athanasios, was a quiet and gentle man. He was a cantor in the church and known for his knowledge of the Scriptures. He also had a nickname (this was a common practice at that time when family groups were few but many-branched and the same first names used again and again; often these nicknames or *paratsouklia* were also given in jest as in my grandfather's case and over time would become the last names of the family). In his later years he was called Lazarus because his chanting in church had become so weak that he sounded like Lazarus back from the dead. Ironically when my father appeared in the village after a thirty year absence he was also called Lazarus back from the dead. My grandfather's only brother, a teacher, died young. He was allegedly poisoned in another village by a jealous rival suitor and left my grandfather with five sisters to marry off. Thus, he himself married late in life after giving away most of his lands as dowries. His wife died shortly after the birth of his only child, my father, on October 26, 1889. He later remarried a woman notorious for being a shrew and a mean stepmother, who made life miserable for both husband and stepson. My father remembered that his father was so gentle that he would not even disturb an anthill and as a child watching his father weep and keen over the death of his favorite mare.

About the age of twelve my father left the village with his father's blessing to go to Athens to work for a relative there. He was never to see his father again. Eventually at the age of fourteen he got himself appointed to the Naval Cadet School on the island of Poros. These were among the happiest years of his life and he never forgot them.

Finishing the school in 1909 and deciding he could have no career in the Greek navy without the right connections (which he did not have), my father went to England and shipped out as an able-bodied seaman on British commercial freighters. In 1912, however, with the outbreak of the Balkan Wars, he returned voluntarily from England to rejoin the Greek navy where he served on the light destroyer, *Sphendone*. He was present at the liberation of Thessalonica on October 26, 1912 which fell on the Feast Day of St. Dimitrios (the patron saint of both Thessalonica and of my father), an event of which he was extremely proud.

Completing his tour of duty, my father returned to England in 1914 just before the beginning of the First World War to sail out again as an able-bodied seaman. Finding himself in Canada after the war had actually begun, he decided he was not prepared or willing to risk his life for the British and he soon found work with American shipping on the Great Lakes. Following America's entry into the war in 1917, he continued working on American merchant ships and thereby gained his citizenship.

Leaving the seaman's life in 1923, he ended up in Hagerstown, Maryland where he partnered in the restaurant business with some fellow villagers whom he had tracked down there. In 1930 after an absence of almost thirty years he returned to the village, inspired to marry by a photograph of my mother.

In 1930 my mother was twenty-two years old, and though registered in Theodoriana she had actually been born in a cane hut down on the plains at the winter pastures near Katouna in Xeromero (west central Greece) on January 18, 1908. When she was born, Greece was still observing the old Julian calendar, which means that there is a thirteen day difference in dates, that is, January 18 is today January 31. My mother remembered when in 1923 Greece officially changed calendars that many in the village were distraught and fearful about losing 13 days out of their lives. Some refused to accept the decision and to this day in Greece there is a small schismatic, somewhat fundamentalist church of "Old Calendar" believers.

A teenage contemporary of the flapper of the Roaring 20s, my mother was still dressed in homespun clothes covering her arms and reaching to her ankles, wore no make-up, did not smoke and certainly did not date nor had ever danced with a man. She was considered one of the belles of the village, known for her spirit and winsome ways. Years later an old man accosted me in the village square during my first visit demanding to know who I was. When I told him who my father and mother were, he replied, "oh, you're Vasilo's son; she was the moon of the village and all the young men were heartbroken when 'the American' took her off."

My mother early on demonstrated her independent ways. Chafing at the drabness of dress in the village, she caused gasps when she appeared in church at the age of fifteen (about 1923) outfitted by a reluctant mother in a new self-designed slightly shorter home-woven skirt dyed in an eye-catching red and black plaid pattern. This was complemented by a matching red blouse. Up to this time all the women of the village were decked out in dark blues or black. This was the traditional dress code going back to Turkish times when, according to the explanation passed down over generations, Christian women in the villages, even if not in mourning, dressed in dark colors so as not to draw attention to themselves lest they be kidnapped or taken as captives. In less than a year all the young girls were wearing similar colorful plaid patterns.

The old ways changed slowly, however, if at all during my mother's growing up. Boys and girls interacted in school, at work in the fields, at social and religious events such as weddings and baptisms but there was always an inculcated sense of restraint and distance dictated by a code of honor and shame. Women, for example, did not ever frequent the *kafenia* alone or linger too long in the square; both places were considered almost total male preserves. No doubt these restrictions may have caused frustration and stress but they also acted as inspiration for the depth of feeling found in the songs of the village, especially the love songs. The latter are often characterized by metaphor and innuendo but the intention and intensity are quite obvious.

In my mother's days there were some 300 houses in the village and about 1600 inhabitants. The houses were built of stone and covered with slate roofs. They had no window panes (except for the house of the doctor) or inside plumbing and toilet facilities. Water had to be carried and was primarily a woman's chore. There was no electricity and the houses were heated by fireplaces, the wood for which was also usually collected and carried by women. The houses of the better-off were two-storied with the ground floor or lower part used for storage, for the loom or for the animals during the winter. There was usually one big room, maybe two where the family lived and slept as well as a smaller room for cooking. The less fortunate made do with small one-room stone structures.

The village had no streets only stony, unpaved paths along the sides of which often ran irrigation ditches or streams. There was a large and capacious *plateia* or square with the handsome stone church of St. George and a well-constructed school house of six grades on one side, three small one-room, dirt-floored general stores with limited merchandise and several *kafenia*, coffee shops, on another. There was also an an engaging view of the valley and the mountains on the third. In the middle of the *plateia* was a gigantic plane tree over 150 years old. There was no hotel or inn and the houses of the more prominent and more well-off families served that purpose. My mother's dwelling was one such house, as had been her great-grandfather's during the Turkish period. There was no bakery, drug store or store selling newspapers and books. There were no radios, telephones, phonographs or cameras.

In fact, books were so few and highly prized by those who had any that one old tattered book of poems was greedily passed from hand to hand before its owner took it with him when he went off to secondary school. Some of the poems in this collection my mother memorized from that book on the few occasions when she had access to it. My mother early acquired a love of reading, but had few opportunities to indulge herself in her childhood. She made up for that youthful lack only after she came to America and saw her house filled with books and newspapers not only in Greek but also in English, which she taught herself to read.

My mother did not ride in an automobile until her twenty-third year as she prepared to leave Greece in 1931 for the United States. The first time she rode on a train was in the same year when she went from Patras to Athens to confirm her visa at the American Embassy there. The first boat or ship she ever traveled on was the Italian liner, the *Saturnia*, which brought her to the United States that year in a second class cabin. This trip in itself on a luxury liner was a magical experience which she never forgot, even though she suffered a miscarriage as the ship entered New York harbor and she lost her first child. She did not see her first movie until after she arrived there.

As she often said, her childhood did not last long and already by the age of five she was fetching water, knitting socks and doing other household chores. Soon enough she was milking, hoeing, weeding and reaping with the other women and girls and out looking for firewood, mountain greens and herbs. She learned to spin about the age of eight. She wove her first *flokoti**, the heavy blanket for which Epirus is famous, at the age of thirteen and went on to weave *mandanies* and *pandes*, tapestry-like bed coverings and hangings. Eventually she also learned to embroider and to sew. The acquisition of a Singer sewing machine with money sent from an uncle in America and supplemented with funds from the sale of some of her mother's dowry sheep was a major event in her life; it enabled her to become the first seamstress in the village to use a treadle sewing machine.

My mother started school at the age of six with her one pencil, one piece of

---

*Although called *flokati* by city-folk, this word more correctly refers to the woolen great coats worn by shepherds while *flokoti* refers to the blanket itself.

chalk, one small slate, one copybook for the entire year and, of course, her daily piece of firewood for the school stove. After a few months she was promoted to second grade and the teacher, a dedicated taskmaster, singled her out as one of his most promising students. She stopped school towards the end of her third year, however, because of an unfortunate incident.

One May afternoon she was doing some homework, sitting out of doors in the family courtyard. Her doting father was sitting with her and she was asking him how to spell the word "May" which in Greek is *Maios* and then required a di-airesis over the 'i'. Her beloved but sometimes irascible grandfather had awak-ened from his siesta and asked her to make him his afternoon coffee. In her concentration, she forgot all about the request. He got impatient and began muttering that educating girls would make them forget their household duties. Her father overheard his father complaining and apparently thought that he was being criticized for spoiling his daughter. In anger, he impulsively tore up my mother's precious copybook. My mother was crushed and shamed. She re-fused to go back to school again. Given that the family had already decided (as was often the case) to focus its limited resources for education on her younger brother, my mother would more than likely have only been allowed to complete at most the six years of grammar school. But who knows. She was showing great promise and the schoolmaster was strongly encouraging her. The family might have relented, but this is doubtful in the context of the dowry obligations her father then had. My mother was well aware of this fact. While she forgave her father and grandfather (he died in her arms), she regretted her lack of educa-tion all of her life.

She continued to try to learn as much as she could by secretly reading her brother's lessons but the press of work soon put an end to that. Her father only learned that she could read and write several years later when she wrote to warn him that his letters to the family from Patras, where he was working, were being opened and read by a relative. He wept that she had not been able to con-tinue her studies.

This was a typical fate for girls at that time in the poor mountain villages and in other parts of Greece as well. The expectation was that they would be mar-ried off at an early age. As indicated above, at that time one of the major prob-lems in this regard, among so many others, facing families was the question of a dowry. Ideally, dowries were given in gold and silver coins when they were available. In the Tzoumerka it was usually land and livestock. Fathers and broth-ers lamented, if they had many daughters and sisters as this could mean im-poverishment, socially unsuitable bridegrooms or old maids. Daughters and sisters lived with the sense of being a burden to the family and the fear of spin-sterhood. This was potentially the case in my mother's family with one sister al-ready married with a dowry, but with three unmarried sisters and three daughters rapidly approaching the age of marriage.

Thus, two of my mother's paternal uncles left for America in the early 1900's to make money to send back as dowries for their sisters. It was commonplace for younger sons to emigrate for this purpose and many a man spent years abroad working to help his father and older brothers to marry off his sisters (sometimes nieces and cousins as well) in order that he might then be able to get married himself. The custom was that younger brothers were expected not to marry until all their sisters were married. Quite a number never married because they were too old by the time their obligations to family were fulfilled. My two godfathers in America were among them.

To the relief of my mother's family my father asked for no dowry, declaring that a man who wished to marry should be willing and able to take on the responsibilities of a husband and father without rendering his wife's family poor in the process. Without questioning my father's magnanimity, it must be said that he had no sisters or nieces. Knowing him I am certain, however, that he too would have faithfully carried out his responsibilities to any that he might have had.

At that time the village was almost self-sufficient in terms of meeting its basic food needs and material for clothing. Many items, however, such as rice, sugar, coffee, salt, olive oil, wine, fruit (other than plums, cherries and local grapes used primarily to make a potent liquor), tools, needles, thread and any other foreign or luxury goods, had to be hauled up to the village by mules or on the backs of people, often on those of women.

My mother, along with several other young girls, was once caught in a blinding snowstorm. They were carrying over the main pass into the valley seventy-pound chests of the new-for-the-village French dyes desired for the weaving of dower chest finery and other special cloths. If they had not turned back they would all have perished.

There were, of course, professional muleteers, who performed this service on a regular basis for a price and weather permitting. There was a regular postal service with the postman coming on foot on a weekly basis from the nearby larger village below. Finally, by the late Teens there was also a doctor, who was originally from the village and who at least spent his summers there.

My mother's life centered around the extended family and the many work and religious activities of the village. As mentioned earlier, that life was often harsh and brief. Women often died in childbirth; children and adults from tuberculosis, pneumonia and malaria. There was near starvation and death during the Allied Blockade of Greece in 1915. Many died during the Spanish flu pandemic of 1919, including one of my mother's younger brothers. Others succumbed to snakebite and rabies. Still others were killed by falling off narrow mountain paths while carrying loads of wood and still others in bloody land disputes. Locust swarms could devour a year's crop of wheat and corn and landslides could carry away valuable fields and pastures. Sheep rustling was common, contraband smuggling frequent and bandits roamed the mountains.

Yet, life did have its pleasures in three-day wedding festivities, in baptisms and saint's feast day celebrations. The nameday, or saint's day, of your father or grandfather was one of the big events of the year. The house would be open to any and all who wished to express their best wishes or to pay their respects. Birthdays were not celebrated, although it was the custom to name a child after the saint on whose day he might be born, if that saint was considered a major one. Thus, one could remember the birthday as well. For example, my father was named Dimitrios because he was born on October 26, St. Dimitrios day, rather than Konstantinos, his grandfather's name, which would have traditionally been the case. Women as a rule did not celebrate their namedays.

Above all there was a major village festival, which relatives and friends from surrounding villages would attend and where, if you were a girl of marriageable age, you wore your finest traditional finery to be shown off by a proud father or brother. There were the spontaneous good times the young girls and boys would have at reaping and harvest times with dancing, albeit separately, on threshing floors by the light of the full moon. There was the weaving of floral wreaths on May Day while cuckoos and nightingales sang. There were miracles to be sought at the nearby monastery of St. Kyriaki, where my mother's mother walked barefoot over the rocky mountain paths to be successfully cured of a paralyzed arm caused by the Spanish flu. There was the evil eye to contend with and holy moisture from miracle-working icons to drink in order to confound it. There were dreams to relate in the morning and to interpret. There was on holidays roast meat of goat and lamb along with good cheese to savor and always pure water to drink and boast about to strangers. There were dyes to be prepared from various natural sources: walnut leaves gave brown; oak leaves, red; ash leaves, blue and sorrel leaves, yellow or green. There was wool to card and wool to spin. There were long and tedious hours at the loom weaving colorful blankets and wall coverings. There was work at home, work in the fields and work with the flocks, but all was relieved by songs you had learned and songs you composed yourself.

The songs in this collection, therefore, reflect that life, those dangers and activities. Many of these songs date back to the eighteenth century and the Ottoman occupation, others to the Greek War of Independence in 1821. Others were composed by her father, by herself and by relatives and friends. These concern work, absent family members and love. These latter ones might, as was often the case, be built on existing songs and then reinterpreted, recast and expanded. Improvisation of both music and lyrics was integral to the art of the Greek folk song but all within the context of a traditional oral and musical canon.

None of these songs was written down but all were passed down orally and from one generation to the next. They often employ a well-known word grouping or formula to begin the song and then take the theme in a more personal direction. Most, but not all, follow the traditional fifteen-syllable line pattern. Some rhyme and many more do not, relying on rhythm for effect. The songs in the collection by my mother's father and by her are typical of this approach and this oral tradition. Her vivid memory of them and her ability to make up new songs in this manner in her late nineties at the beginning of the 21st century place her at the end of what was once (but regrettably no longer is) a living and wide-spread, age-old oral tradition in the villages of Greece.

Some of the songs in the collection are well-known throughout all of Greece; some are rare and scarcely known. Others are from Epirus, which has its own distinctive corpus of folk songs and music, and some are restricted to the village. Songs of love, songs of death, songs of war, songs of bandits, songs of work, songs of prayer, songs of satire, songs of children, songs of fun and songs for lullabies. Many are dance songs, while others are only meant to be sung and were known as songs of the table–*tou trapeziou*. All of these songs reflect a life that is now long gone.

My mother once said, "These songs and poems were our books, our radio, our movies, and our television. On those snowbound winter nights when the cold wind howled outside and it seemed as if Kostilata itself were about to fall down upon us, we clustered around the kerosene lamp and warmed ourselves before the fireplace. We would be knitting, spinning, embroidering, gossiping, singing old and improvising new songs and reciting poetry to calm our fears and take us out of ourselves to another place, even if only for a short time."

For us today with the panoply of the entertainment and information age at our beck and call it is difficult, indeed, to envisage a time when only the direct, spoken and sung word could provide entry into the realm of family and communal enjoyment and pleasure. No books, no movies, no television, no radio, no phonograph to act as stimulants for the outer and the inner eye, or as movers of the spirit within. I hope that my mother's memories of songs and poems (even if read from a book) will also provide the reader, as they did for her on those wintry nights so long ago, a diverting entry into a time and place that can now only be imagined through these "simple but heartfelt" lines.

I have called this collection, *A Weft of Memory*, with the subtitle, *A Greek Mother's Recollection of Folksongs and Other Poems*. The weft is the cloth or material formed by the thread which the weaver passes back and forth by the shuttle across the warp of the loom. My mother spent many hours spinning wool and then sitting before the loom to weave blankets and tapestries. To pass the time she sang and recited songs and poems. Some were old familiar ones while others she composed herself. This collection might well be called her last *flokoti*, her last tapestry woven from the memory of those songs of her childhood and youth.

Along with the *flokoti*, which she wove at the age of thirteen and which we still have, her memories were the only things she brought with her to her new homeland. She did not even take her dower chest full of finery, which she had woven, knitted, embroidered and sewn over her childhood years, leaving it behind for her two still unmarried sisters.

My mother never saw her father again or one of her brothers and one of her sisters. It would be almost thirty-three years before she would see her mother and her remaining three siblings. In the new world, she and her husband worked hard and long to rear her family of a daughter and two sons and give them the education she was unable to acquire. She never forgot her distant native village but equally she loved the new country, which welcomed and accepted her.

If my mother had ever acquired the education that she pined for all of her life, doubtless she would have collected and published these poems and songs herself. There is a poem in this collection, written in her 99th year as she was lying in a hospital bed, which tells her story. It is a story not unique to my mother alone but shared by many other young Greek brides (and brides from other countries as well), who came to America with similar bittersweet memories and limitless hopes for a better life.

It is to them and, above all, to my mother that my translations of the songs and poems in this collection are dedicated.

xxvi

Note on Translation

Translation is always a challenge – how to convey meaning and equivalence from one language to another without producing a screed of literal opaqueness on the one hand or an opus of too liberal an interpretation on the other. This is especially true of poetry. In attempting to translate the Greek folk songs and poems found in this collection, I have tried to convey in contemporary, yet poetic English the meaning as closely as possible of the original without being literal, forced or outdated. At the same time, however, there are many words in the Greek, which do not have an exact equivalent in English or do not even exist as a concept in the latter language – *xenitia*, for example, which I have loosely translated as "foreign land" or "foreign shores." In these situations the translator must meet the challenge as best he can, but above all he must remain true at least to the sense and spirit of the original, if not to the literal or exact meaning.

In this regard it is important to note that the Greek in these works is simple, direct and colloquial. Even after more than two centuries, these poems still speak to the contemporary Greek in an idiom and vocabulary that are alive and accessible. In fact a significant number of these songs is still being sung and heard on the radio and television as well as at the festive gatherings of families and villages. Of course, there are words and phrases, which are no longer current and which sound archaic, quaint and dialectal. Where appropriate, I have tried to convey this sense as well in the English. Yet, these songs still have the power to move the modern-day Greek listener and reader.

Fortunately for the translator, many of the songs do not have rhyme and are in free verse, relying in great part on meter and rhythm to achieve a poetic effect. The Greek folk song usually expresses itself in a fifteen syllable line which is not always easy to replicate in English, given the difference in the stresses and intonations of each of the languages. Whenever possible I have tried to follow that fifteen syllable pattern of meter but I have tried not to force the issue. Hearing my mother in my childhood sing or recite these songs (because they are as often recited as they are sung), their meter in Greek had the same effect on me as when I heard Longfellow's "Hiawatha" or "Evangeline" in English. Another parallel experience in my childhood was learning about and hearing the Scottish border ballads (in the seventh grade) as well as the music and songs of

Appalachia (in my time and in central Pennsylvania it was called hillbilly music) along with the songs of the slaves of the South.

This is the overall effect I am striving to achieve in the English – to give both the meaning as well as the feeling of these Greek folk songs and poems, which emerged in times and conditions often similar to those facing the Border Scots, their latter-day Appalachian cousins and the African-American slave. Thus, I have paid particular attention to capturing and rendering the meter whenever possible, while at the same time hewing to the sense and tone of the the text. In some instances, where there was rhyme in the Greek I tried to convey it in English, but only if the emerging rhyme flowed in a natural manner and did not appear strained. In other cases, to maintain the meter in English I have augmented the Greek text, but always confining myself to additions which adhere to the meaning and context of the words or phrases in question. My aim above all has been to achieve a result that will stand on its own as good diction in English as well as acceptable poetry in English.

My hope is that the reader will in some measure be moved by and respond to my translations, as I and many others have been moved by and responded to their Greek prototypes, sung and recited over the centuries by unbowed and passionate folk like my mother.

To learn more about the history and the technical aspects of Greek folk poetry, I strongly recommend Roderick Beaton's book, *Folk Poetry of Modern Greece* as well as *The Greek Folk Songs* by Niki Watts, both of which are listed in the bibliography.

Thomas J. Scotes
Belesi, Poros
2007

Acknowledgments

During the past three years while working on this book, I have been fortunate to have had the generous help and encouragement of family, friends and colleagues. My daughters, Eleny and Athena, were from the beginning unfailingly supportive. Both read the succeeding versions of the translations, as they emerged, and either in person or by phone gave me perceptive and critical feedback. My son, Demetry, helped me locate many of the books cited in the bibliography and commented usefully on the translations as they developed. My sister, Anna Scotes Haydon, and my brother, Lt. Col. (USMC ret.) Theodore J. Scotes along with his wife, Nathalia, were among the first to read my initial English renderings and urged me to continue. My sister also spent many hours assisting me in collating the original versions of the poems in Greek and in English. Equally important has been her devoted care of our mother during this time and over the years enabling our mother to remain in her home in her last days.

Special thanks is due to my friend and relative, Rigas-Georgios S. Skoutelas, who has written (among other histories and novels) the definitive book on Theodoriana and who after reading my manuscript gave me the perfect title for the collection. My mother's brother, Dimitrios Papachristos, his wife, Maritsa, and my cousins, Vasiliki, Lamprini and Christos, also provided further useful information regarding the family. Another distant cousin, Stavros Skoutelas, helped track down information regarding family and family friends. I am particularly grateful to Professor Edmund (Mike) Keeley who graciously took the time from a busy schedule to read the manuscript and to give me valuable and much appreciated guidance and counsel. Professor J. N. Kazazis and his staff at the Centre for the Greek Language in Thessalonica were most helpful in researching some of the obscure material found in the text. Thanks as well to Dimitri Stergioulis for his assistance in locating photographs as well as Giannis Papagiannis. To doctor Monroe E. Trout and his wife Sandy deep appreciation-for their steadfast support over many years of fraternal friendship. Thanks is due to my old colleague and friend U. S. Ambassador (ret.) John Condon (my "uncle from Koroni") and his wife, Nancy, who spent a long August afternoon in my house above the lemon orchards of Poros listening to my first translation attempts and giving me their enthusiastic approval along with objective criticism based on their deep knowledge of Greek and English.

This book would never have gone beyond the initial translation stage without the full and unstinting support of the Hellenic American Union under the dynamic leadership of its president, Chris Spirou, who is not only a fellow and passionate Epirote, but a good friend as well. His knowledge of the songs and traditions of Epirus gives full expression to the love and longing which the Epirotes of the diaspora have for the land of their forebears. Prof. Evangelos Sorogas, also a fellow and committed Epirote and Public Affairs Advisor at the Hellenic American Union, was always ready and willing with his valuable contacts, knowledge and advice. Dimitra Dimitrakopoulou, Chief Librarian at the Hellenic American Union Library, and her staff were indefatigable with their prompt, courteous and reliable service. Kyriaki Kondylopoulou, the President's secretary, was the first to begin the arduous task of typing the manuscript. In addition, however, she never failed to meet any request for assistance both with regard to the book or to logistics in general. Aliki Douli, Executive Office secretary, is in many ways the real heroine of the project, because it was she who had to type and retype some seven times the ever-growing manuscript, as my mother provided more poems and as I transcribed them in often undecipherable Greek and English renderings.

Without Tom Cody, a friend since high school days, my computer would never have been up and running, nor its capabilities harnessed by the likes of me. My deep thanks to Michael Vovakes, the worthy son of a boyhood friend, and his wife Mary for taking the time from a busy schedule to photograph my mother and her *flokoti*. Thanks, too, to Manos Marinatos and his energetic staff at the Hellenic Library and Archive for their immediate and useful replies to my questions regarding authorship questions. I would also like to thank A. I. Tzamtzis, Captain (ret.) Hellenic Navy, for the picture of the old Italian liner, *Saturnia*, from his personal archive of ships and naval vessels. In addition deep thanks to Dinos Giotis, a relative and an accomplished photographer and journalist, for providing the pictures of the village, whose beautiful scenery and landscapes he captured in his handsome coffee-table book, *Theodoriana*.

Finally, I must express my heart-felt and sincere gratitude to Aristide Caratzas, my erudite and limerick-reciting publisher and scion of a proud Epirote lineage, to his competent and discerning wife and editor, Christiane Lange, and to their lovely and able daughter and assistant, Anastasia. Their unwavering commitment to this project, their judicious advice and guidance along with their cherished friendship and camaraderie were essential to its professional realization and timely completion.

Εύφραινε φίλους

Publisher's Note
on Transliteration

The transliteration of Modern Greek into Latin characters can be a problematic and confusing matter. A number of systems compete in the newspapers, periodic literature and books of the English-speaking world. Lately the lack of serious education in Classical or English literature and in history has forced editors and journalists to rely on transliterations provided by Greek-speakers who may have a formal and stilted knowledge of English, and who usually have little sensitivity about the infelicities of ugly or humorous renditions of names, toponyms or other terms transliterated from one language to the other. The road-, street- and store signs throughout Greece, often so imaginatively rendered into English, provide an endless source of bewilderment and amusement, but certainly are no guide.

Given the absence of a generally accepted transliteration system for Modern Greek, this House has adopted the following approach in maneuvering between, on the one hand, the Scylla of phonetic reproduction and the Charybdis of traditional orthography, and, on the other, the plenitude of Greek personal names, toponyms and terms that have become part of the English language and cultural vocabulary over the last half millennium.

1. The basic guide is the Library of Congress system (see Georg F. von Ostermann, *Manual of Foreign Languages*, 4th edition, New York: Central Book Company, 1952, reprinted 1970, p. 109ff; also, *A Manual of Style*, 14th edition, Chicago: The University Press, 1993, p 349ff). It is based on the established practice for transliterating the classical language. Its main merits include practicality and integrity. It is practical because it is based on the concept of direct equivalence between Greek and Latin characters; thus α (alpha) is *a*, γ (gamma) *g*, δ (delta) *d* etc. It is faithful, furthermore, to the orthography of the ancient language, which has been preserved over two millennia, and which can be found in large part even in the modern language. Certain conventions derive from longstanding transliteration practices from Greek to Latin, i.e. φ (phi) is *ph*; the initial ρ (rho) is *rh*, unless the recently–adopted monotonic system prevails in the original; the rough breathing is retained as an h, again unless the Greek original conforms to the monotonic system; and, χ (chi) is *ch*, and sounds as in the German *ich*.

2. Some modifications to the Library of Congress system have been made to

conform more closely to phonetic changes from classical to modern Greek. Most common in this book is the rendering of *η* (ēta) as *i*, not the more usual but forbidding *ē*. Another such departure from the system's conventions, the diphthongs *αυ*, *ευ* and *ου* (alpha, epsilon and omicron with upsilon), which ordinarily are rendered as *au*, *eu* and *ou* respectively, have been rendered to approximate more closely the modern phonetics, where such rendering was deemed necessary especially for the sake of poetic euphony; hence Evdokia not Eudocia

3. Toponyms, i.e. names of regions, cities, towns and geographical features, that have existed in literature have been graced by the felicitous English rendition, as in Athens, Olympus, Epirus, Macedonia, not Athina, Olymbos, Ipiros, Makethonia and other such abominations. In instances where toponyms do not occur commonly in English literature, then the practice outlined above applies. The same principle holds for any terms or personal names that have a history in Anglophone literature. Examples of this are the use of klepht and klephts rather than *klephtis* and *klephtes* or the spelling of Ρήγας Φεραίος as Rhigas Pheraios although the Greek text is not polytonic.

Κλέφτικα και Ληστρικά
Klepht and Bandit Songs

A view of the mountains where the klephts had their haunts.

Ο Όλυμπος κι ο Κίσσαβος

Ο Όλυμπος κι ο Κίσσαβος, τα δυο βουνά μαλώνουν,
το ποιο να ρίξει τη βροχή και ποιο να ρίξει χιόνι.
Ο Κίσσαβος ρίχνει βροχή κι ο Όλυμπος το χιόνι.
Γυρίζει ο γερο-Όλυμπος και λέγει του Κισσάβου,
– Μη με μαλώνεις, Κίσσαβε, κονιαροπατημένε,
που σε πατάει η Κονεριά κι οι Λαρσινοί αγάδες.
Εγώ είμ' ο γερο-Όλυμπος, στον κόσμο ξακουσμένος,
που έχω σαράντα δυο κορφές και εξήντα δυο βρυσούλες.
Κάθε κορφή και φλάμπουρο, κάθε βρύση και κλέφτης.
Και όταν έρχετ' η άνοιξη κι ανθίζουν τα κλαράκια,
γεμίζουν τα βουνά κλεφτιά και τα λαγκάδια σκλάβους.
Έχω και τον χρυσόν αετό, τον χρυσοπλουμισμένο.
Πάνω στην πέτρα κάθεται, και με τον ήλιο μάλωνε και με τον ήλιο λέει,
– Ήλιε, για τί δεν βαρείς από ταχύ, βαρείς το μεσημέρι
να ζεσταθούν τα νύχια μου, να γίνουν τα φτερά μου;
Και σα 'ρθουν τ' άλλα το πουλιά, μαζί τους να πετάξω.

This is one of the oldest and best known of the klepht songs with several versions. My mother's is one of the oldest variants. The theme of mountains quarreling with one another goes back to ancient times and can be found in a fragment ascribed to the poetess Corrina, of the 5th century B.C. In latter day Greek folklore the song can involve mountains other than Olympus and nearby Kissavos or Ossa, its classical Greek name.

In the latter days of the Turkish occupation, the populated lower reaches of Mount Olympus were one of the primary haunts of outlaws and rebels. It would have been difficult to survive on the upper reaches, but life was not easy anywhere on the alpine flanks of the mountain, as the last lines of the song clearly indicate.

The Koneria people, were Muslim and originally from the Konya region (ancient Ico-

Olympos and Kissavos

Olympos and Kissavos, the two mountains in a quarrel,
Which of them to cast down the rain and which to cast the snow.
Kissavos casts down the rain and Olympos the snow.
Old Olympos then turns and says to Kissavos the mountain,
– Don't quarrel with me, Kissavos, trampled by Konerians.
Koneria tramples over you and aghas from Larissa.
But I am old man Olympos, throughout the world known and praised
With peaks that number forty-two and springs of two and sixty.
Each high peak with its battle flag, each cold spring with its brave klepht.
And when the spring-time does arrive and branches start to blossom,
The mountains fill up with bands of klephts, the hollows fill up with slaves.
I have a golden eagle, too, all bedecked with golden hues.
He sits alone upon the rock, scolding the sun while saying,
– Sun, why don't you beat down sooner, but wait to beat down at noon,
So that my claws can warm themselves, so that my wings be stronger?
And once the other birds come again, with them I can fly away.

nium) of Asia Minor. They had been settled in the area of Larissa, the main city of Thessaly near Mount Kissavos, immediately after the Turkish conquest in the latter part of the 15th century. There was constant fighting between them and the Greek klephts, who had no compunction about and relished the taking of Muslims if not for slavery, then certainly for ransom. Most of these people died in a plague in 1742 and this song must, therefore, date to before that time. *Agha* was an Ottoman military and landowner's title.
Having climbed to the top of Mount Olympus in July of 2001, I did not count forty-two peaks but there were certainly many springs as well as large stands of handsome beech trees and a great variety of wild flowers.

Ο καημένος πλάτανος

Τι έχεις, καημένε πλάτανε, και στέκεις μαραμένος,
με τις ριζούλες στο νερό και τη δροσιά στα φύλλα;
– Έχω μαράζι στην καρδιά και πικραλιά στα φύλλα.
Ο Αλή-Πασάς επέρασε με δέκαοχτώ χιλιάδες.
Κι όλοι στον ίσκιο μ' κάθισαν κι όλοι στη δροσιά μου.
Και στο σημάδι μ' έβαλαν όλοι με την αράδα.
Άλλοι βαρούν στα φύλλα μου κι άλλοι βαρούν στους κλώνους.
Κι αυτός ο γέρο Αλή-Πασάς βαρεί μες στην καρδιά μου.

The plane tree figures in many Greek folksongs. It needs water and its shade is particularly prized and praised for its coolness. Many towns and villages in Greece have plane trees growing in their main squares. My mother's village is one of them. This table song may refer to a plane tree near the famous bridge of Arta (see page 58) under whose shade once sat Ali Pasha, according to the tradition.

Ali Tepelenli was born in Tepeleni, Albania circa 1744. His father and his grandfather were bandits and he followed the family profession. Through guile and skill he got himself appointed the pasha of Ioannina, initially by forging a *firman* or decree from the Ottoman sultan. Taking advantage of the weakened position of the central government, he soon had ambitions to establish himself as an independent ruler of all of Greece. At first he was successful and conquered or acquired by arms and diplomacy large areas of the country where he appointed his sons as local rulers. He conspired or battled against fellow Muslims, while also engaging in bitterly fought wars with the independent Greeks of Souli (see notes on pages 8-11) and Parga.

Parga is a beautiful town on the Ionian Sea and for several centuries was under the pro-

The plane tree

O poor plane tree, what's the matter and you're standing dried and withered,
When your roots are in the water and the dew clings to your leaves?
– I have sadness in my heart and bitterness among my leaves.
Ali Pasha passed by this day with eighteen thousand warriors
And all of them sat in my shade; all sat beneath my coolness.
And they made of me a target, each one standing in a row.
Some shoot their guns up at my leaves and others hit my branches,
While that old Ali Pasha shoots straight into my heart.

tection of the Venetians. In 1819, the town was transferred to Ali Pasha in a perfidious transaction by the British, who had assumed the protecting role formerly held by the Venetians. The people of Parga in defiance and in desperation abandoned their homes for the island of Corfu, taking with them even the bones of their ancestors. Those brave but doomed struggles of the Souliotes and the Pargans inspired Byron to write, "On Suli's rock, Parga's shore, exists the remnant of a line such as the Doric mothers bore." *(Don Juan* 86.B.) Byron also recorded his impressions of Ali Pasha in his long and epoch-making poem, *Childe Harold's Pilgrimage,* written in 1809-11 during Byron's peregrinations of Greece. The outbreak of the Greek revolt on March 25, 1821 was timed to take advantage of Ali Pasha's growing unruliness. Thereupon, the Ottoman sultan sent a large army to depose him and to deal with the Greeks. Ali Pasha was killed on January 25, 1822. His head was cut off and sent to the sultan in Constantinople where later all his sons and grandsons were also executed. Many klepht songs relate the bloody and treacherous encounters the klephts had with Ali Pasha and his minions. A few of these are found elsewhere in this collection.

Του Κίτσου η μάννα

Του Κίτσου η μάννα κάθεται στην άκρη στο ποτάμι.
Με το ποτάμι μάλωνε και το λιθοβολούσε.
– Ποτάμι μ', για λιγόστεψε, ποτάμι μ', στρίψε πίσω
για να περάσω αντίπερα πέρα στα κλεφτοχώρια,
πόχουν οι κλέφτες σύναξη και κάνουν πανηγύρι.
Τον Κίτσο τον επιάσανε και παν να τον κρεμάσουν.
Χίλιοι Αρβανίτες παν μπροστά και δυο χιλιάδες πίσω,
στη μέση πάει ο Κίτσος μου, τα χέρια τού δεμένα.
Και η μάννα του του φώναξε και η μάννα του του λέει,
– Κίτσο, που τα 'χεις τ' άρματα, που έχεις το ντουφέκι;
– Μάννα μ', δεν κλαις τα νιάτα μου, δεν κλαις τη λεβεντιά μου,
που με ρωτάς για τ' άρματα, το έρημο ντουφέκι;
Μάννα μου, τα παράτησα, στον πλάτανο στη ρίζα.

This one of the most popular of the old klepht songs. Kitsos, an affectionate form of the name Christos, was a famous klepht who fought in the uprising of 1770. Kitsos was captured by Ali Pasha and executed some years after the uprising. The "they" who captured Kitsos were the Turco-Albanians and not the klephts of whom Kitsos was a leader.

Kitsos's mother

Kitsos's mother's sitting out by the river's edge.
And she was railing at the river; she was stoning it as well.
– River, lessen your waters now; river, backwards turn and flow,
So I can cross to the other side, to the klephts and to their villages,
Where the klephts are now gathering and having a celebration.
They have gone and captured Kitsos and they're taking him for hanging.
In front march a thousand Albanians and two thousand in the rear
And in the midst of them my Kitsos walks, his hands well bound and tied.
And his poor mother called to him and his poor mother asks him,
– Kitsos, where have you put your arms, where did you leave your musket?
– Mother, you're not weeping for my youth or for my gallantry?
You only ask about my arms and my abandoned musket?
I left them all, my dear mother, at the plane tree in its roots.

Χορός του Ζαλόγγου

Στη στεριά δε ζει το ψάρι κι ανθός στην αμμουδιά.
Έτσι και οι Σουλιώτισσες δεν μάθαν για να ζούνε στη σκλαβιά.
Έχετε γεια βρυσούλες, λόγγοι, βουνά, ραχούλες.
Έχε γεια, καημένε κόσμε, έχε γεια γλυκιά ζωή.
Έχε γεια και συ γλυκιά πατρίδα, έχε γεια παντοτινή.
Σαν να παν σε πανηγύρι, σαν ανθισμένη πασχαλιά,
μες στον Άδη κατέβαιναν, όλο γέλια και χαρά,
μες στον Άδη κατέβαιναν με τα παιδιά στην αγκαλιά.

This song is sung and danced throughout all of Greece. Although the poem itself was written in the 1840s, it was soon being sung as a folk song and immediately became part of the national folk heritage because of the tragic historical event it commemorated. Souli was a collection of mountain villages in Epirus in northwestern Greece, which had managed through inaccessibility and bravery to maintain its freedom during the centuries of the long and oppressive Turkish occupation.

In 1788, however, a Turco-Albanian freebooter managed to be appointed by the weakening and increasingly corrupt Ottoman central government as pasha or military governor in Ioannina, main city of Epirus. This was the notorious Ali Pasha, whose craftiness and cruelty became a byword of the time. Very soon he had pretensions to increasing his power and authority, but Souli stood in his way. Over the next decade or so beginning

The dance at Zalongo

A fish cannot live on dry land nor flowers on sandy shores.

So, too, the women of Souli did not learn to live as slaves.

Farewell to you springs of water, dales, mountains and high ridges.

Farewell to you poor, wretched world; farewell to you, life so sweet.

Farewell to you, our dear homeland; farewell to you forever.

As if bound for a festival, like a blooming lilac bush,

To Hades they were descending all laughter and all joy.

To Hades they were descending, and in their arms the children.

with the first attempt in 1791 followed by a major defeat in 1792, Ali Pasha was not to be deterred. Another attempt in 1800 failed. In 1803, however, after a long and bitterly fought siege and with the help of a traitor Souli fell in the winter of that year.

The surviving Souliotes broke up into several bands fleeing for their lives. One such group of women, children and some men reached Zalongo, a mountain some thirty miles south of Souli. Here they were surrounded and after the men were all killed fighting to protect them, it became obvious that the women would be captured and taken into slavery. Whereupon, they took their children in their arms and singing and dancing hurled themselves from the cliff.

Today a monument marks the place of their martyrdom. The monument can be reached after a climb of some hundred or so steps. My mother made that climb in her ninetieth year.

Κορίτσια από τα Γιάννενα

Κορίτσια από τα Γιάννενα, νυφάδες απ' το Σούλι,
τα μαύρα να φορέσετε να λεροφορηθείτε.
Το Σούλι θα χαρατσωθεί, χαράτσι θα πληρώνει.
Τζαβέλαινα σαν τ' άκουσε, κόρες και νύφες κράζει.
Και παίρνει και ζώνει τ' άρματα και παίρνει το ντουφέκι.
Και πήρε δίπλα τα βουνά, δίπλα τα κορφοβούνια.

Many folk songs describe the story and the exploits of the people of Souli, both men and women, in their doomed struggle with Ali Pasha of Ioannina. Among these heroic people was Moscho Tzavelaina, the wife of Lampros Tzavelas, one of the outstanding leaders of the Souliotes. She fought in a major battle in July, 1792. Leading a group of 400 women (referred to in the song) Tzavelaina helped turn the tide against the 12,000-man army of Ali Pasha, which was marching towards Souli.

You girls from the town of Giannena

You girls from the town of Giannena and you brides who come from Souli,
Put on your mourning clothes of black, put on rags drab and dirty.
For Souli will be overcome; and 't will be paying the head-tax.
On hearing this, Tzavelaina calls daughters and wives of her sons.
She then girds herself with weapons and takes down her musket
And goes up along the mountains, up along the mountain peaks.

When mourning, women put on black dress, in many cases never to stop wearing it. It was also the custom to present an unkempt and unwashed appearance, certainly during the first days and weeks of the mourning period.
The head tax or *charatch* was levied on all non-Muslim subjects of the Ottoman Turks, without exception for age, gender or class. It was often collected in a manner contrived to humiliate and degrade the person paying the tax and it was greatly resented.

Του Κατσαντώνη

Εσείς Τζουμέρκα κι Άγραφα, παλικαριών λημέρια,
αν δείτε τη γυναίκα μου, αν δείτε και τον γιο μου,
πέστε τους πως με πιάσανε και στον Πασά με πάνε.
Αρρωστημένο μ' εύρανε, ξαρματωτόν στο στρώμα,
σαν το μωρό στην κούνια του, στα σπάργανα δεμένο.
Κι ακούς ν' αχοβολεί του ντουφεκιού του ο βρόντος.
Εύγε σου, Κατσαντώνη.

This is an excerpt from a series of songs about one of the bravest and most famous klephts, who was active in the early 19th century. He was the son of a leading Sarakatsan
sheep-herder named Giannis Makrygiannis, and born in a small village near Ioannina, the
capital of Epirus in the days of Ali Pasha. He was one of three sons, who in time had differences with Ali Pasha and were obliged to take to the hills and the life of outlaws and
rebels against the depredations and cruelties of the Turco-Albanian tyrant.
For several years he and his brothers carried out successful raids and encounters against
the forces of Ali Pasha, during the most famous of which he killed one of Ali's most
trusted and favored henchmen, Veligekas. He was finally captured on his sickbed hiding
in a cave along with one of his brothers (as related in the above song). The two were
taken to Ioannina where on September 23, 1808, they were both beheaded in the pres-

Katsantonis

You, O Tzoumerka and Agrapha, the haunts of many heroes,
If you ever see my wife and if by chance you see my son,
Tell them that I've been captured and they're taking me to the Pasha.
Sick and ill they found me, unarmed lying on a pallet,
Like a baby in its cradle well wrapped in swaddling clothes.
Then his musket can be heard, booming out like thunder.
Well done, O Katsantonis.

ence of the European consuls after all of their bones had been broken systematically by the executioner using a hammer. Their remaining brother was murdered in 1815 by an assassin in the employment of Ali Pasha.

He came to be called Katsantonis by the combination of the word *katse* or "sit still" with his given name, Antonis. According to tradition, while still a young boy, his mother observed that he was high-spirited and impatient to join the klephts in the mountains. With concern and foreboding she would say, *kats'Antoni* or "sit still Antonis," and hence the name, which obviously had no effect on his subsequent career. As he was being taken to Ioannina he asked his captors if he could hold his musket for the last time. His wish was granted and Katsantonis took the musket and smashed it against a rock to prevent Ali Pasha from having it. This is the reference in the last line in the song above.

Ο Κατσαντώνης και ο Βεληγκέκας

– Αντώνη μου, τι σκέπτεσαι; Τι 'σαι συλλογισμένος;
– Παιδιά, μη μου βιάζεστε και θα σας 'μολογήσω.
Εψές μου 'ρθαν τα γράμματα από τον γερο-Δήμο.
Ο Βεληγκέκας, το σκυλί, κι ο άπιστος ο σκύλος
μου πήρε τη γυναίκα μου και το μικρό παιδί μου
και στον Πασά τα παει.

This is a well-known klepht song. The story of Katsantonis is told on the previous page.
The wife and son were eventually freed. In a later battle Katsantonis killed Veligekas,
who was one of the chief lieutenants of Ali Pasha, the pasha mentioned in the last line.
This event is recounted in several klepht songs.

Η κυρα-Φροσύνη

Χίλια καντάρια ζάχαρη να ρίξουμε στη λίμνη
για να γλυκήνει το νερό να πιεί η κυρα-Φροσύνη.
– Τι ήθελες, Φροσύνη μου, και βγήκες στο σεργιάνι;
– Τι ήθελες και βγήκες με το λαχούρικο φουστάνι;

These are a few lines from a famous song telling the tragic and true story of Frosyni (form
of Euphrosyne, which means literally delight), the beautiful wife of Dimitrios Vasiliou, a
prominent trader of Ioannina in the days of Ali Pasha. The former was often away on
long trips. While he was away Frosyni became involved in an affair with one of Ali Pasha's
sons. Whether freely or by force is not clear.
In any case, at some point in the relationship her lover gave her a unique and valuable
ring belonging to his wife. Being in financial difficulty during one of her husband's ab-
sences, Frosyni was eventually obliged to sell it. The jeweler then took the ring, whose
stone was apparently of considerable size, and tried to sell it to its original owner, the
son's wife. Furious, she went to Ali Pasha, her father-in-law, seeking revenge.

Katsantonis and Veligekas

– Antonis, what are you thinking and why so deep in thought?

– Don't rush or hurry me, my boys, and I will tell you everything.

Yesterday letters came to me from old man Dimos, my dear friend.

Veligekas, that dirty dog, that unbeliever of a dog,

Has gone and carried off my wife and captured my little boy

And he is taking both of them off to the Pasha.

Lady Frosyni

A thousand tons of sugar let us drop into the lake,

So its water will be sweetened and of it Lady Frosyni drink.

– What were you seeking, Frosyni, when you went out for a stroll?

– What were you seeking venturing forth, dressed in cloth from Lahore?

On the night of January 11, 1801, before the eyes of her young children Frosyni was dragged out of her bed by Ali Pasha's soldiers. After several days in prison, together with seventeen other women of alleged ill repute, she was put in a sack and thrown into the freezing waters of the Lake of Ioannina. The bodies were recovered and buried in a nearby church, where Frosyni's grave attracted mourners over the years. In time she came to be considered a saint and martyr. The Lahore cloth refers to the dress of fine Indian material that Frosyni wore on the day that Ali Pasha's son first saw her and was smitten by her. The mention of Lahore cloth is a good indication of Frosyni's wealth and station, as well as of the wide-ranging commercial activity of Greek merchants in the latter part of the 18th century.

Εγώ είμαι η βλάχα η όμορφη

– Εγώ είμαι η βλάχα η όμορφη, η βλάχα η παινεμένη,
πόχω τα χίλια πρόβατα και πεντακόσια γίδια.
Λύκος να φάει τα πρόβατα και τσάκαλος τα γίδια.
Εγώ θα πάω στα Γιάννενα στου Μπέη τα σεράγια,
– Γεια σου, χαρά σου, Μπέη μου! – Καλώς τη βλάχα που 'ρθε.
Εσύ είσαι η βλάχα η όμορφη η βλάχα η παινεμένη;
– Εγώ είμαι η βλάχα η όμορφη, η βλάχα η παινεμένη.
Πόχω τα χίλια πρόβατα και πεντακόσια γίδια.

This is a variant of a song well-known in Epirus and is probably based on the story of the seizure by Ali Pasha of Despo Liakatas (see also the note for the following song), daughter of a very rich sheep-herder; this can be inferred from the wish in the song that a wolf and jackal eat the flocks, which in addition to her beauty were doubtless another reason for

Ξύπνα καημένε Αλή-Πασά

Ξύπνα, καημένε Αλή-Πασά και βγάλε το φακιόλι
να δεις την κυρα-Βασιλική, σκλάβα την παν στην Πόλη.

This couplet relates the fate of Vasiliki, the last wife of Ali Pasha of Ioannina. She was in her late teens when Ali Pasha, then 72, seized and married her in 1816. In the same year he had seized another young girl, Despo Liakatas, daughter of a rich sheep-herder, but she died after only a few weeks in his harem. His first wife, Emine, mother of some of his children, died of fright many years earlier when he knocked on her door to ask for forgiveness after trying to murder her.
Ali Pasha apparently really loved Vasiliki and she was often able to take advantage of her position to help her fellow Christians. Famed for her beauty and good deeds, many folk songs were composed about her. After her husband's overthrow and death in 1822, she

I am the pretty shepherd girl

– I am the pretty shepherd girl, the girl so widely praised.

The one who has a thousand sheep and five hundred goats as well.

May a wolf attack and eat the sheep and a jackal eat the goats,

For, I am off to Giannena, to the seraglio of the bey.

– To your health and happiness, my bey! – Welcome to the shepherd girl.

Are you the pretty shepherd girl, the girl everyone has praised?

– I am the pretty shepherd girl that everyone has praised.

The one who has a thousand sheep and five hundred goats as well.

the attraction of the rapacious bey. In the other variants the girl refuses the advances of the bey, a Turkish military title used to identify Ali Pasha in the song. She goes on to say that she would rather die than have his lips touch hers. This is what actually did happen, as Despo expired (presumably from grief and shame) after a few weeks in Ali Pasha's harem.

Wake up, poor Ali Pasha

Wake up, poor Ali Pasha, and take off your turban
To see Lady Vasiliki taken a slave to the City.

was taken prisoner to Constantinople. She was later freed and ended her days in 1835 in a small village in the newly established Greek state, a poor but still respected woman. The Greeks to this day still call Constantinople, "the City." This usage refers both to the meaning of the name itself, which in Greek means the city of Constantine and also to the fact that for over a thousand years as capital of the Byzantine Empire this was *the* city *par excellence* in Europe. Under the Ottoman Turks it was also the major city of that empire and of the region. In fact, the modern name Istanbul is the Turkish pronunciation of the Greek phrase *eis tin polin* or "to the city," answering the question, "where are you going?"

Σαράντα παλικάρια από τη Λιβαδειά

Σαράντα παλικάρια από τη Λιβαδειά,
όλα καλά κι αρματωμένα πηγαίνουν για κλεψιά.
Στο δρόμο που πηγαίναν όλο έλεγαν,
– Να 'χαμαν κι έναν γέρο για την ορμηνιά.
Σαν βάησαν και τον βρήκαν σε μια ριζοσπηλιά,
που έλουε τ' ασήμι και έκανε κουμπιά.
– Καλημέρα, γέρο, μπάρμπα-γέρο. – Καλώς τα, τα παιδιά.
– Σήκω, γέρο, μπάρμπα-γέρο, άστα τα κουμπιά,
βάλ' τα τσαρούχια σου, πάμε για κλεψιά.
– Δεν μπορώ, παιδιά μου, σας λέω παραγέρασα.
Περνάτε από τη στάνη μου κι από τα πρόβατα
και πάρτε τονε γιο μου, τον Νικηταρά,
που έχει λαγού ποδάρια και σταυραετού φτερά.
Ξέρει τα μονοπάτια και όλα τα σύρματα.
Ξέρει και τις βρυσούλες, που πίναμε νερό.
Ξέρει και τις κουμπάρες, που παίρναμε ψωμί.

This is an old klepht dance song in the *tsamikos* rhythm, dating back to the 18th century and the Ottoman Turkish occupation. It is known throughout mainland Greece. Another version continues the story with the old man warning the young bucks not to be distracted by girls along the way. They don't listen and tarry with a group of fair maids who get them drunk. They are caught by the Turks and the old man has to come to their rescue.

The "boots" in the translation were really *tsarouchia*, low hand-cobbled leather shoes with pompoms, still to be seen on the presidential guard at the Tomb of the Unknown Soldier in Syntagma Square in Athens. The "godmothers" refers to the fact that the general population often gave aid and succor to the so-called brigands or klepths.

Livadia is a small town in east central Greece on the road to Delphi. The surrounding mountainous region and especially nearby Mount Parnassus (also called Liakoura) were

Forty young men from Livadia

Forty brave and bold young men from the town of Livadia,
All well armed and well equipped are going out to raid.
As they were going on their way, they said to one another,
– If we only had an older man for counsel and advice.
As they moved along, they found him in a low-lying cave.
He was melting silver there, to shape and make some buttons.
– Good day to you, old-timer. – A good welcome to the boys.
– Get up, old man, old-timer; leave off your button-making.
Put on your boots and join us; let's go out upon a raid.
– I can't, my boys, I must tell you that I've grown too old.
But go there by my sheepfold, pass by where I keep my flocks
And take with you my son, my son Nikitaras,
Who has the swift feet of a rabbit and the wings of a royal eagle.
He knows well the pathways and knows all the trails.
He knows, too, the springs where we drank the water.
He also knows the godmothers where we would get our bread.

stomping grounds of many well-known klephts. One of these was Lampros Katsonis (1752-1804), who fought on land and by sea against the Turks in the Russian-inspired unsuccessful revolt of 1769. He fled to the Crimea in 1770 where he and his followers were given lands by Catherine the Great. He named his new settlement Livadia after his hometown, and the palace that was built there was the scene of the Yalta Conference in 1944.

Nikitaras means "man of victory" and as a proper name was carried by several klephts. The most famous was Nikitaras, the so-called Turk-Eater or *Turkophagos*. With about 2500 men under the leadership of Theodoros Kolokotronis on July 22, 1822, he played a great role in inflicting a major defeat with severe losses on a Turkish force of some 30,000 at the narrow pass of Dervenaki in the Peloponnese.

Πολλή μαυρίλα πλάκωσε

Πολλή μαυρίλα πλάκωσε, μαύρη σαν καλιακούδα.

Ο Ομέρ Βρυώνης έρχεται με δεκαοχτώ χιλιάδες.

Και το Διάκο τον επιάσανε, στο δρόμο τον πηγαίνουν.

Κι ο Ομέρ Βρυώνης μυστικά στο δρόμο τον ρωτάει,

– Γίνεσαι Τούρκος, Διάκο μου, την πίστη σου ν' αλλάξεις;

Να προσκυνήσεις στο τζαμί, την εκκλησιά ν' αφήσεις;

Κι εκείνος τ' αποκρίθηκε και στρίφτει το μουστάκι,

– Πάτε εσείς κι η πίστη σας μορτάδες, να χαθείτε.

Εγώ Γραικός γεννήθηκα, Γραικός θε να πεθάνω.

Όσο είν' ο Διάκος ζωντανός, Τούρκους δεν φοβάται.

Τον Διάκο τον επήρανε και στο σουβλί τον βάλαν,

ολόρθον τον εστήσανε κι αυτός εξεφωνούσε,

– Για δες καιρό που διάλεξε ο Χάρος να με πάρει

τώρα π' ανθίζουν τα κλαριά και βγάζει η γης χορτάρι.

This is one of the most famous of the klepht songs (especially the last two lines). It commemorates the savage but heroic death of Athanasios Diakos who was impaled and roasted alive on April 22-23, 1821, in the first days of the Greek revolt, after his defeat and capture at the battle of Alamana in central Greece at the hands of Omer Vryonis, the Turkish commander. Athanasios Diakos started off to become a priest, hence his sobriquet, The Deacon. At a young age and after killing a Turk who tried to seduce him, he took to the hills and became a klepht. Until his death, he was one of the fiercest fighters against the Turks.

From the first appearance of the Turks in Asia Minor in the 11th century there was much

Great blackness pressed upon the land

Great blackness pressed upon the land as black as is the jackdaw.

Omer Vryonis is on the way with a host of eighteen thousand.

They have caught and captured Diakos, and on the road they take him.

On the road Omer Vryonis in secret goes and asks him,

– Diakos, will you become a Turk and change your religion

To pray and bow down in a mosque and leave the church behind you?

Diakos answered him by saying, while twirling his black moustache,

– May you all and your religion go to hell, you scoundrels.

I was born and bred a Greek and as a Greek I will die.

As long as Diakos is alive, he has no fear of Turks.

Then, they took and seized poor Diakos and on a skewer put him.

And upright they stood and placed him, while he shouted out and said,

– What a season Death has chosen to come and take me from here,

Now that the branches are in bloom and the earth brings forth green grass.

pressure on the Christians to convert to Islam. By persuasion or by force, many Christians succumbed in order to retain their lands or save their lives. Those, who did not convert, often suffered martyrdom. Impaling was a common and much used form of execution by the Turks. The barbaric treatment, which the Turks meted out to the Christians over many centuries engendered a hatred and a desire for revenge among the subject peoples. This treatment led to bloody and often similar reprisals when the Christians finally began to get the upper hand during the uprisings of the Greeks, Serbs and Bulgarians during the 19th and 20th centuries.

Του Μάρκου

Τρία πουλάκια κάθονταν στου Μάρκου το κεφάλι.

Κι όλα του Μάρκου έλεγαν και όλα του Μάρκου λέγαν,

– Σήκω Μάρκο να φύγουμε στον τόπο μας να πάμε.

Και ο Μοριάς σου τούρκεψε, τον πήραν οι Αραπάδες.

– Φωτιά να μπει μες στο Μοριά, φωτιά στους Αραπάδες.

Εγώ σας λέγω δεν μπορώ, σας λέγω θα πεθάνω.

Έχω δύο βόλια στην καρδιά, δύο βόλια στο κεφάλι,

και ανάμεσα στα δίπλατα τρεις σφαίρες περασμένες.

Παιδιά μου, μη μ' αφήσετε εδώ σ' αυτά τα μέρη.

Πάρτε με και θάψτε με σε μια ψηλή ραχούλα

για να αγναντεύω τ' Άγραφα, να βλέπω τα Τζουμέρκα.

This is a table song. It may refer to the famous Souliote hero of the Greek War for Independence, Markos Botsaris who was killed fighting the Turks in August, 1823. His loss was mourned by all the Greeks and his fame was captured by poets in Europe and America like Byron and Fitzgreene Halleck.

Many klepht songs begin with the formula of three birds talking, exhorting or warning. Moria or Morea is the medieval Greek name for the Peloponnese, which according to some etymologies derives from "land of the mulberry tree." Mulberry leaves fed the silkworms which were the basis for the silk-manufacturing industry of the Byzantines and in later times.

The term "black Arabs" refers to the Egyptian troops of Mehmet Ali, an Albanian freebooter then ruling Egypt in the name of the Ottoman Turkish sultan. At the sultan's desperate request, he sent his son, Ibrahim Pasha, with a French-trained army to the assistance of the Turks in 1825 following the outbreak of the Greek revolt in 1821. Ibrahim was able to reconquer most of the Peloponnese from the badly trained, outgunned, out-

Markos

Three little birds were sitting, close by the head of Markos.
All three were telling Markos and all three were speaking to him,
– Get up, O Markos, let us leave and go to lands we call our own.
For Turks have taken your Moria; black Arabs have seized it all.
– Let fire fall on the Moria and fire upon the Arabs.
I tell you that I cannot move; I tell you that I'm dying.
I have two shots deep in my heart, another two in my head,
Right between my shoulder blades three rounds have made their passage.
My friends, don't go and leave me here in these forsaken places,
But take me now and bury me, high upon some mountain ridge,
So I can see the Agrapha and gaze at the Tzoumerka.

manned and quarreling Greeks before his fleet was defeated by the combined fleets of the British, French and Russians at the battle of Navarino in October 1827.

Before his defeat and until his departure from Greece in 1828, however, his troops caused much destruction and took many slaves. So many were taken that, according to local chroniclers, the hitherto high price for a Greek slave decreased by more than half in the Cairo slave market. To this day there are Egyptian families, which acknowledge having a Greek female ancestor, more than likely one of those cheap and unfortunate slaves.

The word Agrapha means "the unwritten" with mountains or regions understood. The term refers to the southern reaches of the Pindus Range located in northwestern Greece, which together with the Tzoumerka in the same range to the north were not written up in the Turkish tax rolls for direct taxation. These regions along with Mani in the southernmost part of Greece enjoyed a high degree of non-interference by the Turks and early became the refuge of those fleeing the Turks as well as the haunts of bandits, outlaws and eventually of freedom fighters.

Λάμπουν οι στράτες στο Μοριά

Λάμπουν οι στράτες στο Μοριά, λάμπουν και στα ντερβένια
από τους κλέφτες τους πολλούς, τους Κολοκοτρωναίους,
που 'χουν τ' ασήμια τα πολλά και τα χρυσά γαϊτάνια.
Καβάλα παν, στην εκκλησιά καβάλα προσκυνάνε,
καβάλα παίρνουν αντίδωρο απ' του παπά το χέρι.
Ο Θεός μας καταράστηκε και θέλει να μας χάσει
από την περφάνια την πολλή που 'χουμε εμείς οι κλέφτες.

This is one of twenty or more songs, which relate the deeds of the Kolokotronis clan. This was a powerful family in the western Peloponnese from the beginning of the 16th century. Theodoros Kolokotronis, the Old Man of the Morea, as he is called in Greek folklore and history, is considered the bravest, most effective and outstanding Greek leader in the struggle for independence against the Turks, although at times he could be greedy, brutal and narrow-minded. His equestrian statue stands in front of the old parliament building

Αντρούτσος

Αντρούτσο, που ξεχείμαζες τον περσινό χειμώνα,
που 'ταν τα χιόνια τα πολλά και τα βαριά χαλάζια;
Στην Πρέβεζα ξεχείμαζα μες στ' αγγλικά καράβια.

Odysseas Androutsos was an outstanding but controversial commander during the war for independence. He was born on Ithaca, hence his first name, in 1788 but came from a family originating in Pthiotis in east central Greece where his father had been a klepht. As a young man, he entered the army of Ali Pasha of Ioannina and eventually became an officer.
In 1818 he entered the struggle against the Turks by joining the secret revolutionary society, the *Philiki Etaireia*. He fought bravely on many occasions, notably at the critical battle of Gravias in 1821 and was made commander-in-chief of the Greek forces in the Roumeli region in central Greece.
In 1822, however, he was stripped of his command on the charge of dealing with the enemy. He was subsequently imprisoned in a cave on the Acropolis of Athens where he was executed on June 5, 1825. This act was condemned by many at the time and the folk

In the Moria the highways gleam

In the Moria the highways gleam, they gleam at the mountain passes
From the band of many klephts, the men of Kolokotronis,
Who wear clothes with silver trappings, with trimmings of shiny gold.
On horseback they go to church; on horseback they go to worship.
On horseback they take blessed bread from the hand of the holy priest.
God has cursed us and condemned us and wishes to destroy us
For the great vanity and pride, which we the klephts possess.

in Athens with the inscription, *Teaching all peoples, through the ages, how slaves become free.*
Most of the variants of this song end on a more positive note with a prayer asking for
Christ's blessing. My mother's version may reflect the hardships and the trials of this family over the years of their struggles against the Turks as well as his fierce and at times over-
weening pride. Of thirty-six first cousins of Kolokotronis only eight survived, which gave
rise to the saying that "there is not place in the Morea where a Kolokotronis is not buried."

Androutsos

Androutsos, where were you wintering during the year that passed,
When the snows were thick and many and the hail was heavy, too?
I was wintering in Preveza aboard the English ships.

memory of Androutsos deemed him innocent. Androutsos captured the imagination of
many foreigners, especially the British, as a romantic brigand-cum-freedom fighter. Edward John Trelawny, one of Byron's eccentric friends and a fellow philhellene, has left a
colorful account of his time spent with Androutsos.
In this context it is noteworthy that the short extract my mother remembers from the
song about Androutsos has him wintering on English ships. Preveza is a seaport on the
Ionian coast in Epirus. A good description of Androutsos as well as an account of the role
of the European and American philhellenes who came to participate in the Greek Revo-
lution can be found in the book by David Crane, listed in the bibliography. The book by
William St. Clair, *That Greece Might Be Free*, also relates the story and exploits of the philhellenes.

Του Πανουργιά

Σαράντα μέρες περπατώ να βρω παπά πνευματικό.
[Γεια σου, Πανουργιά.]
Κι απάνω στις σαράνταδυο τον ευρήκα τον πνευματικό.
Σκύφτω, φιλώ το χέρι του, κάθησα στο μπεντέρι του.
Του λέγω,– ξομολόγα με, τα κρίματά μου ρώτα με.
– Τα κρίματά σου είν' πολλά δεν συγχωριούνται μια φορά.
[Γεια σου, Πανουργιά.]
Δεν συγχωριούνται μια φορά.

This song is about Panourgias (1759-1834), a famous klepht in the region of Mount Parnassus. Originally serving under Ali Pasha as an *armatolos* or local peace-keeping irregular, he had a falling out with Ali over the appointment of a rival and took to the hills as a bandit. With the outbreak of the Greek uprising against the Turks in 1821 he joined the struggle, participating bravely in many battles.

Ένας αετός περήφανος

Ένας αετός περήφανος, ένας αετός λεβέντης,
από την περηφάνια του, από τη λεβεντιά του
δεν πήγε στα κατώμερα να ξεκαλοχειμάσει.
Μα μένει πάνω στα βουνά, ψηλά στα κορφοβούνια.
Και πέσαν χιόνια στα βουνά και κρύσταλλα στους κάμπους.
Και παγώσανε τα νύχια του και πέσαν τα φτερά του.
Και τώρα ήρθε η άνοιξη και λιώσανε τα χιόνια.
Γύρισαν τ' άλλα τα πουλιά, γύρισαν και τ' αηδόνια.
Γύρισαν και οι αετοί και τον περιγελούνε.
Και αυτός στην πέτρα κάθεται χωρίς φτερά και νύχια.

This is an old klepht song. Although in this song it is the proud and bold klepht who decides to remain high up on the mountains during the harsh winter months, this was not what usually happened for obvious reasons. This song may be interpreted more as warning to the klephts rather than an example to be emulated.

Panourgias

Forty days have I been walking to find a confessor priest.
[Your health, Panourgias.]
And on the forty-second day I found me a confessor.
Bowing, I kiss his hand and I sit with him in his tower.
I tell him, – take my confession; ask of me my sinful deeds.
– Your sinful deeds are quite many; they can't be forgiven all at once.
[Your health, Panourgias.]
They can't be forgiven all at once.

This song, however, refers to his earlier bandit exploits, which apparently were not so heroic. Confession is one of the seven mysteries or sacraments of the Orthodox church and is required at least once a year, although it is expected that the believer resort to it more often. Traditionally, one goes to confession during Lent not to the parish priest but rather, if available, to a priest or monk especially trained and dedicated for this purpose.

An eagle proud and lordly

An eagle so proud and lordly, an eagle so brave and bold,
Because of his pride and haughtiness because of his bold ways and manner
Did not go down to the lowlands to pass the wintertime with ease.
But stays high up on the mountains, high up on the mountain peaks.
And snow fell upon the mountains and ice crystals on the plains.
And frozen became his talons and fallen were his feathers.
Springtime has come back again and all the snows have melted.
The other birds have all returned and with them the nightingales.
The eagles have returned as well and they deride and mock him.
And on a rock he sits alone without feathers, without talons.

Κάτω στον κάμπο τον πλατύ

Κάτω στον κάμπο τον πλατύ, που είναι οι κλέφτες οι πολλοί.
Κάθονται και τρων και πίνουν και την Άρτα φοβερίζουν.
Πιάνουν και γράφουν μια γραφή, χέζουν τα γένια του κατή.
Γράψανε και στο Κομπότι, προσκυνάν' και τον δεσπότη.

During the long centuries of the Turkish occupation, there were revolts and attempts to fight back against the oppressor. This song dates to the major uprising against the Turks of 1769-70 inspired by the Russians, which failed after the latter did not sustain their support of the Greek rebels. The revolt was suppressed after considerable resistance. Many of the rebel leaders had been Turkish appointed *armatoloi*, or local peace-keeping irregulars. In the southern Epirus region with Arta, the administrative seat, they were

Χορεύουν τα κλεφτόπουλα

Χορεύουν τα κλεφτόπουλα, γλεντάνε τα καημένα.
Κι ένα μικρό κλεφτόπουλο δεν παίζει, δεν γελάει.
Μόν' τ' άρματά του 'τοίμαζε και το σπαθί τροχάει.
– Ντουφέκι μου περήφανο, σπαθί μου παινεμένο,
πολλές φορές με γλίτωσες κι απόψε τούτη ώρα
θα σε στολίσω μάλαμα, θα σε σμαλτώσω ασήμι.

This is an old song with several variants. It is danced to the *tsamikos* rhythm. It briefly but rather romantically depicts the life of the klephts as being one of carousing and battle. While certainly there is truth to this picture, the reality was often much harsher and more dangerous, a sense also conveyed by the penultimate line.

Down on the plain so wide and broad

Down on the plain so wide and broad there are bands of many klephts.
They are sitting, eating, drinking and frightening the town of Arta.
Then they up and write a letter and in it shit on the *qadi's* beard.
They also write to nearby Kompoti and bow before the bishop.

only able to regain their power and influence by threatening reprisal raids, as the song indicates.
A *qadi* is a Muslim judge and in the Turkish period was one of the most important officials in the Ottoman administration. A reference to the *qadi's* beard in this manner was the ultimate insult. The seemingly more respectful tone taken with the bishop did not hide the fact that pressure was being put on him as well to cooperate.

The klephts are all out dancing

The klephts are all out dancing, the poor boys are at a feast.
But one, a young and youthful klepht, does not play nor does he laugh.
He's only readying his weapons and he's sharpening his sword.
– O my proud and peerless musket, O my sword admired and praised,
Many times have you saved me and tonight at this very hour
I shall embellish you with gold; with silver I will coat you.

Παιδιά μ', σαν θέλετε λεβεντιά

Παιδιά μ', σαν θέλετε λεβεντιά και κλέφτες για να πάτε,
εμένα να ρωτήσετε πώς τα περνάν οι κλέφτες.
Δώδεκα χρόνια έκανα στους κλέφτες καπετάνος.
Σε στρώμα δεν κοιμήθηκα, ούτε σε μαξιλάρι.
Το χέρι μου προσκέφαλο και το σπαθί μου στρώμα.
Κι αυτό το ντουφεκάκι μου το βράδυ καραούλι.

This is my mother's version of a very old klepht song, which shows the less glamorous side of the life of these bandits-cum-freedom fighters.

The life of a klepht

Since you want gallantry, my boys, and to become like klephts,
Ask me and I will tell you how those klephts pass their days.
For twelve years I was a captain among those bands of klephts
And all that time I did not sleep on a mattress or a pillow.
My hand was pillow for my head and my sword was my mattress.
And at night with my dear musket I had to stand alone on guard.

Παιδιά απ' τη Σαμαρίνα

Εσείς παιδιά κλεφτόπουλα, παιδιά απ' την Σαμαρίνα.
[Μωρέ παιδιά καημένα, κι ας είστε λερωμένα.]
Αν πάτε κατά τον τόπο μας, κατά τη Σαμαρίνα,
[Μωρέ παιδιά καημένα, κι ας είστε λερωμένα.]
ντουφέκια να μη ρίξετε, τραγούδι να μη πείτε.
[Μωρέ παιδιά καημένα, κι ας είστε λερωμένα.]
Και σας ακούσει η μάννα μου και η δόλια αδερφή μου,
[Μωρέ παιδιά καημένα, κι ας είστε λερωμένα.]
κι έρθουν και σας ρωτήσουνε, για μένα να μη πείτε.
[Μωρέ παιδιά καημένα, κι ας είστε λερωμένα.]
Μη πείτε πως σκοτώθηκα, μη πείτε πως εχάθη.
[Μωρέ παιδιά καημένα, κι ας είστε λερωμένα.]
Να πείτε πως παντρεύθηκα εδώ σε τούτα μέρη.
[Μωρέ παιδιά καημένα, κι ας είστε λερωμένα.]
Πήρα την πέτρα πεθερά, τη μαύρη γη γυναίκα.
[Μωρέ παιδιά καημένα, κι ας είστε λερωμένα.]

Samarina, a town in Epirus, was known for its klephts. The refrain refers to the "boys" returning from battle, begrimed and dirty. The verb in Greek "to kill" literally means "to put somone in darkness," a view of death going back to the days of Homer, both as a concept and as a poetic turn of phrase. The Greeks have been Christians for almost two thousand years, but many of the old ideas persist and are nowhere more evident than in the folk way of talking about and dealing with death.

Death is personified as Charos, a slightly changed form of Charon, the ancient mythic ferryman across the river of the death, the Styx. Although it is God who sends him, he often appears almost as an independent force coming to take the person not to paradise, but away from the pleasures and beauty of the world above to the cheerless world of darkness below. Once he was sent by God to take a child away and the weeping parents begged him to spare it. Death took pity on the parents and did so. God was so angered by

Young klephts from Samarina

You boys, you young klephts and boys, who come from Samarina,
[O you poor unlucky boys, no matter that you're dirty.]
If you're heading towards our homeland, going on to Samarina,
[O you poor unlucky boys, no matter that you're dirty.]
Don't shoot off your guns and muskets, don't sing or break out in song,
[O you poor unlucky boys, no matter that you're dirty.]
And my dear mother hears you and my poor sister hears you, too,
[O you poor unlucky boys, no matter that you're dirty.]
And they come and ask you questions; don't you speak to them of me.
[O you poor unlucky boys, no matter that you're dirty.]
Don't go and tell them I've been killed; don't go and say that he is lost.
[O you poor unlucky boys, no matter that you're dirty.]
Just tell them that I've married here, here in these far-off places.
[O you poor unlucky boys, no matter that you're dirty.]
As mother-in-law I took the stone, the black earth I took as wife.
[O you poor unlucky boys, no matter that you're dirty.]

Death's insubordination that he blinded him and made him deaf. That's why Death can not see or hear our weeping and show any mercy.
The Greek church service for the dead is a beautiful and poignant reaffirmation of life after death as it bids farewell to the soul on its final journey to a place of repose and peace with God. Yet, the traditional keening songs or lamentations, *moirologia*, describe a much bleaker picture, reflecting more the view of Homer than that of Jesus. In Greece, the dead are usually buried within 24 hours and are not embalmed. Because space is limited, graves are constantly being reused and bones are exhumed after three years to be placed in an ossuary, usually in the church attached to the graveyard. When I went to my ancestral village for the first time in 1956, I wanted to pay my repects to the graves of my two grandfathers. I was told their bones had long since been cast into the common ossuary of the village and that "in death as in life everybody was together."

Παλιά μου χρόνια και καλά

Παλιά μου χρόνια και καλά, καλά και περασμένα,
πίσω να γυρίζατε και πάλι να ξαναρθείτε.
Να γίνω δεκαοχτώ χρονών πάνω στο Είκοσι-ένα.
Να πάρω σκλάβους δώδεκα και σκλάβες δεκαπέντε.
Οι πέντε να με ξυπνάνε το πρωί με γλυκά τραγούδια.
Και πέντε το απομεσήμερο να με κερνάν να πίνω.
Και πέντε το αποβραδίς να στρώνουν να κοιμάμαι.

This song dates to the time after the Greek War for Independence, which started in 1821. The theme may appear cruel and self-indulgent to the modern reader but after centuries of similar unremitting Turkish behavior some of the Greek freedom fighters may have thought that it was now their turn and expressed it accordingly.

Θ' ανέβω πάνω στα βουνά

Θ' ανέβω πάνω στα βουνά, ψηλά στα κορφοβούνια.
Και θα σφυρίξω κλέφτικα να μαζευτούν οι κλέφτες,
κι όλα τα κλεφτόπουλα και οι καπεταναίοι
να τραγουδήσουν κλέφτικα και το χορό ν' αρχίσουν,
για να βουΐξουν τ' Άγραφα, να σιώνται τα Τζουμέρκα.

A variant composed by my mother on a klepht theme. The Agrapha and the Tzoumerka are regions in the southern part of the Pindus Mountains in northwestern mainland Greece. and were famous as the haunts of bandits and of freedom fighters (see also page 22).

My good old years

Good old years of mine so happy, good but long since gone and past,
I wish you could return once more and come back to me again.
If I could become eighteen again in the year "Twenty-One,"
To raid and take away twelve slaves and capture fifteen slave girls.
Five to awaken me at dawn with songs sweet and tender.
And five at the midday hour to pour wine for me to drink.
And five when the night has fallen to make a bed for me to sleep.

I'll go high up on the mountains

I'll go high up on the mountains, high up on the mountain tops.
There I will whistle like a klepht so all the klephts can gather,
Together with the young ones along with their brave captains,
That they might sing the songs of klephts and then begin the dancing,
So the Agrapha will resound and the Tzoumerka tremble.

Εβγήκα δίπλα στα βουνά

Εβγήκα δίπλα στα βουνά, δίπλα στα κορφοβούνια,
στη Λιάκουρα της Λιβαδειάς που 'χουν τις καταβόθρες.
Ήταν λημέρια των κλεφτών και των καπεταναίων.
Βρίσκω λημέρια έρημα, βαριά χορταριασμένα.
Με πήρε το παράπονο και άρχισα να κλαίω, βαριά αναστενάζω.
Πού 'σαι καημένη κλεφτουριά, καημένα παλικάρια;

The first line is a traditional formulaic beginning employed in many klepht songs. This song was composed by my mother's father in the style of the klepht songs, which was still a living traditional style in the mountain villages of Epirus during the later part of the 19th century. Liakoura is another name for Mount Parnassus, which was a major center of banditry and rebellion during the Turkish period. Livadia is a town on the eastern approaches to Mount Parnassus, (see note on page 18).

Ο γερο-Δήμος

Γέρασα, μωρέ παιδιά, θέλω να ξαποστάσω,
να γείρω να αποκοιμηθώ, λίγο να ξανασάνω.
Ποιος ξέρει απ' τον ύπνο μου τι δέντρο θα φυτρώσει.
Και αν φυτρώσει πλάτανος, στον ίσκιο από κάτω
να 'ρχονται τα κλεφτόπουλα τ' άρματα να κρεμάνε.

My mother composed this song in the klepht style as a young girl working on one of the family fields called Tziouka. It was common practice for the fields and plots of land, which were usually widely dispersed, to have names. Tziouka was one such large piece requiring four to five days of plowing. It was also difficult to prepare for planting because of the claylike nature of the soil. While the major work was done by the plowman and the oxen,

I ventured out by the mountains

I ventured out by the mountains, out by the mountain peaks,
To Liakoura of Livadia where huge caverns can be found.
These were the haunts of the klephts, of their chiefs and of their captains.
I found the haunts all deserted and heavily grassed over.
Sorrow at once overcame me, and then I began to weep and deeply I gave a sigh.
Where are you, O bands of klephts; where are you, my poor brave boys?

Old man Dimos

I've grown old and grey, my boys, I want to sit and rest my feet,
To lie down and fall asleep and refresh myself a bit.
Who knows what tree will then appear and grow out of my slumber.
And if a plane tree starts to grow, beneath its shades and shadows,
All the young klephts can then come forth and hang up their weapons there.

people (mostly women and girls and usually barefoot) had to follow along behind and break up the clods. My mother in exasperation cursed it. It was carried away by a major landslide years after she left in 1937. Old man Dimos was a semi-legendary klepht hero, who figures in many folk songs. Dimos is a form of Dimitrios.

Τρεις σταυραετοί καθόντανε

Τρεις σταυραετοί καθόντανε σε τρία μαύρα λιθάρια,
και κλαίγανε τα ντέρτια τους και τα παράπονά τους.
Ο ένας κλαίει που μέθυσε, ο άλλος κλαίει τ' αεταίρι.
Ο τρίτος κλαίει που γέρασε και πέσαν τα φτερά του.
– Εσύ, αετέ μ', που μέθυσες, πάλι θα ξεμεθύσεις,
και εσύ που κλαις το αεταίρι σου, αεταίρι παίρνεις κι άλλο.
Κρίμα σε με που γέρασα και πέσαν τα φτερά μου.
Τα γέρα να πουλιόντανε ν' αγόραζα τα νιάτα.

This is a table song to be sung and not danced. In Greek the words for old age and youth are in the plural, imparting a layered sense of the many inescapable and unfair woes of old age as compared with the many happy but transient pleasures of youth. This was a typical klepht theme.

Να 'ταν τα νιάτα δυο φορές

Να 'ταν τα νιάτα δυο φορές, τα γηρατειά καμία.
Να ξανανιώσω, μάτια μου, να γίνω παλικάρι.
Να βάλω το φεσάκι μου και να βγω στο παζάρι
και να πουλάω γηρατειά και ν' αγοράζω νιάτα.

This is an old klepht song sung throughout Greece.

Three royal eagles

Three royal eagles were sitting on three black rocks together
And weeping over their troubles and over their many woes.
One wept for having gotten drunk; the other wept for his lost mate.
The third wept because he had aged and his feathers had all fallen.
– You, my eagle, who's gotten drunk, once again you will be sober.
And you who weep for your lost mate, you can go and take another.
Pity me, who has gotten old and my feathers have all fallen.
If only old age could be sold off and I could buy back my youth.

If only youth could happen twice

If only youth could happen twice and old age not even once,
To be young again, my love, to be a brave young man.
To put on and don my little fez and go out in the bazaar.
And there to sell off my old age and buy up the time of youth.

Τ' ανδρειωμένου τ' άρματα

Τ' ανδρειωμένου τ' άρματα δεν πρέπει να πωλούνται.
Πρέπει μέσα στην εκκλησιά εκεί να λειτουργούνται.
Πρέπει να κρέμονται ψηλά σε πύργο αραχνιασμένο.
Να τρώει τ' άρματα η σκουριά και η γη τον ανδρειωμένο.

Γρίβα μ', σε θέλει ο βασιλιάς

– Γρίβα μ', σε θέλει ο βασιλιάς, όλος ο κόσμος και ο ντουνιάς.
– Σαν τι με θέλει ο βασιλιάς, όλος ο κόσμος και ο ντουνιάς;
Αν με θέλει για καλό, ν' αλλάξω και να στολισθώ.
Κι αν με θέλει για φυλακή, να 'ρθει μόνος να μου το πει.
– Για πάρε, Γρίβα, το σπαθάκι σου, πάρε και το ντουφεκάκι σου.

This is a well-known song and dance in the *tsamikos* rhythm. Theodoros Grivas was a fighter against the Turks during the war for independence. After independence was achieved, Grivas wanted Greece to be a republic and was not pleased with the appointment by the major European powers of the Bavarian prince, Otho, to the throne of Greece. As the years went by Otho and his Bavarian advisers ruled Greece in an increasingly ar-

The brave man's arms

The brave man's arms must not be taken out to be bought and sold.
They must be taken to the church and there be blessed and hallowed.
And then they must be hung on high in a tower full of cobwebs,
So rust will eat away the arms and earth devour the brave man.

The king wants you, Grivas

– The king wants you, my dear Grivas; everybody and everyone as well.
– And what does the king want of me and everybody and everyone as well?
If he wants me for something good, I'll change and put on my best.
And if he wants me to go to jail, let him come himself to tell me.
– Take up your sword, my dear Grivas, and take up your musket too.

bitrary manner, leading Grivas to mount several abortive revolts in 1844 and 1847. He
died on October 24, 1862 at Mesolongi after being informed of the final overthrow of the
King and as he was preparing to march on the capital. Unfortunately for Grivas and others who shared his republican views, a new king was installed over the Greeks, as a result of negotiations between the European powers.

Του κλέφτη ο τάφος

Να θάψτε το κορμάκι μου σε μια ψηλή ραχούλα.
Και απ' τη δεξιά μεριά αφήστε παραθύρι
να μπαινοβγαίνουν τα πουλιά, της άνοιξης τ' αηδόνια.

Springtime was the season when after lying low among friends on the plains the klephts would take themselves back up to their mountain eyries to begin anew their life of brigandage and later of fighting against the Turks.

Βαριά στενάζουν τα βουνά

Βαριά στενάζουν τα βουνά κι ο ήλιος σκοτιδιάζει.
Το δόλιο το Μορίχοβο και πάλι ανταριάζει.
Που 'σαι, βρε Λούκα άπιστε, Βουλγάρε Καρατάσιο;
Δεν έχεις γέρους άρρωστους σήμερα για να σφάξεις,
ούτε κορίτσια ανύπανδρα για να τα υποτάξεις.
Έχεις μπροστά σου σήμερα τον Κώστα τον Γαρέφη.

My mother heard her uncle, her father's brother, singing this song in 1912 when she was four years old. He had returned to Greece to participate in the Balkan Wars, from the United States where he had gone as an immigrant some years before. Inspired by patriotic fervor many Greeks from America and elsewhere in the diaspora, including my father who was in England at that time, voluntarily returned to do the same.

The klepht's last wish

You can bury my poor body on a high mountain ridge
And on the right side of the grave let there be a window,
So the birds can fly in and out, the nightingales of spring.

Kostas Garephis

The mountains are sighing deeply, the sun has darkened over.
Poor unlucky Morichovo again with fog is covered.
Where are you Lukas of no faith, Bulgar Karatasios?
Today, you have no sick old men for you to kill and slaughter.
Today, you have no unwed girls for you to rape and ravish.
Today, you have standing here before you, Kostas Garephis.

Kostas Garephis was a Greek army officer, who died in 1906 at the town of Morichovo in Turkish-held Macedonia fighting Bulgarian guerillas. At that time, Greek and Bulgarian guerillas were fighting one another as well as against the Turks to consolidate control over those parts of Macedonia where their respective ethnic group was in the majority. Both sides accused the other of inflicting indignities on innocent civilians.

Τσετσεμήτσος

Βαρύς αχός ακούγεται και ταραχή μεγάλη.
Μην είν' βουβάλια πολεμάν, μην είν' θηριά παλεύουν;
Ούτε βουβάλια πολεμάν, ούτε θηριά παλεύουν.
Ο Τσετσεμήτσος έρχεται, σκλάβους για να μας πάρει.

This is a dance song sung to the *tsamikos* rhythm. The first three lines are a formulaic phrase, which is found in a number of folksongs describing the arrival or the deeds of some klepht leader or even Turco-Albanian figure. Tsetsemitsos appears to have been a bandit but when is not evident from the song.

Του Κάγγαλου

Το μάθατε τι έγινε μέσα στο Λιδωρίκι;
Τον Κάγγαλο τον πιάσανε και παν να τον κρεμάσουν.
Χίλι' Αρβανίτες παν μπροστά και δυο χιλιάδες πίσω,
στη μέση πάει ο Κάγγαλος σαν μήλο μαραμένος.
Και η μάννα του του φώναζε, και η μάννα του του λέει,
– Πες μου πού έχεις τ' άρματα, πού είναι το ντουφέκι;
– Μάννα μου, δεν κλαις τα νιάτα μου, δεν κλαις τη λεβεντιά μου
που με ρωτάς για τ' άρματα, το έρημο ντουφέκι;
Μάννα μου, τα παράτησα στον πλάτανο στη ρίζα.

This is a bandit song, which is a variant on one of the most famous of the klepht songs, "Kitsos's Mother" found elsewhere in this collection. This reapplication of songs from a klepht protagonist to a later bandit figure was often done. There are many such songs called *listrika*, or bandit songs, dating in great part to the mid and late 19th century and even until the 1920's when common banditry was widespread in the poorly organized newly emergent Greek state.

Conditions were similar to the American Wild West, as my mother would often say pointing to the banditry still occurring in her days. These activities gave rise to similar folk-

Tsetsemitsos

A loud and fearsome noise is heard and then a mighty uproar.
Wild oxen, perhaps, are fighting; wild beasts are, perhaps, at war.
Neither are wild oxen fighting, nor are wild beasts at war.
Tsetsemitsos is coming now to take all of us as slaves.

Kangalos

Have you all learned what happened in the town of Lidoriki?
They captured poor young Kangalos and took him there for hanging.
A thousand Albanians in front, two thousand in the rear
And in the midst of them poor Kangalos, all shriveled like an apple.
His mother was calling out to him, and his mother asks him,
– Tell me, where do you have your weapons; tell me, where is your musket?
– Mother, you don't weep for my youth, my good looks and courage
But only for my weapons and my unlucky musket?
I abandoned them, dear mother, at the roots of the plane tree.

lore and folk music romantization of outlaws. These men were often nothing more than ordinary criminals even if they tried to present themselves as heirs to the klepht or freedom fighter/Robin Hood tradition of the preceeding era. Kangalos was active in the region of Mount Parnassus in the 1850's. He was captured and beheaded (not hanged) in 1860, not by Albanians but by the Greek gendarmerie. Lidoriki is a town in central Greece. My mother characterized this song and the dance that goes with it as "heavy and difficult." She remembered how one of her uncles once danced it in slow, measured steps, while balancing a glass of wine on his head.

Του Χρήστου Νταβέλη

Επήρε μέρα και αυγή,
[Γειά σου, Νταβέλη αρχιληστή.]
αχ, πήρε το μεσημέρι,
[Γειά σου, αρχιληστή Νταβέλη.]
και πού θα λημεριάσουμε, Νταβέλη, θα μας πιάσουνε.
– Στης Τζιτζιφιάς τη ρεματιά, εκεί θα κάνουμε λημέρι.
[Γειά σου, αρχιληστή Νταβέλη.]

This the is one of the so-called bandit songs, *listrika*. Christos Davelis or Natsos was the son of Sarakatsan nomads from Epirus. He was wrongly accused by a monk at the Petraki Monastery in Athens of stealing and in anger killed him. He took to the hills where he joined up with an uncle and began a career of brigandage.

During the Anglo-French occupation of Athens to ensure Greek neutrality in the Crimean War of 1854-57, he captured a French officer and kept him hostage until the foreigners

Δεν είναι κρίμα;

Δεν είναι κρίμα κι άδικο δεν είναι και αμαρτία
να 'ναι η Βασίλω σ' ερημιά, σε κλέφτικα λημέρια;
Να στρώνει μπάτσες στρώματα κι οξιές για μαξιλάρια;
Ο καπετάνος φώναξε, ο καπετάνος λέει,
– Σήκω Βασίλω μ', κ' έφεξε, σήκω και πήρε μέρα.
Σήκω να πάρεις τον καφέ να πάρεις παξιμάδι.
Την ξαγορά την έφεραν, τρεις μούλες φορτωμένες,
όλο μετζίτια και φλουριά και όλο μαργαριτάρια.

This song tells the story of the kidnapping of Evdokia Averoff and her cousin in the town of Metsovo in Epirus on July 31, 1884, when the area was still under Turkish control. She was the daughter of one of the most prominent men in the town. The family was rich and well known in Epirus and throughout liberated Greece.

The immediate reason for the kidnapping was the anger of a young man, named Flengas. He had been slapped across the face because he dared to pass through the area in the town's square reserved for the village elders. The elder, who administered the slap, was Nikolakis Averoff, Evdokia's father. Flengas sought revenge for this insult and shame by getting in touch with Thymios Gakis, a bandit in the region. Together with twelve men

Davelis, the bandit

Day has come and dawn has broken,
[To your health, bandit chief Davelis.]
O my, midday's already here
[To your health, bandit chief Davelis.]
And where are we going to hide, Davelis, they are going to catch us.
– At the ravine of Tzitzifia, there we'll make our hide-out.
[To your health, bandit chief Davelis.]

left. He was acclaimed a popular hero for this deed but this was not enough to keep him from being surrounded near Delphi and killed by the gendarmes in July 1856. His head was hung in Syntagma Square as a warning to others. Many stories were told of his exploits and he allegedly had affairs with a princess and a duchess; the latter tales are untrue. Tzitzifia is a place near Athens.

Isn't it a wrong and pity?

Isn't it a wrong and pity; isn't it yet a sin
That Vasilo's in a wilderness, in lonely bandit hideouts
And makes her bed from reeds and brush and her pillows from a beech tree?
The leader of the gang called out; the leader speaks and tells her,
– Get up, Vasilo, dawn has come; get up, it's already day.
Get up and take your coffee now and take a dry piece of bread.
They have brought to us the ransom, loaded well upon three mules.
It's all silver coins and gold florins and many, many pearls.

Gakis took Evdokia and her cousin into the mountains and asked for a ransom of Evdokia's weight in gold florins and of her cousin's in silver *mejidies*, Turkish coins of the period.
The ransom was finally paid and Gakis escaped with his share of the loot dressed as a Muslim woman to the city of Smyrna in Turkey where he lived until 1919. He died on July 17 of that year fighting the Turks during the Greek invasion of Asia Minor. In the song the girl is called Vasilo and not Evdokia. Vasilo was often used in Greek folk music as the generic name for a beautiful and well-born woman or girl because of its meaning (royal or queenly) and because it scanned easily.

Του Γιάννη Ρέντζου

Αχ, Λενιώ γιατί να σ' αγαπώ;
Να έρχεσαι τα χαράματα,
να μου λες που πήγαν τα αποσπάσματα.

This an excerpt from a song about the notorious bandit, Giannis Rentzos, who together with his brother pulled off a spectacular hold-up near Arta on June 13, 1926, of a bank car carrying a huge amount of money. In the gunfight six people were killed but one survived to provide the testimony, which later convicted him and his brother. They were executed in 1929 after fleeing to Varna, Rumania, where they were caught.
They initially became outlaws when they killed a group of men to avenge the murder of their father. In the years before their capture they were involved in many robberies and

Βγήκαν οι Φράγκοι απ' τη Φραγκιά

Βγήκαν οι Φράγκοι απ' τη Φραγκιά και οι Τούρκοι από την Άρτα.
Πατήσανε το Χασαπά, την έρημη Φλωριάδα.
Πήραν ασπρά, πήραν φλωριά, πήραν μαργαριτάρια.
Πήραν και μια νεόνυμφη, τριών μερών νυφούλα.
– Γιατί, νύφη μου, δεν περπατείς; Γιατί, νύφη μου, δεν τρέχεις;
Μήπως βαριά είναι τα ρούχα σου, βαριά τ' ασημικά σου;
– Ούτε τα ρούχα μου είναι βαριά, ούτε τ' ασημικά μου.
Μόν' κλαίω για τον άνδρα μου, που οι Τούρκοι μου τον πήραν.
Και Τούρκος το σπαθί του έβγαλε και το λαιμό της κόβει.

This is a variant of an old table song from Epirus. It may well describe a specific event, but such raids and attacks were common occurrences during the troubled late 17th and on into the 18th century. The term Franks was applied to all western Europeans and was often a term of disdain, echoing the oppobrium attached by the Greeks to the western freebooters of the Fourth Crusade who sacked Constantinople in 1204.
During this later period European, specifically Venetian, troops were active from time to time in the area of Greece and particularly in Epirus. It was Turkish and Albanian troops and bandits, however, and Arab pirates who preyed upon the Greek towns and villages, especially those on the plains or near the sea. Chasapa and Phloriada were two such towns. To this day on the coast of Epirus north of the town of Parga there is an isolated inlet called Sarakiniko, the place where the Saracens or Arabs of the North African Barbary

48

The plaint of Giannis Rentzos

O my Lenio, why should I love you so?
That you may come at early dawn,
To tell me where the posses have all gone.

reportedly in some 80 killings. They early acquired a Robin Hood reputation for their
gifts to the poor and for quite a time they enjoyed support among the common folk of
Epirus. This support dwindled after an armed robbery in 1926. In 1914, my mother got a
good look at the two brothers as they were being entertained secretly and undercover at
the encampment of the area's major sheep-herder where her father was the master
cheese maker. Lenio is a form of Eleni or Helen.

Franks and Turks

Out of the west the Franks have come; from Arta have come the Turks
And Chasapa they've trampled on and forlorn Phloriada.
They've taken aspers, florins too; they've taken pearls aplenty.
They've also seized a newlywed, a girl some three days married.
– Why don't you walk with ease, my bride; why don't you run more quickly?
Perhaps your clothes are heavy on you and your jewelry's heavy too?
– My clothes are not heavy on me, nor is my jewelry heavy.
I weep only for my husband, whom the Turks have taken from me.
And then a Turk unsheathed his sword and with it did cut her throat.

Coast would come ashore to raid. There are similar place names elsewhere in Greece.
The villagers there still remember and tell the story of such a raid which one night surprised and enslaved an entire wedding party. Aspers and florins were Turkish and Western European coins respectively, then in wide circulation throughout the eastern
Mediterranean. The tragic bride in this story might, indeed, have been heavily laden with
jewelry, as the custom was to drape over the breast and head of the bride chains of as
many gold and silver coins as possible to demonstrate the wealth of the family.
While the folk muse ends the song with a horrific death not beyond the capability of the
Turk in those days, such a captive would have been worth much more alive than dead,
either in the captor's own harem or better yet at the "white" slave market in Constantinople, where captives were segregated and sold by color.

Αρβανιτάκης ξέβγαινε

Αρβανιτάκης ξέβγαινε μέσα από τα Ζαγόρια.
Και παίρνει σκλάβους δώδεκα και σκλάβες δεκαπέντε.
Επήρε και μια νιόνυμφη, τριών μερών νυφούλα.
– Γιατί, νύφη, δεν περπατείς; Γιατί, νύφη, μου δεν τρέχεις;
Μην είν' βαριά τα ρούχα σου; Μην είν' βαρύ τ' ασήμι;
– Ούτε βαριά τα ρούχα μου, ούτε βαρύ τ' ασήμι.
Βαρύς ο πόνος στην καρδιά, τ' αεταίρι που μου λείπει.

This is a variant of the preceding table song and also comes from Epirus. In this version the poor bride is not slain but chances are she'll never see her mate again. Although captives could be and were ransomed, female captives usually were not that fortunate. The fear of being taken captive and sold into slavery remained among the subject Greek and Balkan populations for a long time.

My mother remembers being told by her mother of an incident that took place in the latter's grandmother's time. That would have been in the early 19th century when Epirus was still under Ottoman control. It seems that a group of young women was gathered, spinning, knitting and gossiping. My mother's great-grandmother was also present but took little part in the gossip because at a 102 years she was almost entirely deaf. At one point, she asked the younger women what they were talking about. One of her daughters-in-law jokingly said, "oh, the Turks are coming." The old woman was frightened but no one took much notice. Later when the family gathered for its evening meal the grandmother was not to be seen. After searching everywhere, they finally found her in a tree which she had climbed in her terror to hide from the Turks. She died a few days later from the shock.

Arvanitakis can be translated the "Little Albanian," as the form of the word in Greek is in the diminutive. The ending "-akis" can be used in an endearing or pejorative way, depending on the intonation and to whom it refers. *Arvanitakis* may have been an Albanian bandit, most likely a Muslim, or a Greek collaborator of the Turks.

Arvanitakis

Arvanitakis was coming forth from within Zagoria lands
And takes with him twelve slaves from there and seizes fifteen slave girls.
He also took one newlywed, a young bride three days married.
– Why can't you walk, my little bride and keep up with the running?
Are your clothes perhaps too heavy and your silver heavy too?
– No, my clothes are not too heavy, nor my silver heavy too.
In my heart the pain is heavy for the mate who's lost to me.

In many instances one can tell from the suffix of a Greek family name where that family hails from. For example, names ending in -akis are associated wih Crete. According to one explanation, the Turks on Crete lorded over the Greeks in many ways, including calling them by the diminutive of their first name as in Antonis, Antonakis. This was in the manner of Southern whites calling their slaves and later their African-American neighbors, "boy." In time the -akis suffix was attached to other forms and adjectives. Thus, Kazantzakis literally means "little cauldron maker."

Another family name suffix and a variant of -akis is -akos, as in Antonakos. This is found in the Mani, a region in the southernmost part of Greece reknowned for its warriors and no doubt was employed in an affectionate manner by the inhabitants themselves, as they were never conquered by the Turks. -Atos as in Antonatos is exclusive originally to the island of Kephalonia and is an Italianate borrowing, thanks to centuries of Venetian control; it is simply a proper noun ending in Italian and Latin. The ending -poulos as in Antonopoulos means "son of" and is common to the Peloponnese but found elsewhere; -idis is an ancient Greek suffix as in Euripides and means "son of;" it is most common among Greeks from the Black Sea region of the Pontos in Asia Minor (Turkey) as in Antonidis. Another form of this suffix is -iadis as in Antoniadis. There is also the Turkish -oglou, meaning "son of" as in Antonoglou. Both of these last two suffixes are common on family names from other parts of Asia Minor.

Κάτω στου Βάλτου τα χωριά

Κάτω στου Βάλτου τα χωριά, φάτε και πιείτε, βρε παιδιά.

Αχ, στα πράσινα λιβάδια, κόρη με τα μαύρα μάτια.

Τούρκα δέρνει τη σκλάβα της, Τούρκα δέρνει τη σκλάβα της.

Αχ, τη δέρνει τη μαλώνει και βαριά τη βαλαντώνει.

– Δείρε με, Τούρκα, δείρε με, δείρε με, Τούρκα, δείρε με.

Δείρε με και μάλωσέ με και όσο θέλεις παίδεψέ με.

Βράδυ σαν έρθει ο 'φέντης μου, βράδυ σαν έρθει ο 'φέντης μου.

Αχ, αν δεν του μαρτυρήσω, Τούρκα σκλάβα δεν θα ζήσω.

– Τι είδες, σκλάβα, και θα πεις, τι είδες και θα μαρτυρήσεις;

– Όλα θα του μαρτυρήσω, όρκο κάνω να μη ζήσω.

Ό,τι είδαν τα ματάκια μου και ό,τι άκουσαν τ' αυτιά μου.

Όλα θα του μαρτυρήσω, Τούρκα σκλάβα δεν θα ζήσω.

My mother's version is a variant of a dance song sung throughout mainland Greece to the *tsamikos* rhythm. Other variants continue the story with the slave girl describing how she caught her mistress in bed with her lover. The punishment for such behavior would have been certain death for the Muslim mistress according to Muslim law. The assumption of the song is that the Turkish mistress would have freed the slave girl to save her-

Down 'mid the Valtos villages

Down 'mid the Valtos villages; eat and drink away, my boys.

Oh, down among the meadows green; girl with eyes so dark and black.

A Turkish mistress beats her slave; a Turkish mistress beats her slave.

Oh, she beats her and she scolds her and she strikes her with heavy blows.

– Beat me, Turkish mistress, beat me; beat me, Turkish mistress, beat me.

Beat me, go on and scold me; as much as you want, abuse me.

Tonight when my master gets home; tonight when my master gets home.

Oh, if I don't tell him everything; I'll not live as a Turkish slave.

– What did you see, slave girl, to tell? What will you reveal?

– Oh, I will tell him everything; I swear by it or live no more.

Whatever I saw with my eyes; whatever I heard with my ears.

Oh, I will tell him everything; I'll not live as a Turkish slave.

self, or she could have had her executed for false testimony, as a Christian's word had little value in a Muslim court.

Valtos is a region on the eastern shore of the Gulf of Arta and means swampy or marsh land.

Παραλογές
Ballads

The Bridge of Arta.

Του Διγενή

Σαν τι να σε βρήκε, Διγενή, και θέλεις να πεθάνεις;
– Συχάσετε, καθήσετε, κι εγώ σας αφηγιέμαι.
Στης Αραβίνας τα βουνά, στης Σύρας τα λαγκάδια,
όπου συν δυο δεν περπατούν, συν τρεις δεν κουβεντιάζουν,
παρά πενήντα και εκατό και πάλι φόβο έχουν.
Κι εγώ μοναχός περπάτησα, μέσα στο σκοτάδι,
νύχτες χωρίς αστροφεγγιά, νύχτες χωρίς φεγγάρι.
Κανέναν δε φοβήθηκα απ' τους αντρειωμένους.
Τώρα ήρθ' ένας ξυπόλητος, πεζός κι αρματωμένος.
Είχε του ρήσου τα πλουμιά, της αστραπής τα μάτια.
Με κράζει να παλέψουμε σε μαρμαρένιο αλώνι
κι όποιος νικήσει από τους δυο, να παίρνει την ψυχή του.
Και πήγαν και παλέψανε σε μαρμαρένιο αλώνι,
Όπου χτυπάει ο Διγενής, το αίμα αυλάκι κάνει.
Κι όπου χτυπάει ο Χάροντας, το αίμα τάφρο κάνει.

This is not a folk song but an excerpt from an epic of the late Middle Ages recounting the deeds of Digenis Akritas, a legendary hero of the Christians in the long struggle against the Muslim Arab raiders and invaders of the Byzantine empire in the 8th, 9th and 10th centuries. The epic is known throughout Greece but more than likely was composed by the Greeks of Asia Minor because the story takes place there. Although presented in a legendary fashion, it appears that the tale is based on the life and deeds of an historical figure whose name was Basileios or Diogenes.

According to one historian he was killed in 788 A.D., fighting the Arabs in the passes of the Taurus Mountains in Asia Minor, and his tomb was still known and honored until 940 A.D. in the city of Samosata in the same area. According to the same historian, he was a turmarch, which was a high-ranking Byzantine military title, and was renowned for his bravery. His sobriquets in the ballad, Digenis and Akritas, mean "borne of two peoples" and "march warden" respectively. He was "of two peoples" because his father, according

Digenis and death

What has happened to you, O Digenis, and now you want to die?
– Rest yourselves, be seated and I'll you all my story.
At Aravina's mountain tops and Syra's wooded valleys,
Where two don't dare to walk nor three hold conversation,
But even fifty or a hundred are overcome with fear.
Yet, I alone did walk there, where there was only darkness.
Nights without any starlight, nights without a moon.
No one have I ever feared, no one from among the brave.
Now, there approached a man unshod, on foot he was and well-armed.
He had the markings of a lynx and lightning in his eyes.
He calls out to me to wrestle on a marble threshing floor
And whoever of the two will win, he can take the other's soul.
So off they went and wrestled on a marble threshing floor.
Where Digenis strikes a blow, the blood makes a little channel.
Where Death strikes a blow, the blood makes a yawning pit.

to legend, was an Arab prince, who captured his mother, Evdokia, in a raid; fell in love
with her and when pursued by her brothers, surrendered to them; became a Christian
and married her. He was also called Akritas or march warden from the word *akra* meaning border or march land. This title described the fighting men, who were given strate-
gically placed lands on the borders, or marches, of Byzantium from which to meet and
head off the constant Arab raids and invasions, which the Empire experienced for centuries.
The epic tells of his deeds of prowess and his heroic style of living on these vulnerable
and dangerous borders. Aravina and Syra are forms of Arabia and Syria respectively
which would have described the regions to the south of Asia Minor then controlled by the
Byzantines. The above excerpt is one of the best known in the epic and describes his final
struggle with Death.

Της Άρτας το γεφύρι

Σαράντα πέντε μάστοροι και εξήντα μαθητάδες,
ολημερίς εκτίζανε της Άρτας το γεφύρι.
Ολημερίς το κτίζανε, το βράδυ γκρεμιζόταν.
Και μοιρολογούν οι μάστοροι και κλαίν' οι μαθητάδες.
Πουλάκι πήγε κι έκατσε στη μεσινή καμάρα.
Δεν κελαηδούσε σαν πουλί, ούτε σαν χελιδόνι.
Παρά κελαηδούσε κι έλεγε ανθρώπινη κουβέντα,
– Μάστοροι, μη δουλεύετε, μην χάνετε τους κόπους.
Κι αν δεν στοιχειώστε άνθρωπο, γεφύρι δεν στεριώνει.
Και μη στοιχειώστε ορφανό, μη ξένο, μη διαβάτη,
παρά του πρωτομάστορα την όμορφη γυναίκα.
Το ακούει ο πρωτομάστορας, ραγίζει η καρδιά του.
Πιάνει μηνάει της λυγερής με το πουλί τ' αηδόνι,
– Γοργά ντυθείς, γοργά 'λλαχτείς, γοργά να 'ρθείς το γιόμα.
Γοργά να 'ρθείς και να σταθείς στη μεσινή καμάρα.
Να τηνε που ξαγνάντησε από την άσπρη στράτα.
Την βλέπει ο πρωτομάστορας και καίγεται η καρδιά του.
– Γειά σας χαρά σας, μάστοροι, κι εσείς, οι μαθητάδες.
Τι έχει ο πρωτομάστορας και είν' βαρυγκομισμένος;
– Το δαχτυλίδι του 'πεσε στη μεσινή καμάρα.
Ποιος θα κατεβεί και ανεβεί το δαχτυλίδι να βρει;
– Εγώ θα κατεβώ και θ' ανεβώ το δαχτυλίδι να βρω.
Ούτε καλά κατέβηκε, ούτε στη μέση πήγε,
και παίρνει ο πρωτομάστορας και ρίχνει μέγα λίθο.
– Αλίμονο στην τύχη μας, κρίμα στο ριζικό μας.
Τρεις αδερφούλες είμαστε και οι τρεις κακογραμμένες.
Μια έκτισε του Δούναβη, η άλλη του Ευφράτη,
κι εγώ, η πιο στερνότερη, της Άρτας το γεφύρι.
Όπως τρέμει το καρυόφυλλο να τρέμει το γεφύρι,
όπως πέφτουν τα φύλλα απ' τα κλαριά να πέφτουν οι διαβάτες.
– Κόρη το λόγο άλλαξε και άλλη κατάρα δώσε,
γιατί έχεις αδερφό στην ξενιτιά, μην τύχει και περάσει.
– Αν τρέμουν τα ψηλά βουνά να τρέμει το γεφύρι,
κι αν πέφτουν τ' άγρια πουλιά να πέφτουν οι διαβάτες.
Γιατί έχω αδερφό στην ξενιτιά, μην τύχει και περάσει.

The theme of a human sacrifice to stabilize a bridge is found in the folklore of other Balkan peoples like the Serbs, Bulgarians and Rumanians. Some scholars believe that the original version was Greek and it spread to the neighboring countries but this has not been proven conclusively. There are many variants in Greece with several other places being designated as the site of the bridge. Arta is the site of the most well-known of the

The bridge of Arta

Forty-five master builders and sixty young apprentices,
All day long were building it, building the bridge at Arta.
All day long they were building it but at night it tumbled down.
The master builders mourn their work; the apprentices all weep.
A bird appeared and sat itself, at the midmost of the arches.
It wasn't singing like a bird, nor as a nightingale does sing.
But it was singing and spoke out, like a human being.
– Don't go on with the work, o builders, and waste your weary efforts.
Unless you take a human soul, the bridge will not be stable.
Don't go and take an orphan's soul, a stranger's or a traveler's,
The first master builder's pretty wife, hers is the soul to take.
The first master builder hears this and his heart breaks and shatters.
And he goes and sends the nightingale to bid his wife to come,
– Quickly dress yourself; quickly change; quickly come here at noontime.
Quickly come here and stand yourself at the midmost of the arches.
Here she comes and he sees her on the white highway in the distance.
The first master builder sees her and his heart breaks within him.
– Here's to your health and happiness, o builders and apprentices.
What's wrong with the first master builder and he is so deeply troubled?
– His ring has come off and fallen at the midmost of the arches.
Who can climb down and climb back up and find the ring that's missing?
– I can climb down and climb back up and find the ring that's missing.
She didn't get down there very far or reach the midmost of the arches.
When the first master builder hurled down a huge rock upon her.
– Mercy upon us for our fate; pity us for our sad lot.
We were three beloved sisters, all three of us unlucky.
One of us built the Danube bridge; the other the Euphrates,
And I, the youngest of the three, have built the bridge at Arta.
Like a walnut leaf that trembles, may this bridge also tremble,
And like leaves that fall from branches may those who cross also fall.
– My girl, take back and change your words and pronounce another curse,
You've a brother in foreign lands who might pass this way by chance.
– If the high mountains all tremble, then may this bridge tremble too,
And if wild birds fall from the sky, may those who cross fall as well.
I've a brother in foreign lands who might pass this way by chance.

versions. The present bridge dates to 1602-06 built on earlier foundations going back to Roman times. Until recently in the Greek countryside it was quite common to sacrifice a rooster or a chicken over the cornerstone of a house about to be built. I saw this being done in the summer of 1967 in the town of Tolo in the Peloponnese. My mother recited this poem over the telephone to me while I was on Poros in the summer of 2005.

Της Ευδοκιάς

Όλοι έλεγαν κι αντέλεγαν, κι ο Κώστας επιμένει,
– 'Λάτε να την παντρέψουμε την Ευδοκιά στα ξένα.
Για να την έχω γύρισμα στο πάει και στο έλα,
για να 'χει ο γρίβας μου ταΐ κι εγώ καλό κονάκι.
Κι ήρθε καιρός αδίσεκτος και χρόνος οργισμένος,
και χάθηκε όλο το βιός και όλο το πανωπροίκι.
Και η Ευδοκιά εγύρισε στο πατρικό να πάει.
Χτύπησε την πόρτα του σπιτιού και ποιος να την ανοίξει;
Κάποιος την πόρτα άνοιξε και τη ρωτάει, – τι θέλεις;
– Έχετε πανί στον αργαλειό και ξέρω να το υφάνω.
– Ξέρεις να υφάνεις κάμποχο και να μιτώσεις ρούχο;
– Ξέρω να υφάνω κάμποχο και να μιτώσω ρούχο.
Και στον αργαλειό εκάθισε κι άρχισε να τραγουδάει,
– Διασίδι κακοδιάσιτο και κακομιτωμένο,
όταν σε ήδιαζα, οι προξενητάδες ήρθαν.
Κι όταν σε ύφαινα, ήρθαν και με πήραν νύφη.
Η μάννα της την άκουσε και πάει και τη ρωτάει,
– Ποια είσαι εσύ που ξέρεις και το πανί υφαίνεις;
Και γύρισε και λέει, – Η Ευδοκιά, η κόρη σου.
– Κόρη μου, ποιος σ' έφερε και ποιος θα σε πηγαίνει;
– Μάννα μου, ο Κώστας μ' έφερε και ο Κώστας θα με πάει.
Κι η μάννα της τής είπε και η μάννα της τής λέει,
– Κόρη μ', ο Κώστας πέθανε εδώ και πέντε χρόνια.
Αγκαλιαστήκανε και οι δυο και πέσαν και πεθάναν.

This ballad has many variants on the theme of the dead brother bringing back the sister. She has been married off against her will and her mother's to live in foreign lands by the brother for his own interests. In these variants the brother has promised the mother that he will bring back his sister on regular visits but then he dies. The mother is des-

Evdokia

All spoke out and all opposed him, but Kostas was insisting,
– Let us marry Evdokia, somewhere off in foreign lands.
So I can have her to rely on as I go and I come back.
So my grey horse will have its food and I a place for lodging.
And then there came an evil time, a year of wrath and fury,
And lost was all her livelihood and all her dower portion.
Evdokia then returned; to her father's house she came
And knocked upon the door but who was there to open?
Someone opened wide the door and asked her what she wanted,
– Do you have cloth upon the loom, as I know how to weave it?
– Do you know how to weave calico and how to pattern clothing?
– Yes, I know how to weave calico and how to pattern clothing.
And at the loom she sat herself and started into singing,
– O warp of yarn badly sorted and skein so badly heddled,
When I started out to sort you, the matchmakers first arrived.
 And when I wove you, others came and took me off as a bride.
Her mother heard her singing and came and asked her saying,
– Who are you that you know to weave and fashion cloth upon the loom?
To her mother she replied, – I'm your daughter, Evdokia.
– My dear girl, who has brought you here and who shall take you back?
– Mother, Kostas has brought me here and Kostas will take me back.
Her mother then up and spoke to her; her mother then exclaimed,
– My dear girl, Kostas has long since died, already some five years.
And then the two of them embraced and falling down they died.

perate and goes to his grave and either curses him or calls on him to keep his promise, depending on the variant. In all versions, he keeps his promise even in death. Kostas is a form of Konstantinos or Constantine.

Εορτικά
Songs for Holidays

Leading the panegyri in Theodoriana, 1965.
Vasiliki and Tom Scotes are on the far left, dressed in traditional costumes.

Ψηλά στην Κωστηλάτα

Ψηλά στην Κωστηλάτα, στα κρύα τα νερά,
χορεύουν τα κορίτσια μαζί με τα παιδιά.
Πω, πω, πω, πω, τι γένεται και στο ντουνιά δεν φαίνεται;
Πω, πω, πω, πω, τρομάρα μου να μην το μάθει η μάννα μου.

Ψηλά στην Κωστηλάτα, στα κρύα τα νερά,
χορεύουν τα κορίτσια με τα ασημοζώναρα.
Πω, πω, πω, πω, τι γένεται και στο ντουνιά δεν φαίνεται.
Πω, πω, πω, πω, τρομάρα μου αν το μάθει η μάννα μου.

Αν είσαι και δεν είσαι του δήμαρχ' αδερφή,
εγώ θα σε φιλήσω κι ας πάω στη φυλακή.
Πω, πω, πω, πω, ποια είν' αυτή με το γαρύφαλο στ' αυτί;
Ποια είν' αυτή που πέρασε και δεν μας καλησπέρασε;

Ο ήλιος βασιλεύει και η μέρα σώνεται.
Ο νους μου από σένα δε συμμαζώνεται.
Ο ήλιος βασιλεύει μέσα στα ρέματα.
Αλήθεια, μωρ' Βασίλω, δε λέω ψέματα.

Ψηλό μου κυπαρίσσι λυγάει η κορφάδα σου.
Και ποιος θα την γλεντήσει την ομορφάδα σου;

Συ που σέρνεις το χορό, κάνε διπλοκάγκελο.
Είμαι ξενός και θα ιδώ και θα πάω να 'μολογώ.
Και θα πάω να 'μολογώ στα χωριά που θα διαβώ.

Έβγα στο παραθύρι σου κρυφά από τη μάννα σου
και κάνε πως ποτίζεις τη ματζουράνα σου.
Έβγα στο παραθύρι κι εγώ διαβαίνοντας
ρίξε μου το μαντήλι να πάω παίζοντας.

Μες στον πέρα μαχαλά πέθανε μια καλογριά,
και την παν στην εκκλησιά με λαμπάδες και κεριά,
με ένα ξύλινο σταυρό και ασημένιο θυμιατό.

High up on Kostilata

High up on Kostilata where the cold waters run,
The girls are dancing with the boys, with each and everyone.
Oh my, oh my, what's happening and people in town don't see a thing?
Oh my, oh my, I dread and fear; my mother shouldn't find out or hear.

High up on Kostilata where the cold waters run,
All the girls are dancing, silver belts on everyone.
Oh my, oh my, what's happening and people in town don't see a thing.
Oh my, oh my, I dread and fear, lest my mother find out or hear.

Maybe you are the mayor's sister and maybe you are not,
I am going to kiss you anyway and in prison let me rot.
Oh my, oh my, who is this here with a carnation behind her ear?
Who is this girl who passed us by and to our good evening didn't reply?

The sun sets in royal splendor and the day is growing less.
My mind can not forget you and this I must confess.
The sun sets in royal splendor down in the valleys there.
I tell the truth, Vasilo, and not a lie, I swear.

My cypress tree tall and straight your crest is bending low.
And who will take pleasure and enjoy your beauty's glow?

You who lead the dance and sway, make a double roundalay.
I'm a stranger and I'll see, then go and tell of it willingly.
Go and tell of it willingly in all the villages where I'll be.

Come to your window secretly, so your mother doesn't know
And pretend you're watering your marigolds there in a row.
Come to your window and as I pass by on my way,
Throw me your handkerchief and with it I'll go on and play.

Over in yonder neighborhood a nun has up and died,
To the church they take her with tapers and candles alongside,
And also with a wooden cross and a censer silver-embossed.

This song is sung during a large communal dance at the major *panegyri* or festival of Theodoriana on August 15 (feast of the Dormition of the Virgin), commemorating both the feast day and the final acquisition by the village of the pastures of Kostilata in 1883. The first verse of the song is now known throughout Greece. The following verses and couplets are examples of the many which were commonly sung in the village, often composed spontaneously during the dance and then remembered to become part of the village repertory.

The dance takes place in the late afternoon of the feast day following the church service in the morning at the small mountain chapel dedicated to the Virgin and following a midday meal which traditionally marked the end of the fifteen days of abstinence from meat and milk products. The villagers called this day the "Little Pascha" as opposed to the "Big Pascha," which is Easter. It was also called the big *panegyri* to distinguish it from the small *panegyri,* which took place on September 8, the Nativity of the Virgin. The big *panegyri* was the time for matchmaking and the small *panegyri* the time to announce the resulting engagements.

In the time of my mother's childhood the people of the village still wore traditional dress which consisted of long dark black or blue embroidered skirts with dark blouses for the women and a dark kerchief, while the men wore white or dark blue *tsaktsires* or breeches, white shirt and dark waistcoat and a black beret-type hat or *skoufaki*. For the festival, however, many would don more elaborate dress, the so-called *vlachika* or shepherd girl attire for the women and the *foustanella* or kilt for the men. Today only a select group of school children and young people dress that way for the *panegyri*.

In 1956 my sister, Anna, and I joined in the dance dressed along with a large group of others in shepherd girl garb and *foustanella*, which were family heirlooms. The dance consists of two long, open, circular lines with the women, girls and little children in the inner line and the men and boys in the outer line, standing directly behind the womenfolk. The lead woman and man dancers guide the two lines around the huge plane tree

Thomas Scotes dressed in his great-uncle's foustanella *for the* panegyri *in Theodoriana in 1956.*

in the middle of the town piazza. The musicians, usually a clarinet, violin and drum walk along at the head of the lines. From time to time the two lines reverse direction and weave around the tree in the opposite direction doing what is a called a *diplokangelo* or double spoke. This latter maneuvre is choreographed by two or three "directors" of the *panegyri*, who are supposed to keep order and decorum but especially to indicate after a proper interval when the two lead dancers must give way for the next two dancers directly beside them.

Families always dance together and depending on size and composition, you might have one group leading the dance for quite awhile. In the old days fathers and brothers made sure that their marriageable daughters and sisters had a chance to lead the dance as a way of showing them off to prospective suitors. They might have even slipped a drachma note or two into the violin of the lead musician to have the music played louder at that important moment.

The order of appearance is decided by directors, a system my mother remembers was put into effect for the 1918 festival by the village doctor, the then mayor, and her grandfather to put an end to the arguments and at times fisticuffs which often occurred over whose sister or daughter had priority. The directors assure that the leaders of the village (the mayor, the priest, the school teachers) and their families go first after any important outside guests are honored like the regional prefect or a visiting politician. Following them, it's basically first come, first served.

The dance can and does go on for hours until all have had a chance to lead. After the communal dancing is over, individual groups of families and friends repair to the several *kafenia*, (*kafenion*, plural *kafenia*, coffee houses-cum-eateries), which provide food (primarily roast goat and lamb), drink and live music for more intimate parties until the wee hours. If the 15th of August falls on a Friday, the *panegyri* can last three days. In any event it will always last for at least two days, depending on the weather. It can rain in August on the uplands of the Pindus.

Vasiliki Scotes dressed in traditional costume for the panegyri *in Theodoriana in 1965.*

67

Ήρθε ο χινόπωρος

Παιδιά μου, ήρθε ο χινόπωρος και θα 'ρθει ο χειμώνας.
Πέσαν τα φύλλα απ' τα κλαριά, τα φύλλα από τα δέντρα.
Παιδιά μου, θα ξεχωρίσομε και πού θα ανταμωθούμε;
'Λάτε να φάμε και να πιούμε, να αποχαιρετηθούμε.
Ετούτο τον χρόνο τον καλό, τον άλλον ποιος τον ξέρει;
Αν ζούμε, αν πεθαίνουμε, σε άλλο τόπο πάμε.
Ας πιούμε καλή αντάμωση και να συγχωρηθούμε.

This is a table song. It is an old one with variants going back to the 18th century when a version describes the sentiments of the klephts, the Greek rebel-outlaws, preparing to descend from their mountain eyries to the plains and possible danger for the winter. My mother's version expresses the same sentiments but in the context of the annual transhumant trek which took almost two thirds of the village to the plains for the winter months to pasture their flocks or to find work.

Για τη βροχή

Μπαρμπαρούσα περπατεί, τον Θεό παρακαλεί,
– Θεέ μου, βρέξε μια βροχή, μια ψιλή βροχή,
να ποτίσεις τα χωράφια.
Να γίνουν φασόλια και σιτάρια,
να φάνε όλα τα παιδάκια.
Αμήν.

In time of drought, the small children of the village would go from house to house singing this prayer, which is sung in other parts of Greece as well. They would be carrying over their heads like an umbrella the big, broad leaves of the barbarousa plant as if to make certain that the reason for the prayer was clearly understood by the Lord above. The barbarousa is called by other names in the many variants of this prayer. Its botanical name is *Alberosa* and it grows in and by the sides of streams.

Autumn has come at last

My boys, autumn has come at last and winter will soon arrive.
The leaves are fallen from the trees, the leaves from all the branches.
We're now going to part, my boys, and where will we meet again?
Come, let's sit down and eat and drink; to each other say farewell.
This has been a good year for us; who knows what the next will be?
If we live, or even if we die, to another place we go.
Let us drink to good reunions and ask each other's pardon.

Children's prayer for rain

Barbarousa walks around and beseeches God above,
– Dear God, rain down for us a rain, a rain that's like a drizzle,
And water well the land and fields.
So the wheat and beans will ripen,
And the little children all can eat.
Amen.

Νάνι, νάνι, νάνι τού

Νάνι, νάνι, νάνι τού,
και ύπνο στα ματάκια τού.
Ως που να 'ρθ' η μάννα τού
να του φέρει κατιτί,
καραμέλες στο χαρτί.

Nani nani are the quieting nonsense syllables used by mothers to put their children to sleep. Candy wrapped in paper would have been quite a treat in the village in my mother's time.

Lullaby

Nani, nani, nani to the baby,
And sleep cover its little eyes.
Until its mother comes to it,
Bringing with her something nice,
Sweet goodies all wrapped in paper.

Καλήν εσπέραν άρχοντες

Καλήν εσπέραν άρχοντες, αν είναι ορισμός σας
Χριστού την θείαν γέννησιν να πω στ' αρχοντικό σας.
Χριστός γεννάται σήμερον εν Βηθλεέμ τη πόλει.
Οι ουρανοί αγάλλονται και χαίρ' η κτίσις όλη.
Εν τω σπηλαίω τίκτεται, εν φάτνη των αλόγων,
ο βασιλεύς των ουρανώ και ποιητής των όλων.
Πλήθος αγγέλων ψάλλουσι το Δόξα εν υψίστοις.
Και τούτο άξιον εστίν η των ποιμένων πίστις.
Εκ της Περσίας έρχονται τρεις Μάγοι με τα δώρα.
Άστρον λαμπρόν τους οδηγεί, χωρίς να λείψει ώρα.
Χρονούς πολλούς να χαίρεσθε, πάντα ευτυχισμένοι,
σωματικά και ψυχικά να είσθε πλουτισμένοι.

This song is one of a category of songs called *kalanda* or carols. The word *kalanda* derives from the Latin word, *calenda*, and refers to the first day of every month according to the ancient Roman calendar. (Calendar derives from the same Latin word). Traditionally the first days in the month of January were a period of merriment and songs were sung welcoming the New Year. During the Roman Empire the Greeks adopted both the names of the Roman calendar as well as the New Year's Day customs. The Medieval Greeks, as the heirs and preservers of the legacy of the Roman Empire in the eastern Mediterranean maintained both the calendar and many of the customs of the earlier empire. In time the songs themselves came to be called *kalanda*. Similar songs were also sung on New Year's Eve, Epiphany, Lazarus Day (the Saturday before Palm Sunday) and Good Friday. They, too, were called *kalanda*.

In the old days more than half of the population of the village of Theodoriana went down to the plains during the cold and often snow-bound winter months. Therefore, the most popular *kalanda* were those sung at Easter time when the villagers had returned and the milder spring weather permitted the children to venture forth. This custom was also observed in other villages in Epirus and elsewhere in Greece.

There are many versions of this carol, depending on the region. The singers, usually small children, go from house to house striking metal triangles and asking the people of the household, "should we say them," meaning sing the verses of the carol. The reply is of course, "yes, say them." After the song is over and the season's greetings conveyed to

Christmas carol

Good evening kind and noble sirs, if this be what you command
Of Christ's divine and holy birth, I will sing at your house so grand.
Oh, Christ is born for us today in Bethlehem of Judah.
The heavens all above rejoice and the earth cries hallelujah.
For born is he in a lowly cave where cattle have their manger,
The king and maker of heav'n and all comes so poor and as a stranger.
A host of angels laud and sing, "O Glory in the Highest."
And worthy are the shepherds too for their faith is strong and pious.
Three wise men come from Persia's land and bring gifts so rich and rare.
A bright star leads them on their way, lest they tarry too long there.
May you be blessed with many years, always happy, hale and healthy,
And may your souls reap their reward and your household always wealthy.

the master and/or lady of the house, a small coin (sometimes also a sweet) is given in return as a token of good luck and appreciation. Christmas in Greece was traditionally a time for families to get together after church services in mid-morning. There were no midnight church services, no Christmas trees, and no gift giving, which took place on New Year's Day.

As already mentioned, my mother's village was often snow-bound and most of the villagers were down on the plains for the winter, Christmas was, thus, a quiet time with any and all of the family present in the village gathered for a festive meal. The meat of choice for the occasion was pork, if you could afford it. *Pites* or pies, which Epirote women are famous for, were customary, both of meat and greens as well as sweet ones of sugar, eggs and milk. The table was also graced with a special bread called *Christopsomo* or Christ Bread. I remember my mother spending at least a week before both Christmas and later Easter making her own phyllo for her delicious pies as well as *melomakarona* (a honey-soaked cookie)and *kourabiedes* (almond cookies smothered in powdered sugar). Another old tradition involved gathering branches and firewood of the holm oak which when burning makes crackling and mildly explosive sounds. This was done to frighten off the *kalikantzari*, imp-like creatures, who were supposed to be abroad during the twelve-day Christmas season causing trouble and mischief. Rags and other smoke-producing matter were also burnt to keep these beings away.

Αρχιμηνιά κι αρχιχρονιά

Αρχιμηνιά κι αρχιχρονιά,
[Μικρή μου δεντρολιβανιά.]
κι αρχή καλός μας χρόνος,
[Εκκλησιά κι ο άγιος θρόνος.]

Αρχή που βγήκε ο Χριστός,
[Άγιος και πνευματικός.]
στη γη να περπατήσει.
[Και να μας καλοκαρδίσει.]

Αγιός Βασίλης έρχεται,
[Και δεν μας καταδέχεται.]
από την Καισαρεία,
[Συ 'σαι αρχόντισσα, κυρία.]

Βάστα εικόνα και χαρτί,
[Ζαχαροκάντο ζυμωτή.]
χαρτί και καλαμάρι.
[Δες και με το παλικάρι.]

Το καλαμάρι έγραφε,
[Και λόγια δεν του έλεγε.]
και το χαρτί μιλούσε,
[Κι απαντήσεις του ζητούσε.]

–Βασίλη, πόθεν έρχεσαι,
[Και δεν μας καταδέχεσαι.]
και πόθεν κατεβαίνεις
[Κι εξηγήσεις δεν μας κρένεις.]

–Απο τη μάννα μ' έρχομαι,
[Κι εδώ δεν παραστέκομαι.]
και στο σχολειό πηγαίνω.
[Κ' εξηγήσεις θα σας κρένω.]

Πάω να μάθω γράμματα,
[Σαν θησαυρός τα διδάγματα.]
να πω την αλφαβήτα.
[Και θα ζω κύριος με σπίτια.]

There are several versions to this carol, depending on the region. There are also more verses. The actual carol consists of the first and third lines of each verse with the second and fourth lines being antiphonal phrases sometimes in context and sometimes merely interjections to complete the rhyme and follow the melody.

As a child, I had only heard the second and third verses. St. Basil is the Greek version of Santa Claus and comes with his gifts on New Year's Day, which is also his feast day. Traditionally gifts were given on New Year's Day and not on Christmas, which was more a day of family feasting following church services. The gifts were usually in the form of money to symbolize good fortune for the coming year. The carolers expected to be gifted with a symbolic coin after completing the carol. Growing up in America we celebrated Christmas with a tree and gifts as did everyone else but on New Year's Eve my father would always place a silver dollar under our pillows for good luck. My mother also made the traditional sugar-powdered *Vasilopita* or Basil cake with a silver or gold coin hidden in the batter. After our holiday meal, the cake would be cut with the first piece going to Christ, the second to the Virgin and the third to the household and then in order of seniority a piece for everyone present. Of course, we all waited with anticipation to have the coin fall to one of us for the the good luck it would bring during the coming year. If it fell to the household, everyone was to be lucky in the coming year. St. Basil is the patron of scholars and learning, as befits one of the major Church Fathers. He was the bishop of the city of Caesarea in Cappadocia (now Kayseri in Turkey). Greek children are encouraged to emulate him both in piety and in learning, especially the latter, whose rewards the carol makes abundantly clear.

New Year's carol

First of the month and first of the year
[Rosemary tree so small and so dear.]
The beginning of our good year
[Church and throne of God so near.]

In the beginning Christ came along,
[Holy he was and His spirit strong.]
On the earth to walk and preach,
[And us all to heal and teach.]

Saint Basil comes on this holy day,
[And does not deign to look our way.]
From Caesar's ancient city,
[You're a lady, fair and pretty.]

He holds an icon in his hand,
[O sugar candy in shapes so grand.]
And some paper and an inkpen.
[Look at me, pride of the young men.]

The ink pen wrote and wrote all the day,
[And not a word did it utter or say.]
But the paper started speaking,
[Some answers it was seeking.]

–O Basil where do you come from this day,
[And do not deign to look our way.]
Please tell us where you are going.
[So we may be in the knowing.]

–I come to you from my mother so dear,
[With little time to tarry here.]
And to my school I'm going.
[Now you are in the knowing.]

I go to learn all my letters there,
[This is a treasure beyond compare.]
To recite the ABC's.
[If I learn, I'll live a life of ease.]

Του Λαζάρου

Λάζαρος αναστημένος
και με το κερί ζωμένος.
Πες μας, Λάζαρε, τι είδες
εις τον Άδη που επήγες.
– Είδα φόβους, είδα τρόμους,
είδα βάσανα και πόνους.
Δώστε μου λίγο νεράκι
να ξεπλύνω το φαρμάκι
της καρδίας, των χειλέων.
Και μη με ρωτάτε πλέον.

This carol was sung along with the carol on page 78 on Lazarus Saturday. The children, usually little boys, would go from house to house carrying small baskets decorated with spring flowers and singing the two carols. As a reward, they hoped to be given a fresh egg, if available, otherwise walnuts or a small sweet. The eggs were gathered to be hardboiled and dyed the traditional red on Holy Thursday.

Though the imagery of the carol is frigthening, my mother remembers that it was sung in a cheerful manner. The sentiments combine the Homeric view of the bleakness of

Lazarus Day carol

Here's Lazarus resurrected
Candle in hand, once more alive.
Tell us, Lazarus, what you saw
There in Hades where you ventured.
– I saw fear, I saw terror,
I saw torments, as well as pain.
Give me, please, a sip of water
To wash away the bitterness
Within my heart, upon my lips.
And question me no further.

Hades with the Christian view of the punishments of hell. The starkness of this carol was no doubt mitigated in the minds of the little singers and their audience by the anticipation of the joy of Christ's Resurrection the following week.

It is noteworthy that when referring to the dead the term *makaritis*, which means "blessed," is prefixed to the proper name of the person. This term harkens back to the pre-Christian Isles of the Blessed, where good souls might hope to reach in their journey after death.

Καλώς σας ηύρε ο Λάζαρος

Καλώς σας ηύρε ο Λάζαρος και φέτο και του χρόνου.
Και τη Λαμπρή καλόκαρδοι και καλοκαρδισμένοι
με τ' άσπρα, με τα κόκκινα και με τα λουλουδάτα.
Εδώ που τραγουδάμε ημείς, πέτρα νε μη ραγίσει,
κι ο νοικοκύρης του σπιτιού πολλά χρόνια να ζήσει.
Να ζήσει χρόνους εκατό, ν' ασπρίσει, να γεράσει,
να γίνει σαν τον Όλυμπο, σαν άσπρο περιστέρι.
Κι αν έχει κόρη για παντρειά, να χαρεί να την παντρέψει.

A song from the *kalanda* group sung on the Saturday before Palm Sunday commemorating the miracle of the resurrection of Lazarus by Jesus at Bethany near Jerusalem. In 1964 my parents, family and I spent Holy Week at the Orthodox monastery of St. Lazarus there. My mother and father had always expressed the wish to perform a pilgrimage to the Holy Land and once in a moment of youthful, filial affection, I promised them that some day I would take them there. Many years later during a diplomatic assignment to Jordan, my parents visited me and my family. They arrived for Christmas (by the old Julian calendar on January 7 as observed by the Orthodox Patriarchate of Jerusalem) and remained through Pentecost of that year, thus performing a traditional Orthodox pilgrimage in its fullness. This was the year the Ecumenical Patriarch, Athenagoras of Constantinople, had his historic meeting with Pope Paul in Jerusalem and we were privileged to be included in some of the ceremonies organized for that event. During the ap-

May Lazarus on his feast day

May Lazarus on his feast day find you well this year and the next.
And on Easter, too, may you be generous and good-hearted
With clothes of white and clothes of red all bedecked with flowers.
Here where we sing our song, may a stone not cleave or break,
And may the master of this house live on for many years.
May he live to his hundredth year, his hair white and he grow old,
May he become like Olympos, may he be white like the dove.
And if he has a girl for marriage, may he rejoice to see her wed.

proximately half year of my parents' visit, the family performed pilgrimages to many holy sites both in Jerusalem and elsewhere on the then Jordanian-held West Bank.
A major occurrence was our pilgrimage to the site of the baptism of Jesus where my daughter, Eleny, was baptized and the rest of us immersed and blessed (wearing shrouds made for that occasion and for eventual use, as tradition requires) to seal our title as *chatzi* or pilgrim. *Chatzi* is derived from the Arabic *haji* and signifies a person who has performed the pilgrimage to Mecca. Eastern Christians have over the centuries informally and colloquially employed the same term, affixing it as a title to the first name of the person performing the pilgrimage. Thus, I would be Chatzi-Thomas. For prestige reasons, it often became adopted as the last name of the family. It can be found as a prefix to many family or last names in Greece to this day as in Chatzidakis, the famous composer. The penultimate two lines of the carol are a formulaic couplet found in other songs as well.

Σήμερα μαύρος ο ουρανός

Σήμερα μαύρος ο ουρανός, σήμερα μαύρη μέρα.
Σήμερα όλοι θλίβονται και τα βουνά λυπάνται.
Σήμερα έβγαλαν βουλή γραμματείς και Φαρισαίοι,
για να σταυρώσουν τον Χριστό, τον παν στον Βασιλέα.
Και ο Κύριος εθέλησε να μπει σε περιβόλι,
να λάβει ύπνο μυστικό να τον συλλάβουν όλοι.
Σαν κλέφτη τον επιάσανε και σαν φονιά τον πάνε,
και στου Πιλάτου την αυλή, εκεί τον τυραγνάνε.
Κι η Παναγιά, η Δέσποινα, καθόταν μοναχή της,
τις προσευχές της έκαμε για τον μονογενή της.
Φωνή εξήλθ' εξ ουρανών και απ' αρχαγγέλου στόμα,
– Σώνουν, κυρά μ', οι προσευχές, σώνουν και οι μετάνοιες.
Και τον υιόν σου πιάσανε και στον χαλκιά τον πάνε.
– Χαλκιά, χαλκιά, φκιάσε καρφιά, φκιάσε τρία περόνια.
Κι εκείνος, ο παράνομος, βαρεί και φκιάνει πέντε.
– Εσύ, φαραέ μ', που τάφκιασες, πρέπει να μας διατάξεις.
– Βάλτε τα δυο στα πόδια του, τ' άλλα τα δυο στας χείρας.
Το πέμπτο το φαρμακερό βάλτε το στην καρδιά του,
να τρέξει αίμα και νερό να λιγωθεί η ψυχή του.

This song is one from the category of songs called *kalanda* and is sung by groups of children going from house to house on Good Friday.

Today the sky above is black

Today the sky above is black; today is a black day.
Today all people grieve and weep and the mountains all take pity.
Today the scribes and Pharisees have rendered a decision,
To crucify Jesus Christ, they will take him to the king.
And the Lord wished to enter and stay awhile in a garden,
To fall into a holy sleep so then they could arrest him.
Like a thief they captured him and like a murderer take him,
And there at the court of Pilate they torture and torment him.
And our Lady, the Virgin Mary, sat by herself alone,
Praying aloud and weeping for her only begotten son.
Then from the heavens came a voice, from the mouth of the archangel,
– My Lady, your prayers count for nothing, your kneeling is for nought.
For they have captured your poor son and to the coppersmith they take him.
– O coppersmith, make the nails, make three piercing prongs.
And that scoundrel strikes hard the iron and makes not three but five.
– You, master, who have made the nails, you must now instruct us.
– Put two of them in his feet and another two in his hands.
The fifth, the deadliest of all, strike deep into his heart,
So blood and water may flow down and his soul waste away.

Κάτω στα Ιεροσόλυμα

Κάτω στα Ιεροσόλυμα, κάτω στον Άγιο Τάφο,
εκεί δέντρο δεν ήτανε και δέντρο εφυτρώθη.
Το δέντρο ήταν ο Χριστός κι η ρίζα η Παναγία,
κι αυτά τα μικροκλώναρα ήταν οι μαθηταί του,
που μαρτυρούσαν κι έλεγαν τα πάθη του Σωτήρος.

A song from the *kalanda* group of songs sung on Good Friday. Easter was and is the major holy day of the Greeks. Although in recent years Christmas has begun to be observed in a more contemporary fashion with trees and a Santa Claus-morphed St. Basil (the traditional New Year's Day gift bearer), for the Greeks it still does not command the religious and traditional significance of Easter. Spring in Greece is truly an act of resurrection and it is no wonder that both the ancient and modern Greeks would focus their religious and cultural energies on this glorious season.

Growing up in Harrisburg, Pennsylvania in the late Thirties and Forties, I knew nothing about spring in Greece, but the importance of Easter was nonetheless real and immediate. Easter was certainly a far more important and emotional event for us as a family than Christmas. While distant from the land of our parents, we observed the age-old rituals and customs of this holy season with dedication and intensity, perhaps even more intensely than in the land where they originated. We knew the holiday as *Lampri*, the Day of Brightness, although it was also more formally called *Pascha*. New clothes were bought for the entire family. Shopping had to be done at the only Italian grocery store in town for olives, olive oil, and feta cheese, which the grocer stocked for his Greek customers. The house was cleaned from top to bottom. My mother would begin weeks ahead to prepare laboriously and skillfully the many individual thin sheets of *phyllo* (unavailable in grocery stores at that time) for the *pites* and other sweets she would be making. Meanwhile, we observed the Lenten period of abstinence as best we could, staying away from eggs, milk and meat, as prescribed. It was difficult, however, especially after we had begun to eat our lunch at the school cafeteria. We certainly abstained on Wednesdays and Fridays and all during Holy Week with nothing to eat on Good Friday except lentils or greens cooked in water (no olive oil) and bread. Our one treat during this time was halva, which in those days we could only buy at the local Jewish delicatessen.

The church calendar was arranged in such a way as to build a momentum during the period of Lent, culminating in the drama of Holy Week. Thus, the Salutations to the Virgin were chanted every Friday evening during Lent, praising Her, while prefiguring Her Son's salvific role. Then came Holy Week itself with special services every night, which in effect were like acts in a passion play leading up to the explosion of light and joy at the midnight Easter service. We attended all of these services faithfully to their completion and in growing anticipation. On Holy Wednesday was the rite of the Holy Chrismation when the priest would anoint our hands and cheeks with holy oil. Holy Thursday involved the reading of the twelve gospel versions of the trial and the enactment of the crucifixion, and on Holy Friday three beautiful but lengthy lamentations sung around a symbolic bier enclosed in flowers. Beginning at 10:30 Saturday night, the final Easter service would last for hours, as would the services of the preceding days. We usually would not get home from church Easter morning until about 4 AM, carrying and shielding our lighted candles on the bus, much to the perplexity of the bus driver and our few fellow riders.

Down at Jerusalem

Down at Jerusalem, down at the Holy Sepulcher,
There no tree could be found and yet a tree did grow there.
The tree was our Lord Jesus Christ and the root the Virgin Mary,
And all the small branches were his twelve disciples,
Who bore witness to the truth and spoke of the Savior's passion.

What no doubt added to the perplexity was the fact that our Easter rarely coincided with that of the "Americans," so no one had any idea of what we were about at that early hour. Soon as we reached home, my father would draw a cross with the lighted candle on the door sill as we entered to bless and protect the house and family for the coming year.

For the past week we had been totally engrossed as a family in the services and preparations leading to the great holiday. It was as if we had been living not so much outside the present but concurrent with the present in another world, a religious world that seemed as real and as immediate as the present and was experienced in a dimly understood but intuited beautiful language. Our life had been church every night, observing and participating in the unfolding drama of the Lord's passion. We still had to go to school, of course, but our attention was elsewhere. Now, back home after a long church service we would begin to re-enter the secular present. Although we had taken communion Holy Saturday morning at what was called The First Resurrection Service, it was still expected that we continue to abstain from meat and eggs until after The Second Resurrection, as it was called, at midnight. Thus, the first step was to end the Lenten abstinence. This in turn would initiate a series of feasts throughout the day, celebrating and confirming our re-entry into the everyday world.

The opening act centered on partaking of the delights of *mageiritsa*, a soup embellished with a delicious and frothy mixture of beaten eggs and lemon juice poured over finely cut boiled pieces of lamb's heart, liver, kidneys and intestines (eventually my mother stopped adding the intestines because it was so difficult and time-consuming to clean them). Although it may not sound appealing, it is a most delicious soup, especially if you're hungry at 4 o'clock Easter morning and have not had any meat for at least a week, if not the full forty days of Lent. In fact, both the meat and the eggs seemed to have a more intense taste on Easter after a week or so of abstinence and this was certainly one of the gratifying rewards of the season. My father had ordered the spring lamb from the Pennsylvania Dutch butcher in the local farmer's market and it had been specially fed to assure its tastiness. (The farmer always knew when we were celebrating Easter because my father would buy one from him every year.) Along with the *mageiritsa* would be *spanakopita* and *tiropita* and *tsoureki* (spinach pie, cheese pie and sweet bread respectively).

Punctuating these matinal festivities would be the gamelike custom of cracking each other's eggs to the joyous and affirming ritual salutation of "*Christos Anesti-Alithos Anesti*; Christ is Risen-Truly He is Risen." As tradition prescribed, my mother had hardboiled and dyed them on Holy Thursday afternoon. They were always and only red, symbolizing the blood of Christ and the joy of His resurrection. After our early morning repast, then, to bed for a short snooze.

By mid-morning up again and my mother (in time with the active help of my sister) would prepare for the next major repast, which usually took place around 2 o'clock. My father always insisted on having guests for Easter. He made a point of inviting anybody we might encounter at church the night before, who was from out of town and a stranger with no place to go. Sometimes this annoyed us children because we never knew who might be eating with us. My father, however, would say that he knew what it was like to be a stranger alone on Easter and that we would understand someday, if we ever found ourselves in the same position. (Many years later I remembered his words after church one cold Easter night alone in a strange city.) Of course, we also had relatives along with friends as guests and the house was usually full. The meal was truly gargantuan with the centerpiece being, of course, the lamb. Although tradition called for it to be skewered, we were not able to carry out this operation either because of lack of equipment or because of bad weather. So, my mother always roasted it in the oven surrounded by crisp, succulent brown potatoes. Then, there was the fresh, mixed salad of tomatoes, lettuce, scallions, green peppers, laced sparingly with oregano, olive oil and vinegar. Black olives and feta cheese were never ingredients of the salad but savored separately along with sliced pickles, sardines and Roquefort cheese, my father's favorite. There were boiled dandelion greens, enhanced by olive oil and a dash of lemon. There were *keftedakia*, perfectly rounded meatballs of ground beef lightly spiced with fresh dill. There were *dolmadakia*, rice wrapped in grape leaves. There were the spinach and cheese pies from the earlier matinal meal along with the *tsoureki*, sweet bread, as well as regular homemade bread. There was wine and beer and we children were permitted a sip when the various toasts were made to health and good fortune. The red eggs were prominently displayed and were solemnly, if not playfully, cracked at the beginning of the meal after the Easter hymn had been sung and we crossed ourselves and kissed one another. The table was set beforehand with all of the above and the meal was enjoyed with animated talk and singing, especially if my father's friends from Kephalonia were present and would begin singing *kantades*, four-part barbershop-like songs. We also had phonograph records of Greek folk music, which were being played all the while and to which we would dance before and after the meal. The feast would culminate in the sweets which along with coffee (Greek or American, as desired) would mark the end of the meal. There was fruit like fresh oranges and apples as well as the sweets (*ta glyka*). These included *baklava, galaktoboureko* (custard pie), *galaktopita* (a sweet semolina pie) and *koulourakia*, my favorite which was a cookie flavored with masticha (whenever available), the unique sweet-flavoring resin from Chios. Sometimes there was also rice pudding sprinkled with cinammon but always thick yoghurt with honey. The latter was made at home, as it was not available in Harrisburg or perhaps anywhere else in the United States at that time except in the neighborhoods of large cities with immigrants from the Balkans or the Middle East.

Needless to say, we were more than satiated by this time but we usually still had the energy to dance, sing and talk some more, which we did. Later on in the evening we would again sit around the table, more to nibble than to eat, but the food was there for anyone who wished to indulge. At this time, as we picked through the leftovers from the lamb, the shiplike shoulderblade might be cleaned off and scrutinized carefully by anyone present who possessed or claimed to possess the skill of reading the future in the manner of the coffee-cup method. No one took the readings seriously, but with their usually fanciful predictions they added to the merriment of the occasion. My mother had spent weeks preparing everything by herself and now with our help and with that of guests, who were relatives or particularly close friends, she would clean up; this task usually didn't finish until almost midnight. It had been a long and happy day, but one which she and the rest of us would look forward to repeating again the coming year and one which would become a lasting part of the family's memory of the all-embracing and unforgettable joys of Greek Easter.

My mother remembers the Easter of 1913. She was five years old and the family had come down to winter pastures at a place called Romia on the Arta plain. Nearby was the town of Louro, which had been liberated from the Turks in the winter of 1912 during the First Balkan War. The town along with its church had been burned down during the fighting. Together with the few remaining townspeople, the sheep-herding families from my mother's village gathered canes and ferns to build a temporary church where they could celebrate the holy feast of Easter. An old priest dressed in worn and tattered vestments led the devout congregation through the solemnities of Holy Week into the joy of the midnight Easter service, a joy which was made more intense by the departure of the centuries-old oppressors, despite the destruction and poverty. My mother also recalls holding her Easter taper very carefully lest she inadvertently set fire to the ferns with which the walls of the "church" were constructed and which were beginning to dry out. She also remembered a cheese-maker from Corfu, who had lost his only son during the war and who distributed eggs dyed in black, rather than the traditional red.

Της Αγάπης
Songs of Love

Dimitrios and Vasiliki Scotes as newlyweds,
photographed in Theodoriana before setting out for the US.

Μπείτε κορίτσια στο χορό

Μπείτε κορίτσια στο χορό να μάθετε τραγούδια
Να δείτε και να μάθετε πώς πιάνεται η αγάπη.
Από τα μάτια πιάνεται, στα χείλη κατεβαίνει.
Από τα χείλη στην καρδιά και στην καρδιά ριζώνει.

This is an old love song and dance known in other regions of Greece. Dancing was among the favorite pastimes in the village and indulged in whenever the opportunity presented itself. Baptisms, weddings, major feastdays like Christmas and especially Easter and the Virgin's Dormition on August 15, saints' feast day parties (usually that of the male head of the family; birthdays were not observed), arrival and farewell parties, spontaneous after work celebrations like after harvesting and threshing and sometimes simply when the spirit moved them and they had what was called *kefi*, a Turco-Arabic word meaning among other things a mood for good company and a good time.

There were two major dances, the *tsamikos* and the *syrtos*. Both were open ended circle dances. The *tsamikos* was named after a region in northwestern Epirus and was danced in three-quarter time with three steps forward and two back in a slow and serious manner. The leader was expected to execute *figoures* or fancy steps and leaps of his own making but always in rhythm; the dance would culminate in a solo performance by the leader in what was called *ston topo* or in place when the line of dancers would stop and the leader would then in effect put on a final show accompanied and inspired by the musicians, who would also be inspired by the dancer, if he was good. It was the dance of choice of

Ποιος έλατος κρατάει δροσιά;

Ποιος έλατος κρατάει δροσιά και ποια κορφή το χιόνι;
[Πες το, πουλί κι αηδόνι.]
Και ποια κόρη ράβει τα προικιά χωρίς να 'χει βελόνι;
[Πες το, πουλί κι αηδόνι.]
Και ποια μαννούλα γέννησε και δεν την πιάσαν πόνοι;
[Πες το, πουλί κι αηδόνι.]
Ποιος έχει αγάπη στην καρδιά και δεν την φανερώνει;
[Πες το, πουλί κι αηδόνι.]
Μα, χρόνια και αν περάσουνε, η αγάπη δεν παλιώνει.
[Πες το, πουλί κι αηδόνι.]

This love song is sung in Epirus as well as in Macedonia and elsewhere.

How to capture love

Get up and join the dance, my girls, and learn how to sing some songs.
To see and learn how love is caught, how love is caught and captured.
At first it's captured by the eyes and then goes down to the lips
And from the lips into the heart and in the heart puts down roots.

the klephts and was in my mother's time considered primarily a man's dance, although women also danced it but in a more reserved and restrained manner.

The other dance form was the *syrtos* or dragging dance, consisting of nine steps forward and three back. The rhythm varied and in some songs could be faster and in others slower. Both men and women danced the *syrtos* with the leader also performing individual steps but not in the flamboyant style of the *tsamikos*. There was also a third style of dance called *stratos* or marching dance of two steps forward and two back. This was also danced by both men and women and was the type employed at the big village festival or *panegyri*. There was no type of couple dancing as might be found in Greek island dancing nor was there any European dancing.

My sister and I learned the traditional dances from my mother when we were still very young and later joined other children of Greek immigrants at church gatherings, which were our main social affairs. At these events we also learned and enjoyed dances from other regions of Greece, including the *ballos* from the Aegean Islands, the *pentozali* from Crete, the *zebekikos* and *tsiftetelis* from Asia Minor and the *chasapikos* or butcher's dance from northern Greece.

What fir tree can hold fast the dew?

What fir tree can hold fast the dew and which mountain peak the snow?
[Tell it, O bird and nightingale.]
And what girl without a needle has ever sewn her dowry?
[Tell it, O bird and nightingale.]
And what mother has given birth and pain has not beset her?
[Tell it, O bird and nightingale.]
Who has a love deep in his heart and does not wish to show it?
[Tell it, O bird and nightingale.]
Even though many years go by, love never ages or grows old.
[Tell it, O bird and nightingale.]

Για νύχτωσε και βράδιασε

Για νύχτωσε και βράδιασε, και ο ξένος πού θα μείνει;
Να μείνει πάνω σε βουνό, φοβάται από τα χιόνια.
Να μείνει σε ακροθαλασσιά, φοβάται από το κύμα.
Τότε, μια κόρη βγήκε κι έστρωσε μέσα σε περιβόλι,
ανάμεσα σε δυο μηλιές και τρεις νερατζοπούλες.
Και πέφταν τ' άνθη πάνω του και τον αποκοιμίσαν.

Στης μαντζουράνας τον ανθό

Στης μαντζουράνας τον ανθό έγειρα να κοιμηθώ.
Δεν μπόρεσα, δεν πλάγιασα, τον ύπνο δεν εχόρτασα.
Δε μ' άφησαν τα κλάματα, της Βάσως τα αγκαλιάσματα.

This is a very old love song sung and danced in Epirus to the *tsamikos* rhythm. It is sung in other parts of Greece and was known among the Greeks of Asia Minor, but to other music.

The flower in the song, the *mantzourana*, is identified as the marigold in my mother's region. In other parts of Greece it is the marjoram, of which the name in Greek is actually a version of the English. Vaso is a form of the name Vasiliki, which could also more classically be transliterated into English as Basilike, meaning royal or queenly. Because of its

Night has fallen

Dusk has fallen and night has come and where will the stranger stay?
To stay up on the mountainside he has a fear of snows.
To stay along the seashore's edge he also fears the waves.
A girl then came out and in a nearby orchard made a bed,
Among two blooming apple trees and three trees of bitter orange.
And the blossoms fell upon him and they sent him off to sleep.

Where the marigold was in flower

Where the marigold was in flower I lay down to take a rest.
I was not able nor could I lie there; I could not get my fill of sleep
Because Vaso's crying didn't let me, neither did her embraces.

connotations, this name is often used in folk songs generically, even when the name of the girl is known to be different. This practice is analogous to calling the heroine in a fairy tale, "the princess." The name was popular in Epirus and is my mother's name. It is also employed in the form, Vasilo. Greek feminine names usually end in an alpha or an eta (pronounced in modern Greek as "ee") but can end in an omega as in Sappho, Calypso and Clio. This ending is often also employed to show endearment or familiarity, thus Maro for Maria and Lenio for Eleni or Helen.

Βασιλικός θα γίνω

Βασιλικός θα γίνω στο παραθύρι σου.
Κι ανύπαντρος θα μείνω για το χατίρι σου.
Το φεγγάρι κάνει βόλτα στης αγάπης μου την πόρτα.
Το φεγγάρι κάνει κύκλο στης αγάπης μου τον κήπο.

A love song from Epirus. Basil is one of the plants often found potted on window sills in Greece and in fact in many parts of the country it was always used for that purpose and not for cooking. My mother had basil as well as marigolds, another traditional flower, always growing in pots or in her garden in America, her new home. It was and still is employed in churches for decorating icons or as small bunches for the sprinkling of holy water.
Basilikos in Greek means royal. The folk story tells of Empress Helena's (mother of the Emperor Constantine, who recognized Christianity in 323) search for the True Cross in

Περιβόλι μ' οργωμένο

Περιβόλι μ' οργωμένο, μαργαριταροσπαρμένο,
γύρω γύρω έχεις αλτάνες και στη μέση μαντζουράνες.
Έχεις και μια μηλιά στη μέση που βεργολογάει να πέσει.
Πάει ο νιος να κόψει μήλο και μαράθηκε το φύλλο.
– Φύγε, νιε, μην κόβεις μήλο και μαραίνεται το φύλλο.
Τα 'χει ο αφέντης μετρημένα και η κυρά λογαριασμένα.

This is an old love song and danced to the *tsamikos* rhythm with variants known throughout Greece. It tells the story of doting parents who wish to be sure of the intentions of the young man in question.

I shall become a sweet basil

I shall become sweet basil upon your window sill.

I shall remain unmarried for your sake alone.

The bright moon is taking a turn by the door of my own dear love.

The bright moon is making a round in the garden of my own dear love.

Jerusalem. At first she was unsuccessful and prepared to leave in despair after many weeks of searching. On the night before her departure, an angel appeared in her dream and told her to dig where she would see a sign. Upon awakening, she smelled the aroma of the basil and dug there finding three crosses. Not knowing which cross was the cross of Jesus she ordered that a sick man be placed on each until he was miraculously cured on the third attempt and the True Cross identified. From then on, the plant was called *basilikos* or the royal plant.

My well-plowed orchard

O my orchard, well-plowed and tilled, sown with daisies everwhere.

All around are beds of flowers in the middle marigolds.

An apple tree also stands there with branches full about to fall.

A youth went to pluck an apple and a leaf dried up and withered.

– Go away, young man, don't pluck an apple as all the leaves will wither.

The master's numbered all the apples and the mistress has them counted.

Μάννα μ', στα περιβόλια μας

Μάννα μ', στα περιβόλια μας και στις αμυγδαλιές μας
πήγα να μάσω μύγδαλα, πήγα να κόψω τ' άνθη.
Και 'κει καθόνταν τρεις αετοί και τρεις καλοί λεβέντες.
Ο ένας με μήλο με βαρεί, ο άλλος με δαχτυλίδι,
και ο τρίτος, ομορφότερος, μ' ένα χρυσό γαϊτάνι.
Εγώ το μήλο το 'φαγα, το δαχτυλίδι το 'χω,
και αυτό το χρυσογάιτανο, πλεξίδι στα μαλλιά μου.

This is my mother's variant of a well-known old love song.

Λουλουδάκι μου γαλάζιο

Λουλουδάκι μου γαλάζιο, λουλουδάκι μου γαλάζιο.
Πού να πάω να σε φυτέψω, για να σ' έχω να σε γλέπω;
Στα βουνά φυσάει αέρας και στους κάμπους καματώνεις.
Θα σε κάνω κυπαρίσσι, μαρμαρένια κρύα βρύση,
να 'ρχονται όμορφες να πλένουν, μαυρομάτες να λευκαίνουν.
Ήρθε μία, ήρθε άλλη, ήρθε το φτωχό κορίτσι.
Έλαμψ' ο γιαλός κι η βρύση κι η κορφή απ' το κυπαρίσσι.

This love song was sung by my mother's paternal grandmother.

Μωρή κοντούλα λεμονιά

Μωρή κοντούλα λεμονιά με τα πολλά λεμόνια,
[Βισσανιώτισσα και συ Δελβινακιώτισσα.]
Σε φίλησα κι αρρώστησα, μωρή κακιά γειτόνισσα.
Χαμήλωσε τους κλώνους σου να πάρω δυο λεμόνια.
[Βισσανιώτισσα και συ Δελβινακιώτισσα.]
Σε φίλησα κι αρρώστησα και τον γιατρό εφώναξα.

A well-known love song from Epirus where the towns of Vissani and Delvinaki are located.

To our orchards

Mother dear, to our orchards and to our almond trees
I went to gather almonds; I went to cut the flowers.
Sitting there were three eagles, three good and handsome men.
The first gave me an apple; the other gave me a ring,
And the third, the most good-looking, gave me a braid of gold.
The apple I have eaten; the ring I still possess,
And that braid, which is made of gold, is now woven in my hair.

My little blue flower

My dear little flower, of blue; O my flower, dear and blue.
Where can I go to plant you, to keep you so I can see you?
In the mountains blows the wind and on the plains you will weaken.
I shall make of you a cypress, a cold spring hewn from marble,
So pretty girls can do their wash, black-eyed girls can whiten clothes.
One girl came and then another and a poor girl also came.
The seashore glowed as did the fountain and the high crest of the cypress.

O you small little lemon tree

O you small little lemon tree, loaded with many lemons.
[O girl from Vissani and girl from Delvinaki.]
I kissed you and I got sick, O you naughty neighbor woman.
Please, lower down your branches that I may take two lemons.
[O girl from Vissani and girl from Delvinaki.]
I kissed you and I got sick and I called for the doctor.

Λουλούδι της Μονεμβασιάς

Λουλούδι της Μονεμβασιάς και κάστρο της Λαμίας.
Και Παλαμίδι τ' Αναπλιού, άνοιξε να μπω μέσα
να δω τις Αναπλιώτισσες, τις Αναπλιωτοπούλες,
που πλένουν και λευκαίνουνε και λούζουν τα μαλλιά τους,
και μοσχοσαπουνίζουν.

This is a well-known love song. Monemvasia is a fortified town in the southernmost part of the Peloponnese. Lamia is in central Greece and the Palamidi is a fortress overlooking the town of Nafplio or Anaplio, as it was called during the Ottoman period, in the north-eastern part of the Peloponnese. Nafplio was the first capital of the newly independent

Απόψε δεν κοιμήθηκα

Απόψε δεν κοιμήθηκα και σήμερα νυστάζω
γιατί κουβέντιασα πολύ με την παλιά μου αγάπη.
Καινούργια αγάπη και παλιά με βάλανε στη μέση.
Γυρνώ κοιτάζω την παλιά, καινούργια δε μ' αρέσει.

This love song is sung throughout Greece.

Από μικρή σ' αγάπησα

Από μικρή σ' αγάπησα, μεγάλη δε σε πήρα.
Έχω ελπίδα στο Θεό για να σε πάρω χήρα.
Βασιλικός πλατύφυλλος με τα σαράντα φύλλα,
σαράντα σ' αγαπήσανε κι εγώ πάλι σε πήρα.

A love song from Epirus.

Flower of Monemvasia

O flower of Monemvasia, and castle of Lamia.
And Palamidi of Nafplio, open up and let me enter
To see the girls of Nafplio, Nafplio's young girls,
Who are washing and are bleaching and shampooing their long hair,
And bathing with scented soap.

Greek state in 1828 and for a short time the scene of many festivities, particularly after the arrival of the young King Otho and his wife Amalia, whose presence no doubt affected the tone of the parties and the toilette of the ladies.

Last night I did not sleep

Last night I did not sleep and so today I'm drowsy
Because I chatted on too long with my love of old.
My new love and my old have put me in the middle.
I turn to look at my love of old, for the new one does not please me.

O basil plant

I loved you from when you were a child; I did not marry you when grown.
I hope to God I can marry you, now that you've been widowed.
O basil plant with your broad leaves with leaves that number forty,
Forty men fell in love with you but I'm the one who took you.

Μια πέρδικα καθότανε

Μια πέρδικα καθότανε σ' ανατολή και δύση.
Γυαλί κρατεί στα χέρια της, τα κάλλη της κοιτάζει.
Κι έχει τα νύχια κόκκινα και τα φτερά βαμμένα,
και το κορμί της λυγερό, λυγερό σαν κυπαρίσσι.
Και με το νου της έλεγε και με το λογικό της,
– Να 'ξερα ποιος θα σε χαρεί και ποιος θα σ' αγαπήσει.

Birds figure prominently in Greek folk songs where the partridge, turtledove and the duck
are metaphors for women and the eagle and the hawk for men. Swallows, nightingales and
cuckoos also appear frequently as messengers and warners. In Greek the same word is
used for the nails of humans as well as the talons and claws of birds and carnivorous animals. The cypress tree, omnipresent on Greek landscapes, is also a widely used metaphor

Η πέρδικα και ο κυνηγός

Μια πέρδικα καθότανε σ' ανατολή και δύση.
Πώς δεν την είδε ο κυνηγός για να την ντουφεκίσει;
Πάει η πέρδικα να πιει νερό και πιάστηκε στα δίχτυα,
στα δίχτυα τα μεταξωτά κι απ' τα κόκκινά της νύχια.
Και ο κυνηγός την έπιασε και σε κλουβί την βάζει,
να κελαηδεί κάθε πρωί, πρωί να τον ξυπνάει.

Sitting alone, a partridge turned

Sitting alone, a partridge turned towards the east and towards the west.
She holds a mirror in her hands and looks upon her beauty.
She has nails that are red, and feathers of many hues,
Her body's slim and graceful like a slender cypress tree.
And she is saying to herself and in her mind is thinking,
–I wonder who will delight in you and who will come to love you.

for both men and women, as it is in Middle Eastern languages like Persian and Arabic. Mirrors were considered a luxury item. My mother did not see her likeness in a mirror until she was about five years old when her father's brother got married and the new bride was given a mirror as a wedding present. She in turn left it at her in-laws when she emigrated to the United States and my mother finally got to see what she looked like.

A partridge was just sitting there

A partridge was just sitting there facing east and facing west.
How come the hunter did not see her so he could aim and shoot her?
The partridge goes to drink some water and gets caught up in the nets,
In nets all made out of silk, caught by her scarlet talons.
And the hunter went and took her and put her in a cage,
To sing for him every morning, to wake him at the dawn.

Ένας αετός καθότανε

Ένας αετός καθότανε στον ήλιο και λιαζότανε.
Και τσίμπαγε τα νύχια του, τα νυχοπόδαρά του.
– Α, νύχια μου, α, νυχάκια μου και νυχοπόδαρά μου,
την πέρδικα που πιάσατε να μην την εχαλάσατε.
Θέλω να τη βάλω στο κλουβί, να κελαηδεί κάθε πρωί.

This is well-known song, which is danced throughout mainland Greece. The dance is called *tsamikos* and is performed to three-quarter time by dancers holding hands in an open circle. Traditionally considered a man's dance, it was the dance of choice of the klephts or mountain rebels during the Turkish occupation and was, one might say, a kind of war dance. The leader is expected to display intricate steps and leaps of his own devising always in rhythm and especially during the culmination of the song. At that point the line of dancers comes to a stop and the clarinetist or violinist backed by the other mu-

Επέρασα από το Ρόρορο

Επέρασ' απ' το Ρόρορο και απ' τις κρύες βρυσούλες.
[Νεράιδα μου γραμμένη, γιατί είσαι πικραμένη;]
Είδα νεράιδες πόπλεναν και λούζαν τα μαλλιά τους,
και ασπρίζαν σαν τα γάλατα και λάμπαν σαν τον ήλιο.
Να γίνομαν χρυσός αετός και πλουμιστός πετρίτης,
να χύμαγα, να άρπαγα την πρώτη τη νεράιδα.
[Νεράιδα μου γραμμένη, γιατί είσαι πικραμένη;]

My mother read these verses in a newspaper in 1936 and set them to an old melody she knew from the village. Rororo might refer to a spring in the Veligradi village outside Constantinople and famous for the coldness of its water.

An eagle in the sunlight

An eagle was sitting in the sun, sitting and sunning himself.
He was pecking at his talons, his little feet with talons.
– O talons, dear little talons, my little feet with talons,
The partridge, which you two have caught, for my sake do not harm her.
I wish to put her in a cage to warble every morning.

sicians will begin to take the melody into a riff-like improvisation. This is the time for the lead dancer to do his solo performance in what is called "in place" (*ston topo*). If the clarinetist is impressed by the dancing, the two will often be inspired by one another and improvise together, music and steps. This dance is not danced by the Greek islanders with the exception of those on Lefkas, which is in the Ionian and barely separated by a few yards from the mainland with the result that their customs and music are of the mainland.

Rororo

Today I passed by Rororo and by its cold-water springs.
[O fairy, with the pretty face why are you sad and bitter?]
There I saw some fairies bathing and washing their braids of hair.
They were so white, as white as milk, and were shining like the sun.
I wish I were a golden eagle, a many-colored rockhawk,
I'd swoop down on my wings and seize the queen of all the fairies.
[O fairy, with the pretty face, why are you sad and bitter?]

Εννέα χιλιάδες πρόβατα

Εννέα χιλιάδες πρόβατα κι εννέα χιλιάδες γίδια.
Εννέα αδέρφια ήμασταν, όλα από δυο χιλιάδες.
Οι τρεις πηγαίνουν για κλεψιά κι οι πέντε για την κόρη,
και μένει ο Γιάννος πιστικός με δέκαοχτώ χιλιάδες.
Φύλα, Γιάννο μου, τα πρόβατα, φύλα και τα ζυγούρια.
Κάτω στην κρυοβρύση μην πας να τα ποτίσεις,
και στα πλατάνια τα δασιά μην πας να τα σταλίσεις.
Εκεί νεράιδες πλένουνε και λούζουν τα μαλλιά τους,
και το χορό αρχίζουνε με το λαμπρό φεγγάρι.
Φυλάξου μη σε μαγέψουνε, μαζί τους να σε πάρουν.

A song from Epirus. The Greek word translated as fairy is *neraida*, a modern form of the ancient word nereid, the sea nymphs of Greek myth. The *neraides* still haunted until recently the remote glens, woods and streams of the Greek mountains, according to the stories of shepherds and villagers and were feared for their power to to cast spells, as this song relates.

Μια κόρη απ' τα Ζαγόρια

Μια κόρη απ' τα Ζαγόρια, μια Ζαγοριανή,
που αγαπάει τον κυρ-Γιαννάκη, τον ζωγραφιστή.
Όλη μέρα ζωγραφίζει στα σεράγια του,
και την Κυριακή ως το γιόμα πάει στην εκκλησιά.
Κι απ' την εκκλησιά γυρίζει, μπαίνει στον οντά,
την κυρά κρατεί στο γόνα και την 'ξετάζει.
– Θέλω ταίρι να σε κάνω, μαζί να ζήσουμε.

A love song from Epirus. Zagoria consists of a group of villages in central Epirus, which were quite prosperous during the late Ottoman period. For a long time, the villages enjoyed self-government and carried out active trade throughout the region and even farther afield into Europe. Many of the old merchant residences were decorated with painted figures and stylized landscapes on the walls of the reception rooms.

Nine thousand were the sheep

Nine thousand were the sheep and the goats nine thousand more.
Nine brothers were we all told, each one of us with two thousand.
Three of us went off on raids, and five went to fetch the girl,
While Giannis stayed behind to watch over the eighteen thousand.
Giannis, my dear, guard well the sheep; guard well the billy goats.
Don't take them down to drink at the cold water spring.
Don't take them to stand in the shade where the plane trees are like forests.
There the fairies bathe themselves, there they wash and do their hair,
And there they start up and dance when the moon is shining brightly.
Watch, they don't put a spell on you and take you away with them.

A young girl from Zagoria

A young girl from Zagoria, a Zagoria girl,
Is in love with master Giannis, the figure painter.
All day long he is painting, painting in his quarters,
And on Sunday until noon he takes himself to church.
And when he's back from church he goes straight off to her room
And puts the lady on his knee and asks of her some questions.
– I want to make of you my partner, so we can live together.

Της στρομπούλου

Στρομπούλου μου, στ' αλώνια σου κι έξω στα περιβόλια σου
καθόταν νιος κι ανύπανδρος κι ένας πρωτοπαλίκαρος.
Και τη στρομπούλου εξέταζε, χίλια φλουριά της έταζε,
– Για πες μου πού 'ναι η μάννα σου, πού είναι και ο πατέρας σου;
– Η μάννα μ' πάει στην εκκλησιά, ο πατέρας μου στα μαγαζιά,
τ' αδέρφια μου στη ξενιτιά κι εγώ είμαι στον αργαλειό.
Κι εγώ είμαι στον αργαλειό, μα τα ματάκια σου τα δυο!

A love song composed by my mother's father. "My little plump girl" is a term of affection for baby girls but was often applied to young girls of a certain physical tendency without hurting their feelings. It is doubtful if one could get away with it today. The word *protopalikaro*, which has been translated "brave and true," actually is a klepht term for the chief lieutenant of the klepht captain or *kapetanos*. In effect the *protopalikaro* was the latter's right hand man and occupied a position of honor. The word also came to be used in a negative way as a bully in the context of bandit or robber gangs. In this song the sense

Μια ωραία βοσκοπούλα

Μια ωραία βοσκοπούλα με ξανθά μαλλιά
έβοσκε τα πρόβατά της στην ακρογιαλιά.
– Καλημέρα βοσκοπούλα, βοσκοπούλα μου καλή,
πόθεν είσαι, τίνος είσαι, κι είσαι πάντα μοναχή;
– Από μάννα και πατέρα είμαι ορφανή.
Την πατρίδα μου δεν ξέρω, είμαι πάντα μοναχή.
– Ορφανή κι εσύ κυρά μου, ορφανός κι εγώ.
Τον παπά θα πάω να φέρω να σε στεφανωθώ.

A love song composed by my mother. The plight of orphans was never an easy one, as so many folk songs and stories from around the world attest. It was particularly difficult for orphan girls in the Greek villages, if they had no dowry and no family to protect their interests.

The little plump girl

O little girl so plump, out by your threshing floors and orchards
Sat a young and unmarried man, first among the brave and true.
He was quizzing the little plump girl, promising her a thousand florins,
– Tell me, where has your mother gone; where has your father gone as well?
– My mother has gone off to church; and to the shops my father,
My brothers are all abroad and I am sitting at my loom.
I am sitting at my loom; oh, those two eyes of yours, so dear!

is more of a young man, who is the first of the brave, handsome and rich lads of the village and whom the girl is obviously interested in and waiting for.
In the Greek, my mother made a distinction between *kapetanos* and *kapetanios* – the former referring to a klepht or bandit leader and the latter to a sea captain. Both forms derive from the medieval Italian and are sometimes used interchangeably, although the distinction appeared to be more common in the regions and songs of the klephts.

A pretty little shepherd girl

A pretty little shepherd girl with hair long and blonde
Was out grazing her flock of sheep by the seashore's edge.
– Good day to you, my shepherd girl, my good little shepherd girl,
Where are you from and who are your kin, and are you always alone?
– I have no mother, nor a father; I am an orphan child.
Of my homeland I know nothing; I have always been alone.
– You're an orphan, my dear lady; I, too, am an orphan child.
I will go and bring back a priest so I can have you crowned.

The Greek Orthodox wedding service culminates in a crowning ceremony. The expression by a man, "I will cause you to be crowned," *tha se stephanotho*, means "I will marry you." However, the expression "I will crown you," *tha se stephanoso*, means "I will be your best man," *koumparos*, and do the actual crowning during the ceremony.

Αγνάντευα κατακαμπής

Αγνάντευα κατακαμπής, κατακαμπής στον κάμπο,
κι είδα κομμάτι σύννεφο κι είδα κομμάτ' αντάρα.
Αυτό δεν είναι σύννεφο, ούτε κομμάτ' αντάρα,
είν' η Μαρία του παπά, που 'ρχεται απ' τ' αμπέλια.
Φέρνει μήλα στη ποδιά, κυδώνια στο μαντήλι.
Δυο μήλα της εγύρεψα, κι αυτή μου δίνει τρία.
– Δεν θέλω εγώ τα μήλα σου, δεν θέλω τα κυδώνια.
Θελώ τα δυο τα μάτια σου και τα γλυκά σου χείλη,
το λυγερό σου το κορμί που 'ναι σαν κυπαρίσσι.

Priests' daughters figure in many of the folk songs, reflecting their relatively high social standing and often better economic position, as suggested in this song.

Στης Λιβαδειάς στη ρεματιά

Στης Λιβαδειάς στη ρεματιά αντάμωσα μια λεβεντιά.
Ήταν κοπέλα λυγερή, στο χέρι βάσταγε σταμνί.
– Γειά σου, χαρά σου, λυγερή, που πας στο ρέμα μοναχή;
– Πάω στο ρέμα για νερό να βρω εκείνον π' αγαπώ.

This is a love song danced in the *tsamikos* rhythm.

The priest's daughter

I was looking down over the plains, the lowlands and the plains,
And I saw a bit of cloud there, a bit of greying fog.
But this is not a bit of cloud, nor is it a bit of fog,
It's the daughter of the priest, Maria, coming from the vinyards.
She brings apples in her apron and quinces in her kerchief.
Two apples did I ask of her and she up and gives me three.
– Oh, I do not want the apples and the quinces even less.
I only want those eyes of yours and those lips of yours so sweet,
I want your slender body, too, standing like a cypress.

At the ravine of Livadia

At the ravine of Livadia I met up with a stately sight.
She was a graceful, pretty girl and held a jug in her hand.
– Greetings, my dear graceful girl; where to, alone in the ravine?
– In the ravine I go for water and to find the one I love.

107

Σαν κίνησαν τρείς λυγερές

Σαν κίνησαν τρείς λυγερές και τρεις καλές νοικοκυρές
να παν απάνω σε βουνό, μάννα και θυγατέρες δυο,
να μάσουν τον αμάραντο και το μελισσοχόρταρο.
Και εκεί που το μαζεύανε και το εδηματιάζανε,
επείνασε η τρανύτερη και δίψασε η μικρότερη.
Και παν στη βρύση για νερό, τον λαβωμένον βρήκανε.
– Για βγάλτε τα μαντήλια σας να τον κεφαλοδέσουμε,
στο σπίτι να τον πάρουμε.
– Εμείς, κόρη μ', δεν έχουμε, τον ξένον τι τον θέλουμε;
– Μάννα μ', το μεραδάκι μου φτάνει σε με και κείνονε.

A love song that has many variants throughout Greece. In one variant it's her bed that
the girl says is enough for both of them.

Νύχτα ήταν που χορεύαμε

Νύχτα ήταν που χορεύαμε, νύχτα ποιος μας είδε;
Μας είδε τ' άστρι και ο ουρανός και το λαμπρό φεγγάρι.
Μας είδε το κλεφτόπουλο που αγαπάει την κόρη.

This is a love song, which my mother composed for her group of girl friends as they were
dancing by the moonlight on a threshing floor after they had finished the day's work.

Three lovely and graceful women

Three lovely and graceful women, good housekeepers were the three,
Started up to climb a mountain, a mother and her two daughters,
They went to gather amaranth and honeybee grass as well.
And there as they were gathering it and tying it up in sheaves,
The elder began to hunger, the younger began to thirst.
They went for water to the spring and found a wounded man there.
– Remove and untie your kerchiefs so we can bind up his head,
Then, let us take him home with us.
– Daughter, at home we haven't much, why do we want this stranger?
– Mother, my small dower portion is enough for me and him.

It was night while we were dancing

It was night while we were dancing; it was night and who could see us?
The evening star saw us, as did the sky, and also the moon so bright.
The klepht's young son saw us, too, the one who loves the unwed girl.

Η σταυραδερφή

Εψές, προψές επέρασα από τη γειτονιά σου,

[Σταυραδερφούλα μ', γειά σου.]

κι άκουσα πως σε μαλώνανε η μάννα σου κι η θειά σου.

[Σταυραδερφούλα μ', γειά σου.]

Κι αν σε μαλώνανε για με, να μην ξαναπεράσω.

[Σταυραδερφούλα μ', γειά σου.]

Να μην ξαναπεράσω από τη γειτονιά σου.

[Σταυραδερφούλα μ', γειά σου.]

The godsister addressed in this song is actually called in Greek a "cross-sister," but the former term seems the best way to convey at least the sense of the word into English. This word refers to the custom of a group of male friends formalizing and, indeed, sanctifying their ties of friendship in church with a special blessing of a priest and in the presence of a honored lady friend as a sort of patroness. She could be married or unmarried but of a good family and connected with at least one member of the group by blood or marriage.

My mother's mother served as a patroness for one such group of her husband's friends. She was called a cross-sister, because the oath of undying friendship was taken on a cross

The godsister

Last night and the night before I passed by your neighborhood,
[Farewell, little godsister.]
And heard your mother and your aunt scolding and berating you.
[Farewell, little godsister.]
If they were scolding you because of me, I won't pass by again.
[Farewell, little godsister.]
I won't pass by anymore, won't pass by your neighborhood.
[Farewell, little godsister.]

jointly by the group, including her. While not a canonical restriction, marriage was strongly discouraged between the cross-sister, if she was unmarrried, and a member of the group.The oath on the cross was deemed to have established a sacred bond between the parties similar to a blood tie of the second degree (between siblings) and should not be trangressed. Hence, the trouble that the two young people are apparently facing in this song. This restriction, however, with full canonical force was also applied to children of godparents; the son of a godfather, for example, could not marry the girl for whom his father had stood as sponsor at the baptismal font.

Γλυκοχαράζουν τα βουνά

Γλυκοχαράζουν τα βουνά και γλυκοφέγγ' η μέρα.
Παν τα πουλάκια στις βοσκές και οι όμορφες να πλύνουν.
Παίρνω κι εγώ τον γρίβα μου να πάω να τον ποτίσω.
Βρίσκω μια κόρη πόπληνε σε μαρμαρένια βρύση.
– Καλήμερά σου, κόρη μου. – Καλώς τονέ τον ξένο.
– Κόρη, δώσε μας νερό, να πιώ κι εγώ κι ο γρίβας.
Δώδεκα κούπες έβγαλε, στα μάτια δεν την είδα,
κι απάνω στις δεκατρείς την βλέπω δακρυσμένη.
Κι εγώ γυρνώ και τη ρωτώ, – Γιάτι 'σαι δακρυσμένη;
– Έχω άνδρα στην ξενιτιά εδώ και πέντε χρόνια,
κι ακόμα δυο τον καρτερώ και τρία τον περιμένω.
Κι αν δεν έρθει, δεν φανεί, καλόγρια θα γίνω.
– Κόρη μ', εγώ είμ' ο άνδρας σου, εγώ είμ' ο καλός σου.
– Αν είσαι συ ο άνδρας μου και πες να σε πιστέψω.
Πες τα σημάδια του σπιτιού και τότες να πιστέψω.
– Έχεις μηλιά στη πόρτα σου και κλήμα στην αυλή σου.
– Αυτά τα ξέρ' η γειτονιά, τα ξέρ' ο κόσμος όλος.
Πες μου σημάδια του κορμιού και τότες να πιστέψω.
– Έχεις ελιά στο μάγουλο, ελιά στην αμασχάλη.
– Εσύ είσαι ο άνδρας μου κι ο αγαπητικός μου!

Many husbands, sons and brothers stayed away in foreign lands, *xenitia*, for years on end, some never returning. Others left as young boys and young men, returning as unrecognizable old men. My father left at the age of ten to return at the the of forty and not be recognized, and then being dubbed Lazarus back from the dead.

The test

The mountains catch the dawn's sweet light, the day breaks with a sweet glow.
The birds go to their feeding grounds and fair maids to do their wash.
And I take my grey stallion and go to find him water.
I find a girl there washing clothes at a spring hewn out of marble.
– Here's a good day to you, my girl. – Welcome to you, O stranger.
– Dear girl, give us both some water, for me and my grey to drink.
She drew twelve cups out for me, but I didn't look into her eyes,
Yet, when she drew the thirteenth cup I see that she is weeping.
And so I turn and ask of her, – Why is it that you weep?
– My husband's off in foreign lands, for five years he is absent,
And for two more I've expected him and wait another three.
If he doesn't come back and show himself, I'll become a nun.
– I am your husband, my dear girl, the good man that you await.
– If you really are my husband, tell me something to believe you.
Tell me some signs about the house, so then I can believe you.
– You have an apple tree by your door, a grape vine in your courtyard.
– All the neighbors know of these things, everybody in the world.
Tell me of marks on my body, so then I can believe you.
– You have a beauty mark on your cheek and one beneath your arm.
– You really are my husband and the man who is my lover.

Το μαργιολικό

Για ιδέστε το μαργιολικό, τ' αναθηματισμένο,
που σέρνει το φεσάκι του σαν να 'ναι μεθυσμένο.
Μ' αυτό δεν είναι μέθυσμα, ούτε κρασί πιωμένο.
Η αγάπη το βαλάντωσε και είν' βαλαντωμένο,
και σέρνει το φεσάκι του σαν να 'ναι μεθυσμένο.
Σαράντα κίτρινα φλουριά σε μια κλωστή δεμένα
πάρ' τα, Μαρουσώ μ', μια βραδιά κι έλα κοντά σ' εμένα,
να σε γεμίσω με φιλιά, να σε χορτάσω αγάπη.

This love song is sung and danced to the *tsamikos* rhythm. It was one of the dances traditionally danced by the Evzones, the Presidential Guard. While the fez was worn
throughout the Middle East and came to be thought of as Muslim headwear (even the
name comes from the city of Fez in Morocco), in fact it originated among the Greeks.
Until 1826 the Turks and Muslims wore turbans and only adopted the fez as a compro-
mise in their first steps to modernization. Western headwear was unacceptable because

Καράβια παν τη θάλασσα

Καράβια παν τη θάλασσα και κόρη πάει την άκρη
με τα μαλάκια ξέπλεκα στις πλάτες της ριγμένα.
Καραβοκύρη φώναζε, καραβοκύρη λέει,
– Αυτόν τον νιο που 'χεις αυτού, να μην μου τον παιδεύεις.
Δώσ' τον δυο μήλα να κρατεί, να παίζει να γελάει,
και στα ταξίδια που γερνά εμένα να θυμάται.

A love song composed by my mother.

Παραπονιάρικό μου

Παραπονιάρικό μου, τι έχεις κι όλο κλαις;
Τι 'ν' το παράπονό σου σε μένα δεν το λες;
Έλα στην αγκαλιά μου και στα χάιδια μου,
Να βρεις τρελή αγάπη στα φυλλοκάρδια μου.

A love song composed by my mother.

The young fellow

Take a look at that young fellow, that poor, damn, unlucky kid,
Who drags about his little fez acting as though he's drunk.
Yet, this is not from drunkenness nor from drinking too much wine.
Love has really pained and hurt him and he is sad and hopeless,
So, he drags about his little fez acting as though he's drunk.
Take forty yellow florins, all tied and hanging on a thread,
My dear Marouso, take them and come to my side at night,
So I can fill you up with kisses, so I can sate you with my love.

the brims of the hats interfered with Muslim prayer. The Greek form of the fez was usually rather closefitting, round, of soft red wool material and with a long tassel. The Turkish form was also round but higher off the head and of a stiff or firm red material with a
short tassel. It was finally abolished in 1923 by Kemal Ataturk as one of his many steps
towards the further modernization of the Turks.

Ships go out upon the sea

Ships go out upon the sea and a girl goes along the shore
With her hair all unbraided, hanging loosely on her shoulders.
And she's calling to the skipper, to the skipper she is saying,
– That young man you've got there, for my sake do not mistreat him.
Give him two apples he can hold, so he can play and he can laugh,
And on the voyages where he roams, let him remember me.

The complainer

My dear little complainer, what's wrong and you cry so much?
What is your complaint and about it you don't tell me?
Come to my embrace and in my caresses,
You will find a wild love in the recesses of my heart.

Του Δήμου

Αυτά τα μάτια σου, Δήμο μ', τα όμορφα, τα φρύδια τα γραμμένα.

Αυτά με κάνουν κι αρρωστώ και πέφτω και πεθαίνω.

[Γειά σου, αγάπη μ', γειά σου, σε κλαίν' τα μάτια μου.]

Για πάρε, Δήμο μ', το ντουφέκι σου και βάλε τα άρματά σου.

Και πάρε δίπλα τα βουνά, δίπλα τα κορφοβούνια.

[Γειά σου, αγάπη μ', γειά σου, σε κλαίν' τα μάτια μου.]

Κι αν εύρεις 'λάφια σκότωσ' τα, κι αρκούδια μέρεψέ τα.

Κι αν εύρεις την αγάπη μου, ρίξε και σκότωσέ την.

[Γειά σου, αγάπη μ', γειά σου, σε κλαίν' τα μάτια μου.]

Και πάρε και το αίμα της σ' ένα ψιλό μαντήλι,

και πάρ' το και γκιζέρα το σ' όλα τα βιλαέτια.

Κι αν σε ρωτήσουν τι έχεις αυτού, το αίμα της αγάπης.

This is an old song sung in many parts of Greece. Dimos, a nickname for Dimitrios, occurs in many klepht songs and is not necessarily a specific person. Some variants have the girl asking Dimos to kill her directly because of her unrequited love for him. In my mother's version, she wants him to kill the love itself, if he can do it.

Dimos

O Dimos, those eyes of yours so beautiful, your eye-brows so well formed.

They make me sick and weak with love and I fall down and die.

[To your health, my love, your health; my eyes weep much for you.]

O Dimos, take down the musket that you own and arm yourself for hunting.

And go up along the mountains, to the mountain tops so high.

[To your health, my love, your health; my eyes weep much for you.]

If it's deer you find there, kill them and if bear, tame them all.

And should you find my love there, shoot and kill it with your musket.

[To your health, my love, your health; my eyes weep much for you].

Then, with a handkerchief so fine, soak up the blood that's fallen,

And, take it and wander with it, throughout all the provinces,

And if they ask what you have there, it is the blood of love.

Vilaetia in the penultimate line (translated as 'provinces') derives from the Turco-Arabic word *vilayet* which can mean province, state, or district and refers to the administrative units into which the Ottoman Empire was divided.

Ο Μανόλης

Ο Μανόλης κι ο Ντερβίσης κι ο Μενούς Αγάς
σε κρασοπωλείο καθόνταν, τρώγαν κι έπιναν.
'Κει που τρώγαν, 'κει που πίναν και κουβέντιαζαν.
Κάτι πέσαν στην κουβέντα για τις όμορφες.
– Του Μανόλη η γυναίκα είναι όμορφη.
– Πού την είδες και την ξέρεις και την 'μολογάς;
– Χθες την είδα στο πηγάδι πόπαιρνε νερό.
Και της έδωσα και το μαντήλι και μου το πλυνε.
– Σαν την είδες και την ξέρεις, πες μας τι φορεί.
– Κόκκινο μαντίλι είχε και κεντίτι πόδια,
και τριγύρω στα μαλλιά της κίτρινα φλωριά.
Ο Μανόλης μεθυσμένος, πάει τη σκότωσε.
Το πρωί σαν ξεμεθάει, πάει της μίλησε,
– Σήκω πάπια μ', σήκω χήνα μ', σήκω γαλανή,
σήκω, ντύσου και στολίσου κι έμπα στο χορό.
Να σε δουν τα παλικάρια να μαραίνονται,
να σε δω κι εγώ, ο καημένος, να σε χαίρομαι.

This is a well-known and old song from Epirus. The jealous and vengeful husband is a universal theme. In this song, however, the theme is further heightened by the shame and loss of face that a Christian Greek would have experienced, if his wife had willingly engaged in a socially unacceptable act with a Muslim Turk.

The handkerchief played a significant, symbolic role in the interaction between the sexes at that time and figures in much of the Greek folklore and customs of the period. To the jealous and drunk Greek husband the giving and the washing of the handkerchief no doubt initially implied an intimacy between the two parties, either consummated or about to happen. Of course, the poor girl may have been simply civil to a drinking friend of her husband's or so intimidated by the Turk that she went along with the request but no further.

The morning-after scene strongly implies that this was, indeed, the case and that the

Manolis

Once Manolis and the Dervish and Menous Agha
Were all sitting in a wine shop.
They were eating, drinking and conversing.
Something was said, as they conversed, about women and their beauty.
– Manolis' wife is beautiful, beautiful, indeed.
– Where did you see her that you know her and talk of her that way?
– Yesterday at the well I saw her, as she was drawing water,
And I even gave my handkerchief and she washed it for me.
– Since you saw her and you know her, tell us what she wears.
– She had a kerchief that was red and an apron all embroidered,
And round about her hair was a band of golden florins.
Manolis, who by then was drunk, went off and killed her.
In the morning no longer drunk, he went to speak to her,
– Get up, my duck; get up, my goose; get up, my dear blue eyes.
Get up, get dressed, deck out yourself and start up your dance.
So the young men can see you and all pine away;
So I can see you, too, poor me, and delight in you.

husband had tragically misread the situation. The word dervish, as used in the song, had
at that time two connotations. The original one referred to a Muslim holy man or hermit, who had renounced earthly pleasures and ways, or, if not a hermit, at least dedicated to a life of piety and prayer. The so-called Whirling Dervishes of Konya in Asia
Minor come to mind. Dervish, however, could also mean a handsome young blade, who
knew how to have a good time. This is the dervish featured in this song; he would not be
drinking wine and with a Christian, if he were heeding the strictures of Islam. Maybe
that's why the husband had his suspicions.
The other figure, Menous Agha, (agha was a high military and political rank among the
Turks) is also a Muslim breaking his religion's rule against drinking wine. Obviously this
Muslim rule was difficult to observe in a region where the making of and the appreciation for wine had been widespread for thousands of years before the arrival of Islam.

Η Μαρία, η Πενταγιώτισσα

Στα Σάλωνα σφάζουν αρνιά
[Μαρία Πενταγιώτισσα.]
και στο Χρυσό κριάρια.
[Μικρή δασκαλοπούλα.]
Και στης Μαριάς την ποδιά
[Μαρια Πενταγιώτισσα.]
σφάζονται παλικάρια.
[Μικρή δασκαλοπούλα.]

Salona (now called Amphissa) and Chryso are small towns in central Greece near Delphi. Maria Athanasopoulou was born in 1821 in the region of Phokis in east central Greece in the village of Pentagi (the Five Saints), hence her nickname, Pentagiotissa, woman from Pentagi. She was the daughter of a school teacher and had a brother named Athanasios or Thanasis. She was described as beautiful but apparently too headstrong and provocative for the time and place where she lived. She once appeared in church without the traditional headcovering of a white kerchief, causing shock and gossip.
She took a lover named Dimitris Tourkaki, or Little Turk. He was not a Turk, as some variants of the song deduced from the last name, but rather dark like a Turk. Her brother found out about the affair and Tourkaki killed him in an argument over the matter. He

Μωρέ σεβντά, παλιοσεβντά

Μωρέ σεβντά, παλιοσεβντά, πώς μ' έχεις καταντήσει;
[Το δόλιο.]
Είκοσιδυο χρονών παιδί, στα μαύρα μ' έχεις ντύσει.
[Το δόλιο.]
Χορτάριασε ο τάφος μου, έλα να βοτανίσεις.
[Το δόλιο.]
Να χύσεις μαύρα δάκρυα ίσως να μ' αναστήσεις.
[Το δόλιο.]

My mother heard this song of unrequited love being sung by a young man from northern Epirus, when she was about 16 years old.

Maria Pentagiotissa

At Salona they're slaughtering lambs
[Maria Pentagiotissa, Pentagiotissa.]
At Chryso it's rams they slay.
[You little teacher's daughter.]
And upon Maria's apron
[Maria Pentagiotissa, Pentagiotissa.]
Young men slaughter one another.
[You little teacher's daughter.]

then tried to hide the body but it was quickly found because of the smell from the decomposing corpse. He and Maria were both tried for murder in Amphissa. He was convicted and executed. She got off with only two years imprisonment because it was said the jury was smitten by her beauty.

She eventually married and died in 1885 in the village of Krokylio (also called Paleokatouno) near Arta. Several variants of the story have her actually involved in the murder of her brother because he had beaten her in anger over the affair. In these variants she also manages to escape with her lover from prison by seducing the prison guard. These variants are not true. This song is widely sung and to a beautiful melody.

My old dear love

O my dear love, my old dear love, what have you done to me?
[Poor fellow.]
A twenty-two year old boy, you have decked me out in black.
[Poor fellow.]
My grave is covered with wild grass, come and clear away the weeds.
[Poor fellow.]
Shed black tears over me and maybe you'll raise me from the dead.
[Poor fellow.]

Περιβολάκια μου

Εσείς περιβολάκια μου με τα όμορφα λουλούδια,
μην είδατε τον αρνητή, τον ψεύτη της αγάπης;
Όταν μ' εφίλη μου 'λεγε, – γλυκιά που 'ναι η αγάπη.
Και τώρα, μ' απαράτησε σαν καλαμιά στον κάμπο.
Θέλω να τον καταραστώ και πάλι μετανιώνω.
Τα χείλια που μ' εφίλησε, το φίδι να τα φάει.
Και το κορμί που μ' αγκάλιασε, βόλι να το βαρέσει.

An old love song of malediction.

O you orchards fair and pleasing

O you orchards fair and pleasing with your flowers of such beauty,
Have you seen the one who's spurned me, that liar who spoke to me of love?
When he would kiss me, he would tell me, – how sweet is love, O my darling.
Now he has gone off and left me like dried stubble in the fields.
I want so much to damn and curse him and then again I still regret it.
The lips with which he kissed me, may a serpent strike and bite them.
And the body, which embraced me, may a bullet strike and hit it.

Ο δυόσμος κι ο βασιλικός

Ο δυόσμος κι ο βασιλικός,
[Γαϊτάνι, γαϊτάνι,
γαϊτάνι, γαϊτανάκι.]
με πότισε φαρμάκι.

Αυτά μ' αποκοιμήσανε,
[Γαϊτάνι, γαϊτάνι,
γαϊτάνι, γαϊτανάκι.]
και μου 'φυγε η αγάπη.

Περνώ τα όρη ψάχνοντα,
[Γαϊτάνι, γαϊτάνι,
και τα βουνά ρωτώντα.]
με την καρδιά κρατώντα.

Μην είδαν την αγάπη μου,
[Γαϊτάνι, γαϊτάνι,
γαϊτάνι μου πλεγμένο.]
και χρυσοκεντημένο.

Γαϊτάνι, γαϊτανάκι,
με πότισε φαρμάκι.

This is a well-known song. It is danced in the *syrtos* rhythm, which is the most popular of the Greek folk dances. Mint and basil are not only used for cooking but are planted simply for decoration, particularly basil in pots. The braid in the song refers to the gold braid, which was an important part of the embroidery on the traditional dress of many regions of Greece. The word is also used for the maypole, which is a custom that was observed in Epirus and elsewhere.

The mint and the basil

It was the mint and the basil,
[Oh, the braid; oh, the braid.
Oh, the braid, the pretty braid.]
It caused me much bitterness.

The both of them put me to sleep,
[Oh, the braid; oh, the braid.
Oh, the braid, the pretty braid.]
And my love got up and left.

To the mountains I go and search,
[Oh, the braid; oh, the braid.
Asking the hills where she is.]
With my heart held so tightly.

Perhaps, they've seen the girl I love,
[Oh, the braid; oh, the braid.
Oh, the well-woven braid.]
Her braid with gold embroidered.

Oh, the braid; oh, the braid!
It caused me much bitterness.

Άσπρο γαρύφαλλο βαστώ

Άσπρο γαρύφαλλο βαστώ, βουλιόμαι να το βάψω.
Κι αν το πετύχω στη βαφή, πολλές καρδιές θα κάψω.
Θα κάψω νιες, θα κάψω νιους, θα κάψω παλικάρια.
Θα κάψω την αγάπη μου μέσα στα φυλλοκάρδια.

My mother composed this variant of a well-known love song when she was about 14 years old. She was dying wool to prepare for the weaving of a bed cover with an overshot pattern of stylized trees (the first such made in the village). Hitherto, such covers and other woven material had only been done in solid colors. The new pattern for my mother and for the village had been brought from a village in Thessaly executed on a small pillow cover. My mother's task was to translate the pattern into a larger size and work out how

Τρεις μέρες έχω να σε δω

Τρεις μέρες έχω να σε δω, Μήτρο μ', να σ' αντικρίσω.
Μη λάχει άλλη αγάπησες κατά την πέρα στάνη;
Πες το μάνιμάνι
να βρω ποτάμι να πνιγώ, γκρεμό να πάω να πέσω.

My mother's variant of an old love song. Mitros is a form of Dimitrios.

Θέλουν ν' ανθίσουν τα κλαδιά

Θέλουν ν' ανθίσουν τα κλαδιά, κι ο πάγος δεν τ' αφήνει.
Θέλω κι εγώ να σ' αρνηθώ, κι ο πόνος δεν μ' αφήνει.
Χαμήλωσε το φέσι σου και φέρ' το ως τα φρύδια,
να μη φανεί το φίλημα, που σ' έχω φιλημένη.
Σ' αφήνω την καληνυχτιά με την καρδιά καμένη.

The first two lines of this love song are a well-known formulaic beginning, which is found in love songs from other parts of Greece. The last three lines are my mother's father's development of the theme.

A white carnation

I hold an all-white carnation and I intend to dye it.
If with the dye I can succeed, I'll make many hearts burn with envy.
With envy I'll make young girls burn, young fellows and bold men, too.
With desire I'll make my true love burn in the depths of his heart.

it was done. She was successful on her first attempt. She went on to weave several more
bed covers like it for other women in the village who wanted this new pattern for their
dowry chests. She composed this song as she was assembling the brightly dyed wool in
her courtyard to the admiration of her family and friends.
Although the verb "to burn" is used in the Greek in the sense of burning with passion, it
can have other meanings depending on the context.

For three days I have not seen you

For three days I have not seen you, Mitros, to see you face to face.
Perhaps you love another girl at that sheepfold over there?
Tell me straight away the truth, so I can go and find a river
To throw myself in and drown, or find a cliff from which to fall.

The branches want to blossom

The branches all want to blossom but the frost will not let them.
I want to give you up and leave, but the pain will not let me.
Lower a bit your little fez and bring it to your eyebrows,
So that the kiss will not appear where I held and embraced you.
I leave you at night's best hours with a heart that's heavy.

Αυτό το αστέρι το λαμπρό

Αυτό το αστέρι το λαμπρό που πάει κοντά στην Πούλια,
αυτό μου φέγγει και έρχομαι, κόρη μου, στην αυλή σου.
Βρίσκω την πόρτα σφαλιστή, και τα κλειδιά παρμένα.
[Αχ, αλίμονο σε μένα.]
Σκυφτοφιλώ την κλειδωνιά, σκυφτοφιλώ την πόρτα.
[Βάστα, καρδιά μου, δυνατά.]
Και τη γειτόνισσα ρωτώ, πού είν' η κόρη π' αγαπώ;

The first two lines are a formulaic beginning, found in other love songs. The remaining lines are by my mother's father.

Για μια φορά που 'μουν πουλί

Για μια φορά που 'μουν πουλί μ' αγαπούσανε πολλοί,
αχ, και τώρα χελιδόνι, μ' αγαπάν και οι γειτόνοι.
Τώρα μου κόψαν τα φτερά,
[Βάστα, καρδιά μου, δυνατά.]
και πάνω περπατώντα την αγάπη μου γλεντώντα.
Και παίρνω το στρατί, στρατί το μονοπάτι.
[Βάσανα που 'χει η αγάπη.]
Το μονοπάτι μ' έβγαλε στην κόρη που μ' αγάπαγε.
Στης λυγερής την πόρτα, που μ' αγαπά οπώς και πρώτα,
βρίσκω την πόρτα σφαλιστή
[Κάμε καρδιά μου υπομονή.]
και τα κλειδιά παρμένα, αχ, αλίμονο σε μένα.

My mother's variant of her father's variant of an old love song.

That star so bright

That star so bright and gleaming, which goes near the Seven Sisters,
It brightly shines for me, my girl, so I can come into your courtyard.
I find the door is tightly closed and all the keys are taken.
[Oh, what bad luck this is for me!]
I bend low and kiss the door latch, I bend low and kiss the door.
[Be strong my heart, keep yourself strong.]
And I ask the neighbor woman, where is the girl I love?

One time when I was like a bird

Once only was I like a bird, and many then did love me,
But now, dear nightingale of mine, the neighbors love me as well.
For, now they've clipped and cut my wings,
[Be strong, O my heart, be strong.]
So I go about on foot, and revel much in my sweet love.
And I take off for the highroad, the highroad, then the footpath.
[What troubles love has to endure.]
The foot path at last has brought me to the girl, who's always loved me.
At the door of that graceful girl, who loves me as she did in the beginning,
I find the door is tightly closed
[Keep up your patience, O my heart.]
And all the keys are taken; what bad luck this is for me.

Κόρη που υφαίνεις στον αργαλειό

Κόρη, που υφαίνεις στον αργαλειό, μίλα μου μ' αγάπη με καλό.
Υφαίνεις τα μεταξωτά, καινούργια αγάπη και παλιά.
Αχ, υφαίνεις και ξυφαίνεις, την καρδούλα μου μαραίνεις.

A love song composed by my mother as she worked on the loom.
The theme of weaving and unraveling in Greek folklore obviously goes back to Homeric times and is also found in many other cultures.

Η Γκόλφω

– Πού ήσουν Γκόλφω κι άργησες; τα πρόβατα πού τ' άφησες;
Τ' αρνιά βελάζουν στο μαντρί, και η Γκόλφω άργησε να 'ρθεί.
– Ήμουν μάννα, καλή μου μάννα, απάνω στο Χελμό,
πήγα, καλή μου μάννα, τον Τάσο μου να βρω.
Τον Τάσο που με άφησε, άλλη βρήκε κι αγάπησε.

This is a song from a well-known Romeo and Juliette folk story. Golpho is a girl's name once popular among villagers and derives from the word meaning silver breast ornament, *engolpion*. Tasos is the diminutive for Anastasios. Mount Helmos is a mountain in the northern part of the Peloponnese.

Πέρασα απ' την πόρτα σου

Πέρασα απ' την πόρτα σου κι απ' την πορτοπούλα σου,
και είδα το χεράκι σου που έστρεφε τ' αδράχτι σου.
Δαχτυλίδι λάμπισε, και η καρδιά μου ράγισε.
Μη σε αρραβωνιάσανε, μη σε καταπιάσανε.

A love song composed by my mother's father.

O girl, who weaves upon the loom

O girl, who weaves upon the loom, speak to me gently and with love.
You are weaving robes of silk, a new love and one that's old.
Oh, you weave and then unravel; you are breaking my poor heart.

Golpho

– Where were you, Golpho, and you're late, where did you leave the sheep?
The lambs are bleating in the fold and Golpho was late in coming.
– I was high up on Mount Helmos, mother dear, on Mount Helmos,
I went there to find my Tasos, mother dear, to find Tasos.
Tasso who has gone and left me and found someone else to love.

I passed by your door

I passed by your front door and your back door too,
And I saw your little hand, as it turned your spindle.
A ring shone brightly there and my heart broke and shattered.
I hope they have not betrothed you, that someone else has not won you.

Μου 'πανε τα γιούλια

Μου 'πανε τα γιούλια πως δεν μ' αγαπάς,
κι αν δε μ' αγαπάς στο διάβολο να πας.
Πουλάκι που 'χα κι έχασα απ' την κακογνωμιά μου,
του 'χα το βράδυ συντροφιά και το πρωί κουβέντα.

This is a love song, composed by my mother, similar to a blues song.

Εσείς πουλιά πετούμενα

Εσείς πουλιά πετούμενα, πετάτε στον αέρα.
[Τα καημένα, τα παραπονεμένα.]
Κι εγώ η τρυγόνα, η ορφανή,
η τρυγόνα, η παινεμένη, η παραπονεμένη,
θα πάω να στήσω τη φωλιά στου πηγαδιού τα χείλη.
Παν τα κορίτσια για νερό κι έρχονται φιλημένα.
[Τα καημένα, τα παραπονεμένα.]

This a variant of a love song known in other regions of Greece, as rendered by my mother's father.
The turtledove can not fly as high as other birds and is often used to describe, metaphorically, a lonely person seeking companionship.

Της Χάιδως

Δεν μπορώ, Χάιδω μ', δεν μπορώ, κι εσύ θέλεις παιγνίδια.
Κι εγώ να παίξω δεν μπορώ, να παίξω να γελάσω.
Θέλεις στην κούνια βάλε με, θέλεις στη σαρμανίτσα,
και με το πόδι κούνα με και με τη ρόκα γνέσε.
Και με τη γλυκιά σου τη φωνή, πες μου γλυκό τραγούδι,
να μου περάσει ο καημός, να μου περάσει ο πόνος.

A love song composed by my mother's father. Chaido is a girl's name, which appears in the Alexandre Dumas novel, *The Count of Monte Christo*, as Haydee and could be translated as "my pet."

The violets told me

The violets have all told me that you no longer love me,
And if you no longer love me, I say to hell with you.
I had and lost a little bird because I was wrong-headed.
I had it by night for company, in the morning for conversation.

You birds on the wing

O you birds on the wing, you fly high in the air,
[Oh, the poor dears, hurt and heartbroken.]
While I, the turtledove, the lonely one,
The turtledove, who's praised, yet hurt and heartbroken,
I will go and build a nest on the edge of the well,
The girls go there for water, and return home with a kiss.
[Oh, the poor dears, hurt and heartbroken.]

I cannot, Chaido

I cannot, Chaido; I cannot and you want to play games.
I cannot play; I cannot; I cannot play or even laugh.
If you want, put me on a swing; if you want, in a cradle
And you can rock me with your foot, while spinning with your distaff.
And with the sweetness of your voice, sing to me a song that's sweet,
So that my sorrow will all pass, my pain pass away as well.

Ήθελα δένδρο να γίνω

Ήθελα δένδρο να γίνω, ίσα με το μπόι σου,
και από κάτω από το δένδρο αργαλειό θε να σου κάνω.
Θα σου φέρω τα μιτάρια, να υφαίνεις μαξιλάρια.
Θα σου φέρω και το χτένι, να υφαίνεις μεσημέρι.
Θα σου φέρω τη σαΐτα, να υφαίνεις μέρα νύχτα.
Να υφαίνεις, να ξυφαίνεις, παλικάρια να μαραίνεις.
Να υφαίνεις, να ξυφαίνεις, την καρδούλα μου μαραίνεις.

A love song composed by my mother's father.

Σαμιώτισσα

Σαμιώτισσα, Σαμιώτισσα, πότε θα πας στη Σάμο;
Ρόδα θα ρίξω στο γιαλό, Σαμιώτισσα, για να 'ρθω να σε πάρω.
Και μες στην βάρκα που θα μπεις χρυσά πανιά θα βάλω.
Μαλαματένια τα κουπιά, Σαμιώτισσα, για να 'ρθω να σε πάρω.
Σαμιώτισσα, Σαμιώτισσα, με τα γλυκά τα μάτια
έκανες την καρδούλα μου, Σαμιώτισσα, χιλιάδες δυο κομμάτια.

An old popular dance song known throughout all of Greece. Samos is an island in the Aegean lying off the coast of Asia Minor. It is relatively rich in agricultural land and famous for its wine since ancient times.

Ένας ασίκης

Ένας ασίκης διάβαινε στη μέση στο παζάρι.
Έλαμψε ο τόπος, έλαμψε και όλο το παζάρι.
Ώρα καλή, ασίκη μου, καλά να πας και να 'ρθεις,
και στο καλό σου γύρισμα απ' έδω πάλι να περάσεις.

This song was composed by my mother's father, based on a theme found in other songs. "Handsome young man" is a rough translation of the word *asikis*, which comes into Greek from the Arabic through Turkish and means lover. In Greek, however, it has acquired the sense as rendered in the English translation.

I wish I could become a tree

I wish I could become a tree equal to your reach and height,
And under and beneath the tree I would build a loom for you.
I shall bring a pair of heddles, so you can weave pillowcovers.
I shall bring for you the comb, so you can also weave at noon.
I shall bring for you the shuttle, so you can weave both day and night.
For you to weave and unravel and make young men waste away.
For you to weave and unravel; oh, you waste away my heart.

Samos girl

O Samos girl, O Samos girl, when will you go to Samos?
I will strew roses on the shore, O Samos girl, so I can come and take you.
And on the boat that you get in I will raise up sails of gold.
The oars will also be of gold, O Samos girl, so I can come and take you.
O Samos girl, O Samos girl, with your eyes that are so sweet
You have made my poor heart, O Samos girl, two thousand broken pieces.

A handsome young man

A handsome young man was passing through the midst of the bazaar.
At once the place began to glow, all aglow was the bazaar.
Good luck to you, my handsome young man, go and come back in good health,
And, then, upon your safe return pass this way by us once more.

Τσομπανάκος ήμουνα

Τσομπανάκος ήμουνα,
προβατάκια φύλαγα.
Δεν εφύλαγα πολλά,
καμιά πεντακοσαριά.
Καλαμούλα έκοψα,
φλογερούλα έκανα.
Δεν την λάλαιγα πολύ,
καμιά ώρα την αυγή.

The first four lines of this song are well-known throughout Greece. The last four lines were composed by my mother's father. The melody of this song was used as the call signal by the Greek public radio system.

Sheep and goat herding was a major occupation of the inhabitants of my mother's village, with some flocks numbering in the hundreds, but most around fifty or so. To be a *tselingas* or owner of a sizeable flock was a goal ardently pursued by the herders, and to be an *architselingas* with more than a thousand sheep conferred great status. The latter had the privilege of driving their flocks through the main street of Arta, capital of the prefecture, during the spring and fall migrations. My mother remembers being part of one such festive procession, in 1917, of the *architselingas* for whom her father then worked as a

Once I was a shepherd boy

Once I was a shepherd boy
And my sheep I guarded well.
I guarded not so many
Five-hundred as I could tell.
I cut me down a little reed,
And a little flute I made.
I did not play it very much,
An hour before the dawn could fade.

cheesemaker. The following year an epidemic struck the man's sheep and he lost most of them.

My mother also recalls how on another, similar occasion the icon of St. Modestos, the patron saint of domesticated livestock, was carried to the mountain pastures where the horses had been struck with sickness in the hope that the saint would intervene. It was to no avail, but the six horses owned by her father did survive. This apparently caused some envy on the part of a few of the villagers who took the horses off in the middle of the night and hid them in a narrow ravine where they were unable to extricate themselves. Luckily they were found the next day, but one of the horses had backed off the cliff–to its death.

Τα πήρανε τα πρόβατα

Τα πήρανε τα πρόβατα, τα πήρανε και πάνε,
και μας δεν μας ρωτάνε.
Και ο πιστικός αγνάντευε από ψηλή ραχούλα.
[Βλάχα τσελιγκοπούλα.]
Και τα βάλανε στη στρούγγα.
[Βλάχα τσελιγκοπούλα.]
Τ' αρμέξαν, τα ξαρμέξανε,
και τα βάλαν' στο στάλο.
Ν' αξήνεις να σε πάρω.

A love song and dance from Epirus, describing a common occurence in the lawless days of the eighteenth and nineteenth centuries in the mountain regions of Greece.

They've taken away the sheep

They've taken away the sheep; they've gone off with all of them,
And they don't even ask us.
The guard was just looking on, watching from a nearby ridge.
[O shepherd girl, daughter of a master shepherd.]
They put them in a sheepfold.
[O shepherd girl, daughter of a master shepherd.]
They milked them; they milked them all quite well,
And took them off to shady pastures.
Grow up so I can marry you.

Στην κεντισμένη σου ποδιά

Στην κεντισμένη σου ποδιά, μωρέ βλάχα.
[Μωρέ βλάχα, βλαχοπούλα,
Σαρακατσανοπούλα.]

Λαλούν αηδόνια και πουλιά, μωρέ βλάχα.
[Μωρέ βλάχα, βλαχοπούλα,
Σαρακατσανοπούλα.]

Να 'ρθω κι εγώ να πέσω στην ποδιά σου;
[Μωρέ Βλάχα, Βλαχοπούλα,
Σαρακατσανοπούλα.]

Στην κεντισμένη μου ποδιά, μωρέ βλάμη.
[Μωρέ βλάμη, βρε μπαμπέση,
δεν σε χωράει στη μέση.]

Γιατ' έχω μάννα κι αδερφό, μωρέ βλάμη.
[Μωρέ βλάμη, βρε μπαμπέση,
δεν σε χωράει στη μέση.]

The Sarakatsan were the proud and conservative transhumant shepherds from whom my mother's mother descended and who are further described on page 208. They were a strict folk who would not have countenanced bold advances like the ones of the young man in the song, but they certainly could sing about them.
"So-called friend" is a loose translation of the word *vlames* which has several meanings

On your well-embroidered apron

On your well-embroidered apron, O shepherd girl.
[My pretty little shepherd girl,
My Sarakatsana girl.]

Nightingales and birds are singing, O shepherd girl.
[My pretty little shepherd girl,
My Sarakatsana girl.]

Should I also come to fall upon your apron?
[My pretty little shepherd girl,
My Sarakatsana girl.]

On my well-embroidered apron, you so-called friend.
[You so-called friend, you deceiver.
There's no room on it for you.]

Cause I've a mother and a brother.
[You, so-called friend, you deceiver.
There's no room on it for you.]

depending on context. Its original meaning was similar to blood brother and is described on page 110. Its secondary meaning was that of a handsome and dashing young man as well as of a lover. There is also a feminine form, *vlamissa*, for this latter meaning. In the song above, it is used ironically to mean a friend who could not be relied upon and who was, therefore, not a worthy match.

Βλαχοπούλα εροβόλαγε

Βλαχοπούλα εροβόλαγε από ψηλή ραχούλα,
με τη ροκούλα γνέθοντας, τ' αδράχτι της γεμάτο.
Κι ο βλάχος την καρτέρησε σ' ένα στένο σοκάκι.
– Βλαχούλα δωσ' μου φίλημα, δωσ' μου μαύρα μάτια.
– Το πώς να σου δώσω φίλημα και πώς και μαύρα μάτια,
που μ' έχει η μάννα μ' ακριβή, μικρή αρραβωνιασμένη;

A love song from Epirus. My mother was given a beautiful handcarved distaff made by a young boy in the village who thought that she might marry his older brother. She did not, but the two families remained close friends.

One day the older brother came rushing to my mother's house asking for her father. His brother, then about fifteen, had gotten into an argument with his sister's husband over some pasture and when the older man began beating him the young boy stabbed him to death. His older brother wanted help to avert further trouble. The dead man's family and relatives were seeking revenge and were surrounding the house of the boys to burn it down. With the help of the gendarmerie my grandfather was able to bring the situation under control and the boy was eventually sentenced to three years in prison in Athens.

When his time was almost up, suddenly he fell ill and died. The official report was that he died of tuberculosis. He was in good health, however, and the suddeness of his death precluded tuberculosis or any other lingering type of affliction. What was learned a few

A little shepherd girl

A little shepherd girl was coming down from a high ridge in haste,
Spinning away on her distaff with a spindle that was full.
And a shepherd lay in wait for her in a small, narrow lane.
– Little shepherd girl, give me a kiss, give me your black eyes too.
– How can I give you a kiss, how can I give my black eyes as well,
Since my mother values me so and I'm betrothed from a young age?

years later was that the sister of the murdered man had dropped off a box of sweets at the prison without identifying herself and the boy fell ill after eating some of the contents. Nothing could be proven and the case was closed.

When my mother departed for America in 1931, she left her prized distaff along with her hand-carved dower chest filled with a trove of finely-woven contents to her two sisters, Athanasia and Athena. The distaff and the dower chest were both destroyed when her family's house was struck by shrapnel during an aerial bombardment of the village by the Germans during the Second World War. On June 23, 1943 during a second air raid Athanasia and a group of five other young women and girls sought refuge under a tree by a field where they had been harvesting. Out of modesty and shame they refused to join a group of British and Greek commandos hiding in a nearby bunker. The Stuka pilot clearly saw whom he was targeting as he swept over his brightly dressed and frightened victims. No one survived.

Απάνω στην κρυόβρυση

Απάνω στην κρυόβρυση που 'ναι το κρυονέρι,
βλαχούλα πάει για νερό με το ασκί στο χέρι.
Στην στράτα την αντάμωσε ψηλό παλικαράκι.
Για τ' όνομά της την ρωτά, της πιάνει το χεράκι.
Κι αυτή ξεροκοκκίνησε και το κεφάλι σκύβει,
βγάζει το μαντηλάκι της το πρόσωπό της κρύβει.
– Για σήκωσε, βλαχούλα μου, το όμορφο μαντήλι
για να σου δώσω ένα φιλί στα κόκκινά σου χείλη.
– Άιντε λεβέντη μ' στο καλό, άσε με να γεμίσω,
Την Κυριακή παντρεύομαι, τον άνδρα μου θα φιλήσω.

A love song from Epirus, sung to the *syrtos* rhythm.

Μια Γαλαξειδιώτισσα

Μια Γαλαξειδιώτισσα και πανωμαχαλιώτισσα
δέρνει τη θυγατέρα της, κρυφά από τον πατέρα της.
– Αχ, πού 'ν' τα δαχτυλίδια σου, πού είν' κι ο αρραβώνας;
– Μάννα μου, ο Γιώργος τα φορεί από την άλλη Κυριακή.
– Γοργά να πας, γοργά να 'ρθείς, τα δαχτυλίδια σου να βρεις.

Galaxeidi is a lovely town on the Gulf of Corinth with a proud history of merchant sea-faring. This song depicts a case where daughter and parents are obviously not in agreement over her choice of a future mate and the former has taken unilateral action.
It was rare that the wishes of the children in these matters were not considered by the parents but it did happen. My mother remembered a girl literally being dragged to the

A shepherd girl and a young man

Up at the cold water spring where the water runs so cold,
A shepherd girl went for water with a flask held in her hand.
On the highroad as she went, a tall young man met her there,
And asked about her name, while taking her by the hand.
She reddened and she blushed and brought her head down lower,
And taking out her kerchief she quickly hid her face.
– Lift up your pretty kerchief, dear little shepherd girl
So I can give one kiss to you on those red lips of yours,
– Be off with you, my good man, and let me fill up my flask,
This coming Sunday I'm to wed and my husband will I kiss.

A Galaxeidi woman

A Galaxeidi woman from the upper neighborhood
Is thrashing her young daughter in secret from her father.
– Oh, where are those rings of yours and where is your engagement ring?
– George is wearing them, dear mother, since a week ago last Sunday.
– Go quickly and come back as fast, you had better find your rings!

church with her dress trailing through the rain-soaked autumn leaves to be wed to a man she did not want. Soon thereafter, she became pregnant but was so unhappy and embittered that she openly prayed she might not live to hold the child. She died giving birth and never laid eyes on the baby, which survived.

Μαράθηκε η καρδούλα μου

Μαράθηκε η καρδούλα μου για τη γειτονοπούλα μου.
Τόσο μαράθηκε πολύ και ντρέπεται να της το πει.
– Δεν πας, μάννα μ', να της το πεις, «μη λάχει άλλον ν' αγαπείς».
– Μετά χαράς σου, γιόκα μου, να πάρω και τη ρόκα μου.
Κινάει η μάννα τ' να πάει εκεί, βρίσκει την κόρη που κεντεί.
– Γειά σου χαρά σου, κόρη μου, μου τρέλανες τ' αγόρι μου.
– Πες του να κάνει υπομονή ώσπου να έρθει η Κυριακή,
ώσπου να έρθει η Κυριακή, για να με στεφανωθεί.

My mother composed this humorous love song around the age of fourteen as she weaving on the loom. It was her version of a variant also known in other parts of Greece.

Στη παραπάνω γειτονιά

Στη παραπάνω γειτονιά, στην παραπίσω ρούγα,
[Μωρή πιπερόριζα, κοντούλα, νοστιμούλα, για σέν' αρρώστησα.]
εκεί κάθεται μια γριά, κάθεται κι ένας γέρος.
[Μωρή πάπια του γιαλού, παράτησες εμένα κι αγάπησες αλλού.]
Έχουν κι ένα σκυλί κακό, κι ένα μεγάλο φράχτη.
[Μωρή πιπερόριζα, κοντούλα, νοστιμούλα, για σέν' αρρώστησα.]
Θέ μου, ν' αρρώστηνε η γριά, να πέθαινε κι ο γέρος,
[Μωρή πάπια του γιαλού, παράτησες εμένα κι αγάπησες αλλού.]
να μείν' η κόρη μοναχή, δική μου να την κάνω.
[Μωρή πιπερόριζα, κοντούλα, νοστιμούλα, για σέν' αρρώστησα.]

As my mother gave it to me, the lines forming the refrain alternate with each line. Some other variants only give the first refrain to be sung following each line of the song.

My poor heart has pined away

My poor heart has pined away for the pretty girl next door.
It has pined away so much; it's too shy to go and tell her.
– Mother, why don't you go and tell her, "Don't you go and love another."
– With pleasure I will go, my son; I will take my distaff, too.
His mother gets up to go there and finds the girl embroidering.
– To your health and happiness, my girl, you have driven my poor boy mad.
– Tell him to be patient and to wait 'til Sunday comes at last,
'Til Sunday comes at last, so he can have me crowned and wed.

At the upper neighborhood

There at the upper neighborhood, at the lane off towards the rear,
[O you dear ginger rootlet, so small and yet so tasty, for you I've fallen sick.]
An old woman has her house there and an old man lives there, too.
[Little duck from the seashore, you up and left me and elsewhere have found love.]
They also have a vicious dog and fence that's high and long.
[O you dear ginger rootlet, so small and yet so tasty, for you I've fallen sick.]
God, I wish the old woman would get sick and the old man die,
[Little duck from the seashore, you up and left me and elsewhere have found love.]
So the young girl would be alone and, then, I could make her mine.
[O you dear ginger rootlet, so small and yet so tasty, for you I've fallen sick.]

Η Μαλάμω

– Μαλάμω, με τα χαϊμαλιά και με τα ρούσα τα μαλλιά.

Αν πας, Μαλάμω, για νερό, εγώ στη βρύση καρτερώ.

Εγώ στη βρύση καρτερώ να σου θολώσω το νερό,

να σου τσακίσω το σταμνί, να πας στη μάννα σ' αδειανή.

Κι αν σε ρωτήσ' η μάννα σου,– Μαλάμω, πού 'ναι η στάμνα σου;

– Μάννα μου, παραπάτησα, τη στάμνα μου την τσάκισα.

– Δεν είναι παραπάτημα, παρά ανδρός αγκάλιασμα.

Malamo means Golden Girl from the word *malama* or gold. As a name for a girl, it has a rather rustic sound to it. It is also used as a term of endearment and my father would often use it with my mother, jokingly and affectionately.

The good-luck charms mentioned in the song refer to amulets worn to avert the evil eye. Usually they are made of something blue and worn or pinned. Babies and pretty girls are considered particularly vulnerable but no one is safe. Compliments about health or beauty should be accompanied by the phrase, loosely translated, "may you not be hexed" and by a stylized spitting, as comically portrayed in the film, *My Big Fat Greek Wedding*. In 1956, on my first visit to my parents' village I was dressed in my great-uncle's *foustanella* or kilt for the *panegyri* or festival on August 15. As I was being prepared, I noticed

Από την πόρτα μου ξεβγαίνω

Από την πόρτα μου ξεβγαίνω, στην αγάπη μου πηγαίνω.

Βρίσκω κόρες που κεντάνε και όλο εμένα χαιρετάνε.

– Σας παρακαλώ κορίτσια, σας παρακαλώ κορίτσια,

βάλτε με και μες στη μέση να φιλήσω ποια μ' αρέσει.

Να φιλήσω την Αγγέλω, κάπως δεν την παραθέλω.

Να φιλήσω την Ελένη, μου 'χει την καρδιά καμένη.

Θα φιλήσω τη Βασίλω, που 'ναι όμορφη σαν μήλο.

This humorous love song was composed by my mother.

Malamo

– Malamo, with your good-luck charms and with hair of reddish blonde,
Malamo, should you go for water, I'll be waiting at the spring.
I'll be waiting at the spring so I can muddy up the water,
So I can break your water jug, so you go empty to your mother.
And should your mother ask of you, – where's that water jug of yours?
– Mother dear, I tripped and fell and I broke my water jug.
– That's not a stumble or a fall, but rather some man's embrace.

that someone had pinned a very small pouch on the inside of my elaborately embroidered vest. When I asked what it was, there was a lot of rather embarrassed and nervous giggling. When I insisted on knowing, I was told it was to protect me from the evil eye of jealous people. I retorted that I did not believe in such things and started to remove it. There was general consternation. Then my black-clad and deceptively severe-looking Sarakatsan grandmother said, "it doesn't matter; he's an American; since he doesn't believe in the evil eye, it can't hurt him." I removed the pouch and survived the exposure (at least for that day) to whatever eyes may have been "eating" me, as the Greek phrase has it.

From my door I venture forth

From my door I venture forth; to my love I wend my way.
I find girls who are embroidering and only me they see and greet.
– Girls, I plead with you and beg you; I beg and plead with you once more.
Put and stand me in the middle that I may kiss the one I like.
Should I go and kiss Angela? Somehow, I really don't much want her.
Should I go and kiss Eleni? She has broken my poor heart.
I will up and kiss Vasilo, who's as pretty as an apple.

Για μια φορά είναι η λεβεντιά

Για μια φορά είναι η λεβεντιά, για μια φορά είν' τα νιάτα.
Για μια φορά περπάτησα κι εγώ με τους λεβέντες.
Εξήντα κορίτσια φίλησα και τόσες παντρεμένες.
Και παπαδιές και καλογριές λογαριασμούς δεν έχουν.

My mother's humorous variant on a song also sung elsewhere in Greece.

Πολλές νύχτες περπάτησα

Πολλές νύχτες περπάτησα μ' ένα όμορφο κορίτσι,
νύχτες με την αστροφεγγιά, με το λαμπρό φεγγάρι.
Να την φιλήσω ντρέπομαι, να της το πω 'ντεριώμαι,
να την αφήσω αφίλητη, μ' εμένα θα γελάει.

My mother's variant on a well-known old love song.

Τώρα την αυγή

Τώρα την αυγή, τώρα σιμά να φέξει
Πέρασε ένας νιος, ένας καλός λεβέντης και με γέλασε.
Μου 'πε πως θα με πάρει και με φίλησε,
στα μάτια και στα φρύδια και στο μάγουλο,
που 'χα το κοκκινάδι και το χάλασε.

My mother's ironic variant on the song on page 214.

Brave deeds are only once

Only once are brave deeds accomplished and only once is youth.
Once I, also, walked by the side of dashing and quite bold young men.
Then, I could kiss sixty girls and as many who were married.
As for the wives of priests and as for nuns their numbers can't be counted.

I have walked on many a night

I have walked on many a night with a young and pretty girl,
Many a night and by starlight along with the glowing moon.
To kiss her I am embarrassed; to tell her I'm unable,
To leave her and not to kiss her; she will laugh at me for sure.

The dawn has now arrived

The dawn has now arrived; the dawn's about to break.
A young man appeared and passed by, a young and good-looking man.
He tricked me and he fooled me and told me that we'd marry,
And then he kissed me on my eyes and eyebrows and upon my cheek,
Where I had applied some rouge and he made a mess of it.

Ένα κορίτσι στο λαιμό του

Ένα κορίτσι στο λαιμό του είχε κρεμάσει χρυσό σταυρό.
Πάω κι εγώ να προσκυνήσω, να την φιλήσω δεν μπορώ.
Τι φταίει ο δόλιος; τι φταίει η δόλια;
Το κρίμα το 'χει ο χρυσός σταυρός.

This is an old love song from the Ionian Islands, which my father used to sing to my mother. My father left the village as a small boy and eventually went to sea and thus he never really learned the songs of his mountain homeland. The songs and music of Epirus differ greatly from the songs and music of the Ionian Islands, which lie directly across the sea from there. The Ionian Island music was strongly influenced by Italian music during

Ετούτη γη που την πατούμε

Ετούτη γη που την πατούμε, όλοι μέσα 'δω θα μπούμε.
Ετούτη γη με τα χορτάρια τρώει νιες και παλικάρια.
Ετούτη θα με φάει και μένα που 'βαλα σεβντά για σένα.
Να ήμουνα στη γη χαλίκι και στ' αυτί σου σκουλαρίκι,
να ήμουνα στη γη βελόνι, να πατάς να σ' αγκελώνει.

This is a rather somber love song with a mixed message of frustrated eroticism; it is sung throughout Greece.

Για μένα βρέχουν τα βουνά

Για μένα βρέχουν τα βουνά, για μένα ψιχαλίζουν,
για μένα που παντρεύτηκα, μικρή γυναίκα πήρα.
Κάθισα, την ανάθρεψα σαν μάννα, σαν πατέρας,
κι εκείνη με παράτησε και πήγε μ' άλλον άνδρα.

Πέρασε ένα καλοκαίρι

– Πέρασε ένα καλοκαίρι και δεν μου έστειλες χαμπέρι.
– Τι χαμπέρι να σου στείλω που έπιασες καινούργιο φίλο;
– Κι αν τον έπιασα τον φίλο, τον παλιό δεν τον αφήνω.

A girl has hung a golden cross

A girl has hung a golden cross around her pretty neck.
And I go there to worship it for I don't dare to kiss her.
Is it the poor fellow's fault? Is it the poor girl's?
The blame lies with the golden cross.

the many centuries of Venetian control. The typical song of these islands is called a *kantada*, of which the above is an example and which is sung in four-part harmony like a barbershop quartette. My father knew many of these *kantades* and would often get together with some friends from the island of Kephalonia, one of the seven Ionian islands famous for its songs and music, to sing them.

This earth

All of us one day will enter this earth which we tread upon.
This earth with its green grass devours young girls and heroes.
This earth will also devour me for falling in love with you.
I wish I were gravel on the ground or a ring hanging on your ear,
I wish I were a needle on the ground for you step on and to sting you.

Rain upon the mountains

For me there's rain upon the mountains and drizzle on the hills,
For me, who went off and married and took a younger woman.
I sat me down and cared for her, like a mother, like a father,
But that girl got up and left me and took off with another man.

A summer has passed

– A summer has passed, you sent me no news.
– What news should I send, since you've found a new friend?
– And if I found a new friend, old friendships don't end.

Στον Άδη θα κατέβω

Στον Άδη θα κατέβω και στον Παράδεισο,
τον Χάρο ν' ανταμώσω, δυο λόγια να του πω,
– Χάρε, για χάρισέ μου σαΐτες κοφτερές,
να πάω να σαϊτέψω δυο-τρεις μελαχρινές,
πού 'χουν στα χείλη βάμμα, στο μάγουλο ελιά.
Μου καίνε την καρδιά, αμάν, μου καίνε την καρδιά.

My mother composed this song while weaving. The mole was considered a sign of beauty.

Από μικρός ορφάνεψα

Από μικρός ορφάνεψα από μάννα και πατέρα,
και πήγα και ρογιάστηκα σε μια κυρά Βουλγάρα.
Δώδεκα χρόνια δούλεψα και στα μάτια δεν την είδα.
Κι από τους δώδεκα κι εμπρός τη βλέπω δακρυσμένη.
Δώδεκα χρόνια δούλεψα και 'τοιμάσθηκα να φύγω.
– Δώσ' μου κυρά μου τη ρόγα μου, δώσ' μου τη δούλεψή μου.
Μου στείλανε τα αδέρφια μου να πάω να με παντρέψουν.
Γυρίζω, την κοιτώ, τη βλέπω δακρυσμένη.
– Δούλεψε, δούλε μ', δούλεψε κι εγώ θα σε παντρέψω.
Τρεις δούλες έχω στον οντά, και όποια θέλεις πάρε.
Θέλεις τη ρούσα, την ξανθιά, θέλεις την μαυρομάτα;
Θέλεις την τρίτη τη μικρότερη, που 'ναι φλουριά γεμάτη;

An old love song. Variants continue the story with the servant telling his mistress that he does not want the girls but rather the mistress. Other variants have the mistress, who has obviously been interested in him all along, propose marriage. Still others have the servant refuse all offers because he wants to go home.

I shall go down to Hades

I shall go down to Hades and on to Paradise,
There to meet up with Death and tell him a thing or two,
– Death, grant me arrows that are sharp,
So I may shoot two or three brunettes,
Who have crimson paint on their lips and on their cheek a mole.
They are burning up my heart, mercy me, they are burning up my heart.

At a young age

At a young age I was orphaned of my mother and my father,
So I went off and hired myself to a Bulgarian mistress.
Twelve long years I worked hard for her and never looked into her eyes.
And from those twelve years and onwards I see that she is tearful.
Twelve long years I worked hard for her; then, I made ready to depart.
– Give me, my lady, what is my due; give me my hard-worked earnings.
My brothers have now sent for me to go home that I may marry.
I turn and see her tearful eyes; her eyes are full of tears.
– Work, my good servant, work, she said and I shall help you marry.
I have three servant girls in my house; take anyone you wish.
Do you want the blonde and fair one or the one whose eyes are dark?
Do you want the third and youngest, who's bedecked with golden florins?

Πολύ τόπο γκιζέρισα

Πολύ τόπο γκιζέρισα, Βλαχιά και Βουκορέστι,
για να βρω κόρη όμορφη, στα κάλλη να μ' αρέσει,
στα κάλλη και στη λεβεντιά και στη λιγνή της μέση.
Μια κόρη του Χοντζιά-Πασά στραβά φοράει το φέσι
και στο ντερβένι θέριζε όλο το μεσημέρι.
Και εγώ διαβάτης διάβαινα και την καλημεράω,
– Καλημέρα σου, κόρη μου. – Καλώς τον τον διαβάτη.
Διαβάτη πούθε έρχεσαι; Και πούθε μας κοπιάζεις;
– Από τα ξένα έρχομαι, στον τόπο μου πηγαίνω.
Με καρτερεί η μάννα μου, τα δόλια μου τ' αδέρφια.
Ρετζιά σού κάνω, κόρη μου, και σου φιλώ το χέρι,
το παραθύρι τ' ακρινό βράδυ να μην το κλείσεις.
– Κι εγώ για το χατίρι σου όλ' ανοιχτά τ' αφήνω!

This song was sung at harvest time in the fields by the women and young girls, who usually did the reaping. Wheat and corn grew on the large slope, which stretched up behind my mother's village and was bound on each side by two narrow, swift-running streams. This area was called "the middle," that is, in the midst of the streams. Every year the crop grown in "the middle" was switched. One year it would be wheat in "the middle" with corn on the far sides of the two streams, while the next corn with wheat on the far sides. The area was divided into discrete family holdings, some large and some small, measured by the number of days it took to plow the individual plots or terraces. The largest typically took four to five days. Most families usually had one or two large plots and several small ones scattered through the areas of cultivation. The dowry system ensured that there was a constant change of landownership and few pieces of land remained in one family for a long period of time.

I wandered through many places

I wandered through many places in Vlachia and Voukoresti,
To find a pretty girl for me with a beauty that would please me,
With a beauty and a bearing and a waist so trim and slender.
A daughter of Choja Pasha was wearing her fez askew
And at the pass she was reaping all through the noonday hours.
As a traveler I came by and greeted her by saying,
– Good day to you, my girl, good day. – Welcome to the traveler.
Where do you come from, traveler, and where do you aim to go?
– From foreign parts I come and I am going to my homeland.
My mother's waiting there for me and my unhappy brothers.
I beg and ask of you, my girl, and take your hand and kiss it,
The far window at the end there, tonight, please do not close it.
– For your sake and your sake alone, I'll leave all of them wide open!

Vlachia and Voukoresti are present-day Romania and Bucharest. During the Ottoman period, many Greeks, especially from Epirus, went to Vlachia or Wallachia to seek their fortunes. For most of the 18th century Wallachia's Ottoman-appointed governors were aristocratic Greeks, from the Phanari section of Constantinople, who tended to favor their countrymen. Choja Pasha is obviously a made-up figure as the two words are merely titles in Turkish meaning roughly religious leader and military leader. That the Christian, Greek boy in this song would dare approach a Muslim, Turkish girl so openly is of particular interest, as the penalty for such an action would have been death.
This song goes back to the late 18th century period of weakness and decline for the Ottoman Empire. The sentiments, therefore, might well be interpreted as a sign of derring-do defiance on the part of the hitherto long-suffering Greeks coupled with the added insinuation that Turkish women were loose and could easily be compromised.

Κάτω στη Ρόδο

Κάτω στη Ρόδο, στη Ροδοπούλα
Τούρκος αγάπησε μια Ρωμιοπούλα.
Η Ρωμιοπούλα δεν τον θέλει,
και η μάννα της την προξενεύει,
– Παρ' τον κόρη μου, τον Τούρκον άνδρα
γιατί έχει αμπέλια και χωράφια.
– Μάννα μου, εγώ δεν τον θέλω,
κι ας έχει και πολλά χρυσάφια.

A well-known song and dance and also sung by children when playing pattycake. Traditionally marriages were arranged by the families themselves or by employing a marriage broker or *proxenitis*.
While love was not the main criterion, the girl's wishes were usually taken into account, unless the family was desperate or felt some social obligation or pressure. My mother remembers a girl literally being dragged through the lanes of the village weeping as she went to marry a man she did not want. She also remembers cases where families thwarted the wish of their children to marry for love because the girl did not have a significant dowry or the boy was not considered worthy.
The arrangements, concluded in the marriage negotiations, were spelled out and formalized in a document called the "dowry contract" or *proikosymphono*. The dowry items such as land or jewelry were considered the bride's and should there be a divorce (permitted by the Greek Church but socially frowned upon), they were to be returned to her

On Rhodes the island

On Rhodes the island, on the isle of Rhodes
A Turk fell in love with a young Greek girl.
The young Greek girl doesn't want him at all,
Yet her own mother is acting the broker.
– Take him, my girl, take the Turk as your husband
Because he has many vineyards and fields.
– Mother dear, I don't want him at all
Even if he had much gold and treasure.

family. Upon her death they were divided only among her children but returned to her family if she had no children of her own.

The mother in the song above was obviously desperate either for economic reasons or out of fear her daughter would be seized anyway. If the daughter agreed, at least there was the possibility the family would be recompensed. The Turkish and Muslim custom was for the groom to give a sum of money or other payment to the bride's family, the so-called bride price, which the bride could keep should she be divorced. Divorce was much easier among the Muslim Turks, especially the richer and more powerful ones (as the one in the song is). They maintained harems of varying sizes, which were replenished or culled whenever the fancy of the master was diverted. Christian and Jewish girls often provided that diversion because they moved about with their faces usually uncovered and could be spotted more easily and also because there was, no doubt, the element of lording it over subject peoples.

Ένα βράδυ

Ένα Σαββάτο βράδυ, μια Κυριακή πρωί,
βγήκα να σεργιανίσω, [καημένε Μήτσο] σ' εβραίικο μπαχτσέ.
Βρίσκω μια Εβραιοπούλα που χτενίζονταν,
και είχε ασημένιο χτένι, κρυστάλλινο γυαλί.
– Εσύ Εβραιοπούλα, να γίνεις Χριστιανή,
να λούζεσαι Σαββάτο, ν' αλλάζεις Κυριακή,
να πας στην εκκλησιά σαν να 'σαι Χριστιανή;

This song has many variants. In some the girl then asks her mother for permission to
marry the Christian. She replies that she would rather have her daughter be killed by a
Turk than marry a Christian. In others, the lover is set upon by the girl's fellow Jews and
taken to be condemned to death. The girl looks out of her window and tells the boy that
she has the ransom to save him. In other variants it is a Turkish rather than a Jewish girl
who is the object of the boy's desire.
It was extremely rare for Christians, Jews and Muslims to intermarry. Muslim men, how-

One Saturday evening

One Saturday evening, one Sunday morning,
I went out for a stroll in a garden of the Jews. [Poor Mitsos]
I found there a Jewish girl, who was combing her long hair,
In one hand she held a silver comb and in the other a crystal mirror.
– O you little Jewish girl, would you become a Christian,
To bathe every Saturday and on Sunday change your clothes,
To go along to church with me like every other Christian?

ever, often seized, or bought as slaves, Christian and Jewish women and took them into
their harems. Death was the penalty for any Christian or Jew who dared to get involved
with a Muslim woman, unless of course, he converted. This song certainly reflects the all
too human desire for the forbidden as well as perhaps the rare exception to the rule.
Mitsos is the nickname for Dimitrios. The reference to bathing and dressing is not a negative comment on the cleanliness of the Jewish girl but a much used formulaic image in
Greek folk songs of female titivation and disportment.

Τρία πουλάκια παν ψηλά

Τρία πουλάκια παν ψηλά, και το 'να χαμηλώνει.
Τ' άλλα πουλιά του λέγανε, τ' άλλα πουλιά του λένε,
– Αυτού που πας και έρχεσαι, φιλείς τα μαύρα μάτια
[Γιάννο λεβέντη.]
Φυλάξου μην σε πιάσουνε του Μπέη τα παλικάρια,
και στη φυλακή σε βάλουνε, τα χέρια σου δεμένα.
[Γιάννο λεβέντη.]
Και η φυλακή έχει σίδερα και σιδερένιες πόρτες,
έχει και δεσμοφύλακα, στο χέρι του ντουφέκι.

This love song relates the dangerous dalliance of a Christian man with a Turkish woman. The hero of the song is called a *leventis*, which usually means a bold, brave and good-looking young man. In this instance it is loosely translated as "rascal" to convey the sense of amorous derring-do. Such an escapade, if it became known, was punishable by death. Bey is a high Turkish administrative title.

Μπήκαν κορίτσια στο χορό

Μπήκαν κορίτσια στο χορό, ξανθές και μαυρομάτες,
χόρευε η Σέρβω και η Ρωμιά και μια Αρβανιτοπούλα.
Κύριε, να 'μαν κι εγώ Ρωμιός να 'μαν και βαπτισμένος,
να πιάνομαν να χόρευα από Ρωμιοπούλας χέρι.

The protagonist in this song is obviously not a Christian and that's why he wishes he were baptized. The Serbian girl would have been a Christian but the young Albanian girl might have been either. In any case, he wants to dance with the Greek girl. The word used for Greek in the song is *Romios* or Roman. This word was used to mean Greek in the days of the Ottoman occupation and went back to the Byzantines, who called themselves Romans and not Greeks, as they considered themselves the heirs of the Roman Empire in the East. In the Balkans and in the Muslim world at this time it could also mean Christian. The word is still used in modern Greek, conveying a sense of traditional, genuine Greekness.

Three birds

Three birds are flying high above but one bird comes down lower.
The other birds were telling him, the other birds are saying,
– There, where you're going and coming, you are kissing eyes of black
[Giannos you rascal.]
Watch yourself that you don't get caught by the soldiers of the bey,
And they throw you into prison, your hands all bound up and tied.
[Giannos you rascal.]
The prison has heavy iron chains and doors well made of iron,
It also has a prison guard and in his hands a musket.

The girls have started up the dance

The girls have started up the dance, blondes and girls with eyes of black,
A Serbian and a Greek girl and a young Albanian.
Oh Lord, I wish I were a Greek, I wish I were blessed and baptized,
Then I'd stand up and join the dance, holding on to a Greek girl's hand.

My mother first heard this dance song in the *syrtos* rhythm when she was about five years old. She was with a group of older girls, who were dancing to it by the moonlight on a threshing floor near one of her family's fields. While they were dancing, a boy sneaked up and began spying on them. When the girls saw him they began to scold him and tell him to go away, warning him that they would throw stones at him if he stayed. He refused to leave. My mother, thinking she was being helpful, picked up a stone and threw it at him, slightly wounding him on the forehead. He left weeping. The next day his father came to complain but when he realized that his teenaged son had been wounded by a five-year old girl he withdrew in embarrassment.

Μιά χήρα πούλαγε κρασί

Μιά χήρα πούλαγε κρασί και μάργαρε σιτάρι.
– Γιατί νερώνεις το κρασί, κριθάρι στο σιτάρι;
– Έχω κόρη για παντρειά να κάνει τα προικιά της,
να κάνει ζώνη του γαμπρού, ποδιά της πεθεράς της.

Having a daughter without a dowry was a major tribulation, particularly if you were poor. This is just one of the many songs describing this problem. The plight of families with daughters was not confined to traditional Greek society.

This was brought home to me when I was serving as a U. S. diplomat in Baghdad in 1965. I was waiting at the maternity clinic to be informed of the birth of my second child. It was the custom for newly minted fathers to give a small gift to the person bearing the news. If it was a boy, a generous present was expected; if a girl, depending on the mood of the father, little or nothing. The male attendant who came to tell me the news growled out the word *bint* or girl with obvious displeasure, expecting no reward for this disappoint-

Δυο μάννες

Έχω γιο κι έχω χαρά
που θα γίνω πεθερά.

Αχ, έχω τσιούπρα, έχω πίκρα
που θα δουλεύω μέρα, νύχτα.

In the traditional village scheme of things a hundred years ago, the mother-in-law was a powerful figure co-presiding, if not ruling, over the extended patriarchal family, often domiciled under the same roof. My mother remembered young brides addressing the mother-in-law as mistress, speaking only when spoken to and doing all the heavy chores

The widow wine seller

A widow once was selling wine and adulterated wheat,
– Why are you watering the wine, putting barley in the wheat?
– I have a daughter to be wed and she must make her dowry.
She must make a sash for the groom, an apron for his mother.

ing information. He was genuinely taken aback by my happiness over the news and grat-
ifyingly surprised by my subsequent generosity.
Two years later, the same maternity clinic and the same male attendant. This time he
excitedly bounded into the waiting area shouting for me and all to hear *walid*, or child,
meaning son. (In the Arabic as well as in the Greek vernacular, there are children and
then there are girls). While I was receiving the good news and rewarding appropriately,
I suddenly heard weeping and moaning. I was informed with a combination of pity and
disdain that a woman had just given birth to her fourth daughter and the gathered family, especially the mother, was bewailing its fate.

Two mothers

I have a son and I am happy
That I'll become a mother-in-law.

Oh my, I have a girl and I am bitter
That I'll be working day and night.

around the house. The mother of the bride, on the other hand, in many instances lost not
only a daughter but in the form of dowry had to pay for the loss as well. This song and
others like it reflect this reality.

Μπάτε κορίτσια στο χορό

Μπάτε κορίτσια στο χορό τώρα που 'χετε τον καιρό.

Αχ, ταχιά θα παντρευτείτε, θα σπιτονοικοκυρευθείτε.

Δεν θα σας αφήνουν οι άνδρες σας να πάτε στις μαννάδες σας.

Δεν σας αφήνουν τα παιδιά να πάτε σ' άλλη γειτονιά.

Δεν σας αφήνει η πεθερά να πάτε όπου είναι η χαρά.

Δεν σας αφήνει ο πεθερός να πάτε όπου είναι ο χορός.

– Τους άνδρες τους μεθύζουμε και τους αποκοιμίζουμε.

Και τα παιδιά τα δέρουμε, στον δάσκαλο τα στέλουμε.

Και την κακιά την πεθερά μέρα και νύχτα νηστικιά.

Και τον κακό τον πεθερό τον κλείνουμε στο πλυσταριό.

This song reflects both a reality in the tradition-bound villages of Greece in earlier centuries but also a spirit of change that was coming over the countryside as the 20th century began. Other variants are known from elsewhere in Greece.

Βλάχα πλένει στο ποτάμι

Βλάχα πλένει στο ποτάμι κι άλλη βλάχα την ρωτάει,

– Βλάχα μ', τ' είσαι σκανιασμένη και βαριά βαλαντωμένη;

– Τι να κάνω, η κακομοίρα, με τον άνδρα εγώ που πήρα.

Πήρα άνδρα μαραζιάρη και κουτσό μ' ένα ποδάρι.

Τα τσαρούχια του στη φράχτη, τα ποδάρια του στη στάχτη.

Ώσπου να αποδέσει το 'να βγήκε ο ήλιος πάει γιόμα,

Κι ώσπου να αποδέσει τ' άλλο βγήκε τ' άστρι το μεγάλο.

This a humorous song composed by my mother's father, employing a formulaic beginning found in other songs. Village attitudes to physical infirmities could be cruel and insensitive, as was the case in all cultures until relatively recently. The use of the word

Get up and dance

Get up and dance, my girls, now that you have the time.
Oh my, soon you will get married and housewives you will become.
And your husbands will not let you pay a call on your mothers.
And the children will not let you visit other neighborhoods.
And your mother-in-law will not let you go where there's a party.
And your father-in-law will not let you go where there's a dance.
– We can make our husbands drunk and put them all to sleep.
And our children we can spank and send them off to school.
And the bad mother-in-law, day and night we'll keep her hungry.
And the bad father-in-law, in the laundry room we'll shut him.

At the river

At the river a country girl was washing when another came and asked her,
– My girl, why are you disheartened and why deeply hurt and sad?
– What can I do, unlucky me, with the husband I have taken?
I have taken a sickly husband with one leg lame and limping.
Up on the fence he leaves his shoes and in the dust he drags his feet.
Until he gets a shoe on one foot, the sun has come and lunch is gone.
Until a shoe is on the other, out comes the evening star so grand.

dumb in English to mean stupid or the expression "the village idiot" are examples of a
similar attitude. The girl in this story was obviously married off against her will which
did happen in the days when almost all marriages were arranged.

Μια παπαδιά

Μια παπαδιά στον αργαλειό τα πόδια της κουνούσε
και με το νου της έλεγε και με το λογικό της,
– Δεν τονε θέλω τον παπά τον τράγο με τα γένια,
μόν' θέλω τσοπανόπουλο που παίζει τη φλογέρα.

This dance song is popular throughout Greece.

Στου παπά τα παραθύρια

Στου παπά τα παραθύρια κάθονται δυο μαύρα φρύδια.
Να 'χω 'γω τα μαύρα φρύδια, κι ο παπάς τα παραθύρια.
Στου παπά την πορτοπούλα κάθεται η παπαδοπούλα.
Ο παπάς την πορτοπούλα, κι εγώ την παπαδοπούλα.
Στου παπά την κρεβατίνα κρέμεται μια προβατίνα.
Ο παπάς την κρεβατίνα, κι εγώ την προβατίνα.

A love song composed by my mother's father.

Μανουσάκια

Εμένα η μάννα μ' έστειλε να μάσω μανουσάκια.
[Μανουσάκια, μανουσάκια, όμορφά μου κοριτσάκια.]
Στην αγορά τα πούλησα και πήρα δυο τσαπράκια.
[Μανουσάκια, μανουσάκια, δυόσμος και γαρυφαλάκια.]
Σαν τι τον έχεις τον παπά και κάθησες κοντά του;
[Μανουσάκια, μανουσάκια, μόσχος και γαρυφαλάκια.]
Τον έχει η μάννα μ' αδερφό κι εγώ τον έχω μπάρμπα.
[Μανουσάκια, μανουσάκια, όμορφά μου κοριτσάκια.]

This is a well-known song and dance in the *syrtos* rhythm.

A priest's wife

A priest's wife seated at the loom was swinging her legs to and fro
And she was saying to herself, thinking over in her mind,
– I don't want the priest anymore, that billygoat with his beard,
I only want a shepherd boy, who can play upon the flute.

At the windows of the priest

At the windows of the priest sit two beautiful black eyebrows.
I wish I had the two black eyebrows and let the priest keep the windows.
At the backdoor of the priest sits the priest's pretty daughter .
Let the priest keep his doorway and I'll take the pretty daughter.
On the arbor of the priest hangs a big fat ewe.
Let the priest keep his arbor and I'll take the ewe.

The narcissus

My mother sent me out one day to gather up narcissus.
[Narcissus, O narcissus, pretty girls, O pretty girls.]
I sold them in the market place and bought me two silver pins.
[Narcissus, O narcissus, sweet mint and bright carnations.]
What's your connection with the priest and you are sitting close to him?
[Narcissus, O narcissus, sweet clove and bright carnations.]
My mother claims him as her brother and so I call him uncle.
[Narcissus, O narcissus, pretty girls, O pretty girls.]

Πέρα κει στα καλυβάκια

Πέρα κει στα καλυβάκια
[Τ' ακούς κουμπάρα μου;]
έχω μι' αγαπητικιά
[Κουμπαρούλα μου γλυκιά.]
Και μου λένε να την πάρω.
[Τ' ακούς κουμπάρα μου;]
Θέλει παπούτσια με κουμπιά,
[Κουμπαρούλα μου γλυκιά.]
και μια κεντητή ποδιά.
[Τ' ακούς κουμπάρα μου;]
Μα, εγώ δεν έχω τον παρά.
[Κουμπάρα μου γλυκιά.]

A song composed by my mother and sung to the *syrtos* rhythm. Godmothers and godfathers were often chosen in the hopes that they would help the child later on in life. From the other side people often became godfathers or godmothers to make good alliances or like politicians to gather and assure votes. Traditionally, godparents had the privilege of choosing the name of the child to be baptized without necessarily having to obtain the prior approval of the parents. Usually the family would be consulted and especially if it was the first and only son. In that instance the child was almost automatically named after the paternal grandfather. Boys were never named after the father unless he was dead and neither were daughters after the mother. In addition, if the child was born on a major feastday or saint's day or if the parents had made a vow to the Virgin or to a saint because they were childless, the child would be named accordingly. My father, for example, was born on October 26, St. Dimitrios Day. Although he was an only male child and should have been named Konstantinos after his paternal grandfather, he took the name of his birthday saint, as thanks from an hitherto childless and aging father. Children were usually not addressed or referred to by their names until they were actually baptized, which traditionally took place within the first few months after birth usually within forty days of birth.

In the summer of 1956, on my first trip to Greece and to my parents' village, I was asked if I would "honor" a family, which had close godfathering ties with my mother's family over generations (a tradition highly esteemed amd observed in earlier times) by standing as godfather to their newly-born second son. I agreed. When I asked what name they wished me to bestow on the child, I was told that I might choose any name I wished. My name, my father's name, my maternal grandfather's name. In short, any name would be acceptable. Whatever I decided, however, I was to keep to myself until the day of the ceremony.

The day of the baptism we all met at the church except for the mother who had not yet completed the forty-day lying-in period, prescribed by both the church and custom. She

Over there at the little huts

Over there at the little huts
[Do you hear me, godmother?]
I have a pretty sweetheart
[Sweet little godmother.]
And they tell me I should wed her.
[Do you hear me, godmother?]
She wants shoes with buttons on them,
[Sweet little godmother.]
And an embroidered apron.
[Do you hear me, godmother?]
But I don't have the cash.
[Sweet little godmother.]

was waiting at the house. At the the appropriate time in the service I was asked to give the name and I said "Theophilos." I had always liked this name, learning it from my mother's tales of Byzantium. Gathered at the church door was a group of boys who were eagerly waiting to hear the name of the newly-illumined or *neophotistos*, as newly baptized children are characterized. Soon as the boys heard the name they all rushed out tell the mother, who would reward the first one to give her the news with a small coin for good luck.

After the ceremony, family and guests proceeded to the house for the traditonal feast. Upon reaching the door, I handed over my new godson, whom I had been carrying, to my *koumpara*, the boy's mother who accepted her child while kissing my hand in respect. Once the festivities got under way, the *koumpara* rather plaintively asked me in a low whisper, "what kind of name have you given my son?" I replied in surprise, "what do you mean?" She answered with obvious concern, "Theophovos (God-fearer or Feared by God) is a heavy name to carry in life." The little boys had obviously mispronounced the name as they conveyed it to the mother, never having heard such a name before, I told her reassuringly, "Theophilos is the name and not Theophovos and I am certain God will love and protect him, as the name signifies, all the days of his life." She was much comforted to hear the correct form of the name and even more pleased to learn that he was the only boy in the village, if not in the entire region, with this name.

Children call their godfather and their godmother, *nonos* and *nona* respectively. The terms are from the late Latin and mean foster father and foster mother. The parents of the godchild call the godparents, *koumparos* and *koumpara*, and the latter employ the same terms when addressing the parents of the godchild. These terms also come from the late Latin *compater* through the Venetian dialectal form *compare*, meaning "like a father." This term is used both for those who stand as godparents at baptisms as well as for those who perform the crowning at weddings, in other words the best man or woman.

Μ' ακούτε Αραχωβίτισσες

Μ' ακούτε Αραχωβίτισσες κι Αραχωβιτοπούλες;
Το Μάη κρασί μην πίνετε, κι έξω μην κοιμηθείτε,
γιατί είναι δυο κακά παιδιά που περπατούν τις νύχτες.
Έχουν ψωμί για τα σκυλιά, κρέας για τα λιοντάρια,
σέρνουν και γλυκό κρασί και μεθάνε τα κορίτσια.

Arachova is the name of three villages, one in the prefecture of Nafpaktia, one a picturesque village near Delphi that is popular with tourists and one near Sparta. This song could refer to any of these. In ancient times the one near Sparta was called Karyai. Many of its people have emigrated to the United States and Canada where they have done well. Their hometown association has an annual *panegyri* in the summer at a beautiful mountain site in North Carolina, which they have bought and to which scores of their *patriotes*

Η Βασίλω

Βάτους κι αγκάθια πάτησα, Βασίλω, ώσπου να σ' αγαπήσω,
και τώρα που σ' αγάπησα, μου λένε να σ' αφήσω.
Μα, εγώ κρασί δεν πίνω, μωρέ, Βασίλω,
δεν πίνω να μεθύσω για να σ' απαρατήσω.
Φέτος τ' αμπέλια χάλασαν, χάλασαν, Βασίλω.
Χάλασαν και οι σταφίδες, αλιά για τους μπεκρήδες.
Φέτος τα στάρια χάλασαν, χάλασαν, Βασίλω,
και τι ψωμί θα φάμε στο δρόμο που θα πάμε;
Κρασί δεν πίνω να μεθύσω, μωρέ, Βασίλω,
Δεν πίνω να μεθύσω για να σε λησμονήσω.

A love song in the *syrtos* rhythm.

Πάρε με κι εμένα μπάρμπα

Πάρε με κι εμένα, μπάρμπα, στο κρασοπωλειό που πας.
Να σου τηγανίσω ψάρια, και γλυκό κρασί να πιεις.
Συ να πίνεις ένα, μπάρμπα, μα εγώ να πίνω δυο.

Women from Arachova

Do you hear me, O women and and young girls from Arachova?
Don't drink wine in the month of May or lie down outdoors to sleep,
Because two bad fellows are about, walking there about at night.
They carry bread to give the dogs and meat to give the lions,
They also bring along sweet wine and get the girls drunk and tipsy.

(people from the same region or village) and their offspring, relatives and friends come
from all over to celebrate and dance, even in the rain as I witnessed in 1955. The Greeks
abroad maintain their ties with their *patriotes*, with the regions of their birth or ances-
try and with their hometowns and villages in organizations like the Pan-Epirotic, the
Pan-Arcadian etc. These are both social and benevolent associations.

Vasilo

Vasilo, I walked on brambles and on sharp thorns until I could love you,
And now that I'm in love with you they're telling me to leave you.
But I don't drink wine, my dear Vasilo,
I don't drink to get drunk so I can leave you.
This year the vinyards are all ruined; ruined, dear Vasilo,
Ruined too are the grapes for wine, bad luck for all the boozers.
This year the wheat fields are all ruined; ruined, dear Vasilo,
What bread will we have to eat on the road that we are taking?
I don't drink wine to get drunk, my dear Vasilo,
I don't drink to get drunk, so I don't forget you.

Take me with you too, dear uncle

Take me with you too, dear uncle, to the wineshop where you go.
So there I can fry fish for you while you can drink up sweet wine.
You can drink one glass, dear uncle, but I can be drinking two.

Μωρή κακιά γειτόνισσα

Μωρή κακιά γειτόνισσα, κακιά γειτονοπούλα,
σύμμασ' τα περιστέρια σου που 'ρχονται στην αυλή μου,
μου τρώνε το σταράκι μου, μου πίνουν το νερό μου,
μου παίρνουν και το χώμα μου στα νυχοπόδαρά τους.
Εγώ το χώμα το 'θελα και το νερό το θέλω,
να χτίσω πύργο κι εκκλησιά και μέγα μοναστήρι.
Μέσα θα βάλω καλογραιές κι απ' έξω καλογέρους.
Θα βάλω κι ένα 'γούμενο να τους ξομολογάει.

This is my mother's humorous variant on an old song known in other parts of Greece as
well. The oldest version of this song describes the building of the cathedral of Saint
Sophia in Constantinople.

Πέρα κει στον Όλυμπο

Πέρα κει στον Όλυμπο και στο γαλαρόκαμπο, Γκόλφω μου,
βόσκουν χίλια πρόβατα κι άλλα τόσα γιδερά.
Κόρη ήταν που τα φύλαγε και τα νυχτοβόσκαγε
μ' εκατό βλαχόσκυλα.
Κλέφτες παν να κλέψουνε, και η κόρη τους κατάλαβε
και τα σκυλιά παράβαλε.

This is a shepherd's song from Epirus. Sheep and goat rustling was quite common in my
mother's days and even later. A relative of my mother's, who had many sheep of his own,
was not above going over to neighboring valleys and grabbing a few for an impromptu
feast. He kept track of the number with notches on his shepherd's staff. There was an
old saying, "a stolen sheep tastes better," evoking a lifestyle going back to Homeric times.

Naughty neighbor woman

O you naughty neighbor woman, naughty little neighbor girl,
Gather up your pigeons, which are coming to my courtyard,
And eating up my grains of wheat and drinking up my water,
They are digging up my earth with the talons of their feet.
I had a need for all that earth and I do need the water,
To build a tower and a church and a grand monastery.
Within I'll put some pious nuns and outside some pious monks.
I'll also put an abbot there who will hear their long confessions.

Over there on Olympos

Over there on Olympos, over at the milking field, dear Golpho,
A thousand sheep are grazing and as many goats and kids.
A girl was watching over them and was grazing them by night
With a hundred sheep dogs.
Rustlers tried to take them off and the girl became aware of them
And set the dogs upon them.

Ζαχαρούλα

Σείονται τα δέντρα, σείονται και τα κλαριά.
Σείεται και η Ζαχαρούλα με τα ξανθά μαλλιά.
Παπούτσια και σκαρπίνια και κεντητή ποδιά,
τα βάζει η Ζαχαρούλα να πάει στην εκκλησιά.
Να κάνει το σταυρό της ν' ανάψει δυο κεριά,
το κεινα στον Αϊ Νικόλα, τ' άλλο στην Παναγιά.

This song was composed by my mother's father for the daughter of his best friend, who was also his *vlamis*, (see page 110). Zacharoula could be translated as Sugarlet. Sundays were usually observed as a day of rest with church in the morning, a family meal at midday and visiting or strolling (if the weather permitted) in the evening. Sunday was the day for weddings and baptisms, so the family might be invited to one such event in the afternoon as well.

Preparations for the Sabbath traditionally began on the preceding eve when the vesper bell was rung. At that time the oil in the vigil lamp before the family's household shrine was replenished and the lamp relit. Often the next day's meal was also prepared and the house given a final tidying up, so that no such work would be carried out on the Sabbath. Certainly, household chores like cleaning, sweeping, sewing, weaving etc. were

Zacharoula

Swaying are the trees; the branches are swaying, too.
Blonde-haired Zacharoula also sways to and fro.
Her shoes, her pretty footwear and her embroidered apron,
Zacharoula wears all of them so she can go to church.
There to bow and cross herself and light two waxen candles,
One is for St. Nicholas the other for the Virgin.

strongly discouraged, if not forbidden. (My mother continued to observe many of these customs in America, especially no sewing or cleaning on Sundays.)
Shrewbread or *prosphoron* might be prepared to be taken to the church to be blessed during the liturgy and distributed to the congregation. If you had your own beehives (as my mother's family did), candles might also be made at home to be taken to the church to fulfill a vow or accompany a petition. My mother's paternal grandmother also had the custom of asking her husband's brother, the priest, to come to the house once a year on the day of the departure of her two sons for America to perform a liturgy just for the family and for the family's well-being. At Christmas and Easter she also would make up baskets of food for the poor and deliver them herself at night so that she not embarrass those receiving her charity by having them see her.

Ο Γιάννος και η Παγώνα

Κάτω στον κάμπο στην καλαμώνα
θέριζε ο Γιάννος και η Παγώνα.
Στοίχημα βάζει ο Γιάννος και η Παγώνα,
ποιος θα διψάσει προτού να 'ρθει το γιόμα;
Εδίψασε η Παγώνα προτού να 'ρθει το γιόμα,
– Νερό, βρε Γιάννο, και θα πεθάνω,
και τέτοιο στοίχημα δεν ξαναβάνω.

Σήμερα τα παλικάρια

Σήμερα τα παλικάρια στέκονται σαν τα λιοντάρια.
Σήμερα και τα κορίτσια στέκονται σαν κυπαρίσσια.
Αχ, κι αυτές οι παντρεμένες στέκονται καμαρωμένες.
Αχ, κι αυτές οι χήρες στέκονται σαν κακομοίρες.

This song was composed by Mitselis (Dimitrios) Chaidos, who was known in the village during my mother's childhood as a bon viveur, singer and dancer. He would sing this verse during the *panegyri* festivities. In the late twenties he left the village for Piraeus

Όταν σε βλέπω να 'ρχεσαι

Μακριά μου όταν σε βλέπω να 'ρχεσαι,
σε βλέπω σαν κάμπο με λουλούδια.
Αλλά κοντά μου σαν έρχεσαι,
σε βλέπω σαν κακάβι με φασούλια.

Giannos and Pagona

Down there in the fields amid the stubble
Giannos was harvesting, as was Pagona.
Giannos and Pagona then make a bet,
Who will get thirsty before lunchtime arrives?
Pagona got thirsty before lunchtime arrived,
– Water, O Giannos, for I'm going to die,
Such a bet I will never make again.

Today the young men

Today, all of the brave young men are standing here like lions.
Today, all of the pretty girls are standing like cypress trees.
And the women who are married are standing much admired,
But those poor widow ladies stand unfortunate and sad.

where he opened a taverna and where on October 26, 1932, his name day, he was stabbed
to death by a drunk customer in an argument over a cigarette lighter.

When I see you approaching me

From afar I see you approaching me,
You look like a field of flowers.
But once you have come close to me,
You look like a sooty kettle full of beans.

Αλά γκάρσονι

Τα μαλλιά σου τα κομμένα
τρέλαναν πολλούς και μένα.
Τα 'κοψες α λά γκάρσονι
και η μαμά σου σε μαλώνει.

This little ditty is not a folk song, but was being sung in Athens in the early 20's with the introduction of the Chanel-inspired bobbed hair style from Paris, which was quite shocking to the then very conservative Greek society, whether urban or rural.

My mother recalls the song being brought to the village by young men who had been to the capital and whom her two grandmothers characterized as *manges* or big-city hoods (depending on context *mangas*, the singular, can also mean a cool guy), singing *bournellika* or low-class songs. This kind of song and others which were considered not serious, risqué or indecorous (songs usually coming from outside the traditional canon) were also characterized as *poustika*, a vulgar and insulting word for a catamite. Such a word

A la garçon

Your hair so short and newly cut
Has made me and others act the nut.
You've cut it in a boyish style
And your mother scolds you all the while.

would never have been used by my mother's grandmothers, however. In fact vulgar and coarse language was frowned upon in my mother's family, perhaps because of the family's strong priestly connection over generations. My mother remembers her paternal grandfather not only sharply reprimanding his forty-year old son, her father, for cursing the cross but actually slapping him across the face for his impiety. Greek cursing usually involves the f-word applied to the cross, the Virgin, etc. I, in turn, never heard my father or any of his friends use this kind of language, at least not in the presence of their families.

Η Διαμάντω

Σήκω, Διαμάντω, να πας στο μύλο.
Δεν μπορώ, μάννα μ', δεν μπορώ.
['Αιντε να φέρεις τον γιάτρο,
τον γιατρό και τον σπετσέρη,
με τα φάρμακα στο χέρι.]
Σήκω, Διαμάντω, να πας για ξύλα.
Δεν μπορώ, μάννα μ', δεν μπορώ.
['Αιντε να φέρεις τον γιάτρο,
τον γιατρό και τον σπετσέρη
με τα φάρμακα στο χέρι.]
Σήκω, Διαμάντω, να πας στη βρύση.
Δεν μπορώ, μάννα μ', δεν μπορώ.
['Αιντε να φέρεις τον γιάτρο,
τον γιατρό και τον σπετσέρη
με τα φάρμακα στο χέρι.]

This song describes quite accurately the chores that girls and young women in the village were expected to perform on a daily basis. Diamanto or Diamond is not sick; she's either in love or exhausted. More than likely both.

Beginning in the late teens, my mother's village was fortunate to have a medical doctor resident there at least during the summer. He was from the village and an excellent physician, who in 1930 was awarded a Rockefeller grant to study in Paris. During the winter, however, when many of the people of Theodoriana were down on the plains with the flocks, there was often no doctor available. Then the villagers had to rely on folk medicine, whose cures were usually known to old women.

Once when my mother was about 12, she got a bad infection in her hand, causing it to swell up and start to turn black. She also had a high fever. There was no doctor on hand

Diamanto

Get up, Diamanto, and go to the mill.
I can't, dear mother, I can not.
[Go and bring me back the doctor,
The doctor and the apothecary,
And with him all his medicines.]
Get up, Diamanto, and go fetch some wood.
I can't, dear mother, I can not.
[Go and bring me back the doctor,
The doctor and the apothecary,
And with him all his medicines.]
Get up, Diamanto, and go to the spring.
I can't, dear mother, I can not.
[Go and bring me back the doctor,
The doctor and the apothecary,
And with him all his medicines.]

at the winter pastures where they were that year, near the town of Amphilochia. In desperation, her mother sought out an old woman who assured her that she could cure the child, but also advised her to make a vow to St. Kyriaki. Going to a nearby marsh, the old woman caught a frog which she crushed and applied directly to my mother's hand. During the night the fever came down, and by morning the swelling and discoloration were markedly reduced. In a few days my mother was completely cured. The old woman would not take any payment, but my grandmother fulfilled her vow to St. Kyriaki by having a silver replica made of her daughter's hand and hanging it over the the icon of St. Kyriaki at the monastery church. These kinds of votive offerings, called *tamata* (singular *tama*), for miraculous cures are a common sight in churches throughout Greece.

Μάννα μου, μαντζουράνα μου

Με πάντρεψαν από μικρή
μ' αυτόν τον γέρο, τον μπεκρή.
·Κι εγώ τον πήρα άνδρα μου,
μάννα μου, μαντζουράνα μου.

This is a dance song in the *syrtos* rhythm and known throughout Greece. The word *bekris* in the second line, which I have translated as "boozer" comes from Turkish. Despite the many centuries of Ottoman Turkish occupation, there are surprisingly not that many words of Turkish origin in Greek. Many of the words apply to food, clothing and every-

Απόψε είδα στ' όνειρό μου

Απόψε είδα στ' όνειρό μου μαύρα μάτια στο πλευρό μου.
Αχ, ξυπνάω και δεν τα βρίσκω.
Με τα ρούχα μου μαλώνω, τα ξεσχίζω, τα μπαλώνω.
Ρούχα μου, παλιά μου ρούχα, που 'ν' τα μαύρα μάτια που 'χα;

A love song composed by my mother's paternal grandfather.

Momma dear, my marigold

They married me off when I was young
To that old man, to that boozer.
And so I took him as my husband,
Momma dear, my marigold.

day objects and activities, like *papoutsi* for shoe. Some words have gone from Greek to Arabic to Turkish and then back into Greek, like *makedonision*, parsley, which in Arabic became *magdunis*, then *maïdun* in Turkish and *maïntano* in Modern Greek.

Last night in my dream

Last night in my dream, I saw a pair of black eyes at my side.
Oh, I wake up and do not find them.
I argue with my clothes, I tear at them, then mend them.
O clothes of mine, old clothes, where are those black eyes I once had?

Κυρα-Βαγγελιώ

Ένα νερό, κυρα-Βαγγελιώ, ένα νερό, κρύο νερό!

Αχ, και πούθε κατεβαίνει, Βαγγελιώ μου, παινεμένη;

Ποτίζει, κυρα-Βαγγελιώ, ποτίζει δέντρα και κλαριά.

Αχ, ποτίζει λεμονίτσες, γειά χαρά σας κοπελίτσες.

Ποτίζει και, κυρα-Βαγγελιώ, ποτίζει κι αγιόκλημα.

Αχ, που κάνει το σταφύλι σαν της Βαγγελιώς τα χείλη.

Εγώ θα το, κυρα-Βαγγελιώ, εγώ θα το κόψω κι ας κοπώ,

θα το φάω κι ας πεθάνω, Βαγγελιώ τι να κάνω;

Vangelio is pronounced with a hard 'g' as in "get" with the stress on the 'o' and is one of the diminutive forms of the name Evangelia from which the English Evangeline is derived. This is an old song known throughout Greece. It is sung to a sprightly melody and danced to the rhythm of the *syrtos*. It is one of the songs in this collection that was also sung and danced at our church social affairs in Harrisburg, Pennsylvania during the 30s and 40s. I remember it well, although I never knew all the words or what it was really about, other than it concerned a woman named Vangelio and some water. Unlike the villages in Greece where on festive occasions musicians (often wandering, professional Gypsy bands) would perform the music, we had a gramophone and plenty of the old 78 vinyl phonograph records. Only occasionally was the community able to bring in a musical group from New York to enliven the festivities. The supply of records was always being replenished by visits to New York to the Greek-owned stores there. Surprisingly, the recordings were mostly made in the United States at that time, but also particularly during the Second World War when contact with Greece was broken because of the Nazi occupation. After the war, records began to be brought in from Greece as well and we soon knew all of the Greek popular songs of the day as well as we knew those we heard on the Hit Parade via our local radio station.

Employing the shortened more informal versions of *kyrios* and *kyria* (Lord and Lady; Mr. and Mrs.) as *kyr* and *kyra* with the first name of an older person addressed is a way of showing respect and at the same time intimacy. *Kyra* is only used for married women and widows. While the man in the song might have been addressing a married woman (a risky undertaking at best in the severe traditional patriarchal society of the day) he was more than likely smitten by a widow. If they remained unmarried, widows (especially pretty ones) could become subjects of gossip as well as objects of attention, as depicted by Kazantzakis in *Zorba*. In any case, I have translated the term as "Miss" in this song, following the tradition in the American South of addressing older people as Mister Bill or Miss Pat. In traditional Greek society an unmarried woman would be called by her first name until she reached a certain age and then would be called auntie, *thia/thitsa*, and finally granny, *giagia/vavo*.

Beyond the memory of dancing to this song in the church hall many years ago, for me it also evokes the story of a real Vangelio, whose fate was as tragic as that of the Evangeline in Longfellow's poem.

My mother's father, Christos Papachristos-Kyrtsias, had a brother named Giorgos who had fallen passionately in love with a girl, named Vangelio, in the village. Love was not often a factor in the marital arrangements of that time, although it was hoped that af-

Miss Vangelio

A waterflow, Miss Vangelio, a flow of water icy cold!

Oh, and where does it come down from, my Vangelio, so well-praised?

It waters trees, Miss Vangelio, it waters trees and branches, too.

Oh, it waters small lemon trees; farewell to you, my pretty girls.

It also waters, Miss Vangelio, it also waters a holy vine.

Oh, a vine which produces grapes, like the lips of Vangelio.

I shall cut, Miss Vangelio, I shall cut it and let me be cut,

I shall eat it and let me die; my Vangelio, what can I do?

fection, if not love (*agape*, the word for love also used in the spiritual context), would develop once the marriage was consummated and the couple began its life together. To fall into or marry for *eros* (sensual love) was something always noted and commented upon as out of the ordinary, if not downright dangerous and unpredictable.

My grandfather was the oldest son. By tradition he was expected to marry first among the brothers, after waiting for several of his older sisters to marry before him. This he did in August, 1906. While he knew his intended bride, it was an arranged marriage between one of the village's most important families and a prominent family of Sarakatsan shepherds. Eros played no role in this arrangement, although my grandfather grew to love deeply his proud and handsome mountain bride. Once his brother's marriage festivities were over, Giorgos began insisting that he too wished to marry, but at once. The family was deeply disturbed by this, not because they disapproved of his choice. On the contrary, Vangelio was from a good family, beautiful and well-liked. The reason for the family's concern was the widely held belief that two marriages in the same household during the same calendar year would bring misfortune on one of the couples. Parents, relatives and friends tried to dissuade Giorgos, but to no avail. To their forebodings and misgivings he replied that he would marry Vangelio even if no one of his family would live after him. He married Vangelio in September, 1906.

A few months after they were married, Vangelio became pregnant. Just before giving birth to a son, a beloved brother was killed in an accident. She took the news badly and barely pulled through the ordeal of giving birth. The following year she gave birth to a girl. Her health. physical and mental, had now become so weak that she was advised to have no more children. In 1909 both children died of whooping cough. In 1910 in September, Giorgos died of what was diagnosed of meningitis, although the family attributed his death to a broken heart.

Vangelio was now a childless widow living under the roof of her husband's extended patriarchal family, who still cared for her and were prepared to have her stay. Her kin, however, pressured her to return to her father's house, warning her that she would end up a servant to her in-laws. Vangelio did not want to leave and even proposed that she adopt the youngest sister of her late husband. This proposal was rejected by the family. Eventually her parents convinced her to leave, taking her dowry with her, as was the custom. Soon thereafter she was married off to an innkeeper in a village on the plain where she gave birth to two girls, even though she had been told not to get pregnant again. These births, according to the family's recollection, finally caused Vangelio to lose her mind. In the spring of 1914 my grandfather was taking my mother from the winter pasture on the plains up to the village to enroll her in school. On the way they stopped for food and lodging and to feed their horses at the inn of Vangelio's second husband. While there, they could hear the screams and rantings of a woman during the night. The next morning they were told it was Vangelio. My grandfather at once asked to see her. Initially, Vangelio did not recognize who he was but suddenly she had a moment of lucidity and began calling out to him, "Christos, Christos, take me with you." But, just as suddenly she lapsed back again into incoherence. She was a sorry sight indeed. My mother, six years old at the time, remembered that Vangelio was tied up and confined in a small dark room. My grandfather was told that no medicines had been effective. As a last resort Vangelio was to be taken to the monastery of St. Kyriaki, near her ancestral village and that of her husband, famous locally for its wonder-working icon. There it was hoped that the saint would perform a miracle.

A month or so later, in the spring of 1914, Vangelio was brought to her parent's house in the village prior to be taken to the monastery. She was truly in a bad way, unrecognizable and uncontrollable. That night she was tied even more securely, as her condition seemed to have worsened. Her cries could be heard from time to time throughout the village, pleading that she be taken to the house of her first husband, Giorgos. The next morning the family awoke to find that Vangelio was gone. How she had broken her bonds no one could discover, but gone she was. Her family immediately came to the house of her former in-laws, hoping that she would have gone there but that was not the case. A major search ensued over the following days and weeks with no success.

Vangelio was never seen again, nor was her body ever recovered. It was assumed that she must have fallen into one of the many narrow and inaccessible ravines in the rugged mountains surrounding the village and that scavengers eventually found her. In the years that followed, the story of Giorgos and Vangelio was often recounted with sorrow mingled with dread and cited as an admonition that one would do well to pay heed to the wisdom of the old and not flout custom.

Δίστιχα – Couplets

Ψηλά την κτίζεις τη φωλιά και θα λυγίσει ο κλώνος.
Και θα σου φύγει το πουλί και θα σου μείνει ο πόνος.

You go and build the nest on high and then the branch will bend.
The bird will soon depart from you and leave you only pain.

A well-known couplet of both unrequited love as well as the sorrow for a loved one who is far from home, *xenitiko*.

Ο έρωτας είναι κακός και, αλιά, ποιον θα τον κολλήσει.
Εκόλλησε κι ένα γέροντα και δεν μπορεί να ζήσει.

Love is bad and woe to him whom it afflicts and sickens.
It afflicted an old man and he can not go on living.

Σε τούτο τον κόσμο που 'μαστε, άλλοι τον είχαν πρώτα.
Και μας τον παραδώσανε και άλλοι θα τον πάρουν πάλι.

This world where we now find ourselves, others had it first.
To us they passed it over and others again will take it.

This couplet is known throughout Greece.

Και τα τραγούδια λόγια είναι, τα λέν' οι πικραμένοι
να τους περνάει ο καημός, να τους διαβαίνει ο πόνος.

Songs, too, are just words and phrases, which embittered people say,
So their grief will ease a bit; so that their pain will pass away.

Τα βάσανά μου είναι πολλά, ποιας πέτρας να τα λέω;
Και η πέτρα να μην μου μιλεί, να κάθομαι να κλαίω.

My troubles are many and great; which rock can I tell them to?
The rock does not speak to me, so I sit alone and weep.

Ο βασιλικός κι αν μαραθεί, τη μυρωδιά την έχει.
Η αγάπη μου κι αν μ' αρνηθεί, το νου της σε με τον έχει.

Even if sweet basil dries up and withers, an aroma it maintains.
Even if my love rejects me, thoughts of me she still retains.

Βασιλικός μυρίζει εδώ, τον έχει κόρη στο λαιμό.
Τον έχει η ρούσα και η ξανθιά περιπλεγμένο στα μαλλιά.

There is a scent of sweet basil here; a girl wears it around her neck.
An auburn-haired girl and a blonde, both have their hair braided with it.

A couplet composed by my mother.

Τρεις κοπέλες λυγερές, ματάκια μου, πάνε στο δρόμο μοναχές
Εδώ που πάμε, εμείς οι τρεις, ματάκια μου, να μην έρθει άλλος κανείς.

Three graceful girls, my pretty eyes, are going on the road alone
Here as we go the three of us, my pretty eyes, let no one else come along.

A couplet composed by my mother for her two best friends.

Εσύ που ξέρεις τα πολλά και ο νους σου κατεβάζει,
χίλια καντάρια σίδερο πόσα βελόνια βγάζει;

You, who know so much, and your mind can comprehend,
From one thousand tons of iron how many needles can be made in the end?

This is a riddle with no answer, but used when putting down a know-it-all.

Αχ, αχ, Ελένη, τι καυγάς θα γένει
στη γειτονιά σου για την ομορφιά σου;

Oh, oh, Eleni, what a row will take place
In your neighborhood over your beauty?

Άνοιξε η τριανταφυλλιά, και την πρώτη τους φωλιά
χτίζουνε τ' αηδόνια, χτίζουνε και τα χελιδόνια.

The rose has opened and flowered while nightingales and swallows
Are building and making their first nests up in the trees.

Στην καλύβα μου, ο καημένος, κάθομαν θαραπαυμένος,
φύλαγα τα κερασάκια, μην τα φαν τα κοριτσάκια.

I was sitting in my hut, poor me, quietly and at ease,
Guarding well the little cherries so that the girls would not eat them.

Δυο πουλάκια τα καημένα πάνουν κι έρχονται για μένα.
Το 'να το ταΐζω μέλι, τ' άλλο κόκκινο πιπέρι.

Two poor little birds come and go for me.
To the one I give honey, to the other red pepper.

Τι να την κάνω τη ζωή αν είναι κι άλλη τόση,
ενώ υπάρχει θάνατος και το κορμί θα λιώσει.

What would I do with life even if it lasted twice as long,
When I know that there is always death and the body will melt away.

Πολλές φωτιές με τριγυρνούν, καμία δε με καίει.
Όλες εγώ τις άναψα, κανένας δε μου φταίει.

Many fires gather round me, yet not a one does burn me.
I'm the one who has set them blazing and no one's to blame but me.

Εσένα πάνε, βλαχούλα μ', τα φλουριά
κι όλο πλεξίδες τα μαλλιά.

Florins suit you, my little shepherd girl
And your hair, as well, all braided.

Ώρα καλή στην πρύμνη σου και αέρα στα πανιά σου,
ούτε πουλί πετούμενο να μην βρεθεί μπροστά σου.

Good fortune on your prow and wind in your sails,
May not even a flying bird find itself before you.

A well-known toast.

Αχ, εγώ είδα τη μοίρα μου στο μήλο, στο καρύδι.
Το μήλο ήταν σάπιο και το καρύδι κούφιο.

Oh, I saw my fate and destiny in the apple, in the walnut.
The apple was all rotten and empty was the walnut.

This couplet refers to the custom among the young of the village of picking a ripening walnut or apple on the 6th of August, the feast of the Transfiguration, and cutting it to ascertain the future. This custom is observed in other parts of Greece, as well.

Η θάλασσα με δέρνει, το κύμα με βαρεί,
και ένα μεγάλο ψάρι μου τρώει το κορμί.

The sea beats me, the wave strikes me,
And a huge fish is feeding on my body.

A couplet, describing a drowned sailor composed by my mother.

Μοσχοκάρυδο και κανέλλα
ποια είναι η όμορφη κοπέλα;

Nutmeg and cinnamon
Who's the pretty girl?

Στη θάλασσα θα πέσω, μέσ' στα κύματα,
να πιάσω την ποδιά σου με τα κεντήματα.

I'm going to fall into the sea, among the waves to fall,
To catch hold of your apron with its embroideries and all.

Χελιδονάκι θα γίνω, στα χείλη σου θα κάτσω,
να σε φιλήσω μια και δυο και πάλι να πετάξω.

A little swallow I'll become upon your lips to sit,
To kiss you once, to kiss you twice and again away to flit.

Της όμορφης το μάγουλο,
όταν γελάει, λακώνει.

When a pretty girl laughs,
She has dimples on her cheeks.

Καμάρι, βλαχούλα μ', είσαι του βουνού,
εσύ μου τρέλανες το νου.

You are the pride of the mountain, my shepherd girl,
And you've made me lose my mind, as well.

Πολύ σου πάει, βλαχούλα μ', το τσεμπέρι,
θέλω να σε κάμω ταίρι.

The kerchief suits you and on you looks great,
I want you, shepherd girl, to be my mate.

Μάγια μου 'χεις καμωμένα
και τρελαίνομαι για σένα.

Magic spells you've cast upon me
And I'm crazy over you completely.

Για σένα, μαυρομάτα μου,
αρνήθηκα τη μάννα μου.

For you, my dear black-eyed lover,
I have given up my mother.

Για σένα κι όχι άλλονε
βάλω σεβντά μεγάλονε.

For you and for no other soul
I bear a love, huge beyond control.

Με τρέλανες, να τρελαθείς,
σαν το κεράκι να λιωθείς.

You've made me crazy; be crazy too!
Like a candle, melt without ado.

Με τρέλανε η φούστα σου,
τα νάζια και τα γούστα σου.

I've gone mad because of your skirt,
All of your whims and how you flirt.

Ο καιρός φέρει τα λάχανα, ο καιρός τα παραπούλια.
Με τον καιρό και το δεντρί βγάζει καρπούς και φύλλα.

The right season brings the plants and greens, the right season brings the birds.
And in season also comes the tree with leaves and fruits bestirred.

Εσύ 'σαι κι άλλη μια σε τούτη γειτονιά.
Τα κάλλη σου κυρά μου δεν τά 'χει αλλή καμιά.

But for another girl, in this neighborhood, you're the only one.
Beauty such as yours, my dear, is possessed by none.

Του Γάμου
Marriage Songs

A marriage procession in Theodoriana, 1956.

Της λυγερής το φόρεμα

Της λυγερής το φόρεμα, της νύφης το φουστάνι,
τρία κορίτσια το κεντάν, και τρεις ξανθομαλλούσες.
Η μια κεντάει τον αετό κι άλλη τον πετρίτη,
και η τρίτη, η μικρότερη, του Μάη τα λουλούδια.
– Όσα λουλούδια, νύφη μου, έχει το φόρεμά σου,
τόσα να 'ναι τα χρόνια σου και τόσα τα καλά σου.

This is a Sarakatsan wedding song, sung as the bride was being dressed.

Ασπροσυννεφιά ο ουρανός

Ασπροσυννεφιά ο ουρανός γιατί ξυρίζουν το γαμπρό.
Ξυράφια από τα Γιάννενα κι ακόνια από την Πρέβεζα.
Για σπούδαξε, μπαρμπέρη μου, για σπούδαξε το χέρι σου,
κι έχουμε στράτες μακρινές, ποτάμια να περάσουμε,
την πέρδικα να πιάσουμε.

This song is sung when they are shaving the bridegroom on the day of the wedding. Ioannina or Giannena (as it is called in the local dialect) is the capital of Epirus and Preveza is a seaport on the coast of the same province.

Ας παν να δουν τα μάτια μου

Ας παν να δουν τα μάτια μου πώς τα περνά η αγάπη μου.
Μην ήύρε αλλού κι αγάπησε και μένα μ' απαράτησε.
Ποιος το 'πε, δεντρουλάκι μου, – δεν σ' αγαπώ πουλάκι μου;
Αν το 'πε ο ήλιος να χαθεί, τ' αστέρι να μην ξημερωθεί.
Κι αν το 'πε η κόρη, η ανύπανδρη, τον άνδρα της να μη χαρεί.

This song is sung as the bridegroom's party leaves to go and get the bride.

The dress of the graceful young girl

The dress of the graceful young girl, the gown of the pretty bride,
Three girls are embroidering it, three blonde and fair-haired maids.
One girl embroiders the eagle and the other the rock-bound hawk,
While the third one and the youngest, the blooming flowers of May.
– As many flowers, my dear bride, as can be found on your dress,
So may your years be many, too, and all the good things of life.

The sky is covered with white clouds

The sky is covered with white clouds because it's the groom they're shaving.
The razors come from Giannena, from Preveza the whetstones.
Train yourself well, my barber man and train well that hand of yours,
For long roads have we to travel, rivers have we to ford and cross,
So that we can go and catch the partridge.

Let my eyes now go off and see

Let my eyes now go off and see how my love is doing.
Maybe she's gone elsewhere for love and she has abandoned me.
Little tree, who said it, – I don't love you, my little bird?
If the sun said it, may it get lost; the star, may it not see the dawn.
And if the unmarried girl, may she not enjoy a husband.

Ξύπνα, περδικομάτα μου

Ξύπνα, περδικομάτα μου, και ήρθα στην αυλή σου.
Χρυσά πλεξίδια σου 'φερα να πλέξεις τα μαλλιά σου.
– Σαν ήρθες, καλωσόρισες και έκανες τον κόπο.

This song was sung when the bridegroom's party came to the bride's house to serenade her before leaving for the church. Each region in Greece had its own customs relating to marriage and to other social and religious events as well. Even within regions one could find differences. For the most part the marriage customs in my mother's village were similar to those of other parts of Greece but there were also differences.

In the summer of 1956 my sister and I attended the wedding of my mother's youngest brother and were privileged to participate in what was then still a living traditional wedding celebration. Below is a brief account of such a wedding, as remembered by my mother. Unless otherwise indicated, it is a description of what my sister and I also experienced.

Although people knew that a marriage had been arranged months, if not years, ahead, formal invitations to the wedding itself were usually issued several weeks in advance. Traditionally this was done by young boys who had both parents living. The boys would go to the houses of those to be invited carrying flasks of raki, the Greek version of grappa. Here they would toast the intended guest and orally invite them. While the guests always brought gifts, these could range from money to household items and often included food for the party, like meat and pites.

The festivities began on the Wednesday before the wedding on the following Sunday, (weddings were traditionally always on a Sunday). On that day the dough, prozymia, would be prepared for the baking of the wedding cake, kouloura, a kind of sweet bread. This would be the occasion for the first of the parties associated with the wedding celebration. Actually, two wedding cakes were prepared, one at the bride's house and one at the groom's. The cake was decorated with figures of birds and flowers and a cross. While the cake was being prepared, the bride and groom would be "floured," that is flour would be thrown upon their heads with wishes that they have many children, that they be fortunate and prosperous and that they live long with hair turned white as flour. On Thursday the cakes would be baked amid general merriment. At that time the gifts from the two sides would also be prepared, which could consist of pieces of jewelry or other appropriate items but always a handkerchief of the finest material and workmanship. This was a traditional gift between lovers and figures in many of the folksongs.

On Friday evening, the two cakes and gifts would be exchanged. First the bride's cake was carried to the groom's house where a party would already be underway and then the groom's cake to the bride's. The cakes and gifts were always to be taken by an unmarried young boy and girl, whose parents were both living and preferably cousins. It was considered good luck, if during the respective exchanges, something could be taken by one of the cake carriers from the house of the other family without being caught. Part of the fun of the evening was for the other side to keep watch that this did not happen and to catch them in the act. Saturday would be spent in the more basic preparations for the wedding, especially at the groom's house where the wedding feast was usually held. This would involve among other activities the slaughtering and roasting of the sheep and goats and would be another occasion for a party.

Weddings took place Sunday afternoon. The bride would be dressed in her house by her

Awaken my partridge-eyed girl

Awaken, my partridge-eyed girl, for I've come here to your garden.
I have brought you golden braids to plait into your hair.
– Since you are here, you are welcome for having taken all the trouble.

female relatives and friends who sang special songs for the occasion. If she could afford it, she had two dresses, one for the first day of the wedding and another for the second. The brides had usually made their own dresses or had them made. Traditionally, they did not wear white but rather dresses of various colors with red, the color of life and joy being preferred, as in ancient times and as in other lands like India and China. In 1906 my mother's mother wore a red dress for example. It was only in 1930, the year of my mother's marriage, that two of her friends chose white for the first time. My mother, however, chose a light rose color for her dress, which she sewed herself, because she wanted to refashion it in order to wear it later in America. (In 1956 the white wedding dress was the accepted bridal gown and in the villages, at least, was usually rented with only the veil being bought). While the bride was being titivated and dressed, the groom was being shaved. This procedure was the occasion for singing and gift giving during which the groom sat and held a tray onto which his friends and guests put gifts of money. Once dressed, the groom with his friends would proceed to the bride's house led by a man carrying a flag, *flampouro*, (not done in 1956) and by a young boy of living parents carrying the wedding wreaths on a silver tray. The groom's party would be accompanied by a band of musicians, if he could afford it.

On arriving at the bride's house the song above was sung bidding the bride to come forth but she would not appear. Then the groom played out another custom. As he tried to enter the house to claim his bride, her family would attempt to prevent him from coming in. A stylized struggle would ensue and the groom would have to force himself into the house to try to find her but she would be hidden from him. Finally the groom would give up and depart with his friends but leaving the musicians behind. After his departure the bride would appear at last. Standing in the courtyard of her house or in the door as the case might be, she and the group would sing a song in which she took leave of her family, friends and neighborhood. At the end of the song, her dower chest and its contents (linens, embroideries, knitted, woven and crocheted pieces, etc.) and other household items of her dowry like kitchenware, which had earlier been brought out of the house, would be taken up by female relatives and friends and carried on their heads or backs in display for the admiration of the onlookers through the lanes of the village to the church. This procession was followed by the musicians, the bride, her family and guests.

Reaching the church, the women carrying the dower chest and other dowry items would continue on their way to the groom's house. At the courtyard of the church, however, the groom and his group would be waiting for the bride and her party. The two would come together and join in traditional circle dancing. During the dance the important persons of the party each had a chance to lead, the bride first. Then came the groom, the best man, the fathers, if alive, or oldest brothers or male cousins and the bride's mother but not the groom's mother who would be waiting at his house to greet the bride following the wedding ceremony. After all the important persons had a chance to lead the dance, the groom would take his bride and hand in hand they entered the church. They would be followed by all his friends and relatives and by the bride's father and mother and her relatives and friends. With the completion of the religious ceremony, which is called the crowning or wreathing, *ta stephana*, there would be more dancing in front of the church. After the dancing was over a second time, the bride's family and friends would depart. They were not invited to the subsequent wedding dinner except for one or two of her closest male relatives like brothers or cousins. Traditionally the first day of the wedding was the groom's and only on the second day were the bride's family and friends invited to the groom's to feast together. This event was called the "returns" or the *epistrophia* (in 1956, this custom was no longer observed; the wedding celebration lasted one day and everyone was invited to the dinner).

With the dancing over and the departure of the bride's family, the groom's party would wend its way to his house led by the musicians and singing as it went (in 1956 the bride's family came later, just before the start of dinner). Upon reaching the house the bride would proceed to the door where her mother-in-law was waiting for her. There the bride would kneel and kiss the hand of her mother-in-law, who in turn would give her a gift of a piece of jewelry (usually silver). The bride was then given rice and apples symbolizing fertility and prosperity, which she in sequence cast to the four cardinal directions. Finally she was given two pitchers of wine, which she poured on the ground as she entered the house, crossing over an iron knife lying on the threshold. The knife symbolized good health and steadfastness. In the house she would lead the group to the room which was prepared as the bridal chamber where her hope chest items had been placed and where the groom's friends and relatives would place gifts of money on the bridal bed. Finally everyone would go out to the courtyard, if the weather permitted, where the tables were set and the festivities would begin.

Dimitrios (Jimmy), Vasiliki, Anna and Athanasios (Thomas) Scotes, in a formal portrait taken in America.

In my mother's day and until 1930 the bride was expected to stand by the groom in silence and attendance, bowing from time to time while he and his friends ate and drank. Recently returned to the village after a thirty-year absence, my father would not allow my mother to observe this custom; she was the first in the village not to do so, causing considerable comment afterwards. A few weeks later at another wedding of close friends where my newlywed parents were invited and guests of honor, my father intervened a second time asking why the bride was standing and requested that she sit down. She did and the custom was never observed again.

On Monday, the second day of the wedding celebration, as already mentioned, the groom would entertain the bride's family and friends and the wedding was over. Tuesday following the wedding the groom's family would gather for the first meal as a family with the new bride (in 1956 this custom was no longer observed). At that meal the bride was expected to bring out the piece of the wedding cake, which the groom had previously sent her and which she had put in her dower chest, and offer it to her new family. This was a sign that she was now one of them and would share in all their joys and sorrows. Until my mother's childhood, it was still expected that a new bride speak only when spoken to and do her mother-in-law's bidding. She would also be called by a feminine form of her husband's first name. Thus, the wife of a Giorgos or George would be called Giorgena, the wife of a Thanasis would be Thanasina. Some of the customs described above were already beginning to fall into disuse as my mother grew up. Since the dislocations of the Second World War, the subsequent Civil War and the earthquake of 1967, many of the rest have also been cast aside or forgotten.

The Scotes children,
Anna, Theodore and Thomas,
a few years later.

Μάννα μου, τα λουλούδια μου

Μάννα μου, τα λουλούδια μου συχνά να τα ποτίζεις.
[Μάννα μου γλυκιά.]
Αφήνω γειά στη γειτονιά, σ' όλα τα παλικάρια.
Αφήνω γειά και στις όμορφες, σ' όλες τις μαυρομάτες.
Αφήνω γειά, μαννούλα μου γλυκιά, κι εγώ πάω στην ξενιτιά.
[Μάννα μου γλυκιά.]

A wedding song from Epirus, sung as the bride departed her family's house for the church. While the bride may only have been going to another part of the village, and not to "foreign lands," she was in effect severing her ties with her family and becoming a

Απάνω σ' ένα βουνό

Πάνω σε τρίκορφο βουνό, κορφοανταριασμένο,
πόχει ανταρούλα στην κορφή, καταχνιά στη ρίζα,
εκεί 'ναι πύργος γυάλινος με κρυσταλλένια τζάμια.
Μέσα κοιμάται μια ξανθιά και μιας νεράιδας κόρη.
Και πώς να την ξυπνήσουμε και πώς να της το πούμε;
– Ξύπνα καημένη λυγερή, ξύπνα καημένη κόρη.
Ο καπετάνιος έρχεται μαζί με τόνε γιό του,
Και θα σε πάρουν μακριά να πας να ζεις στα ξένα.

This is a love song, which is sung as the bride leaves her home to go to the church for the wedding ceremony. It is also sung as a song of absence or longing, *xenitiko*, as alluded to in the last line.

Ετούτο το καλοκαιράκι

Ετούτο το καλοκαιράκι κυνηγούσα ένα πουλάκι.
Κυνηγούσα, προσπαθούσα, να το πιάσω δεν μπορούσα.
Στένω τα χρυσόβεργά μου για να 'ρθ' η πέρδικα κοντά μου.

A wedding song sung after the wedding ceremony as the bride and groom make their way to the groom's house.

Please water my flowers often

Please water my flowers often; please water them, dear mother.
[O my sweet mother.]
I bid farewell to the neighborhood, to all the handsome young men.
I bid farewell to the pretty girls and to all those with eyes of black.
I bid you farewell, sweet mother dear, and I leave for foreign lands.
[O my sweet mother.]

member of another family, merging her identity and fate totally with it from now on.
Hence, the sense of final departure expressed in the song.

The glass tower

Up on a mountain of three peaks, a mountain of mist-covered peaks,
Where light mist hangs on every peak and fog sits upon the foothills,
There stands a tower built of glass with windows all of crystal.
Inside there sleeps a fair-haired girl, the daughter of a fairy.
How can we go awaken her; how can we go and tell her?
– Awaken, my poor graceful child; awaken, my poor daughter.
For the captain is coming now, along with his only son,
And they will take you far away to live there on foreign shores.

This past summer time

During all this past summer time I was chasing a little bird.
I was chasing and was trying to catch her but was not able.
I set a snare of golden branches, so the partridge would come near me.

Βιολέτα μ' ανθισμένη

Βιολέτα μ' ανθισμένη με φύλλα πράσινα,
περνάω τον καημό σου με χίλια βάσανα.

Sung by the wedding party after the church ceremony on the way to the groom's house.

Νεραντζούλα

– Νεραντζούλα φουντωμένη, πού είναι τα άνθια σου;
Που είναι τ' άνθια που 'χες πρώτα; Πού είναι ο νιος καρπός;
– Τράβηξε βοριάς κι αέρας, και τα γκρέμισε και τα μάρανε.
– Σε παρακαλώ, βοριά μου, τράβα σιγαλά
για ν' αράξουν τα καράβια τα Ζαγοριανά,
Πόχουν μέσα κοριτσάκια κι όμορφα παιδιά,
για ν' αράξει κι ο καλός μου απ' την ξενιτειά,
και μου φέρει ένα μαντήλι μ' εκατό φλουριά.
Και στην άκρη στο μαντήλι έχει αντίλογο,
– Θέλεις κόρη μου παντρέψου, θέλεις καλογριά.
Θέλεις και στα μαύρα ντύσου και καρτέρε με.

This song has several variants with the ships coming from other parts of Greece, usually one of the islands. Zagoria is an inland region of Epirus, which was a major trading area during the Turkish period, and though it did not have a harbor, its merchants did have

Η Διαμαντούλα

Κάτω στα δασιά πλατάνια, στην κρυόβρυση, Διαμαντούλα μου,
Κάθονταν δυο παλικάρια και μια λυγερή, Διαμαντούλα μου.
Κάθονταν και τρώγαν, πίναν και κουβέντιαζαν, Διαμαντούλα μου.
– Διαμαντούλα μ', τι είσαι τέτοια, τέτοια κίτρινη;
Μην ο ήλιος σε μαραίνει, μην είναι φάντασμα;
– Ούτε ήλιος με μαραίνει, ούτε φάντασμα.
Με μαραίνει η αγάπη, λεβέντη μου, τα μεσάνυχτα.

This is a well-known song of unrequited love, which is also sung after the wedding ceremony on the way to the groom's house.

O my flowering violet

O my flowering violet with your leaves so green,
I endure my longing for you with a thousand torments.

The bitter orange tree

– Leafy bitter orange tree where are all your blossoms?
Where are the blossoms you once had and where is your new fruit?
– A north wind came up and made them fall and withered them all away.
– North wind, I beg of you, blow softly and blow gently
So the ships of Zagoria can drop down their anchors,
The ships that carry pretty girls and very handsome boys,
So my love can also anchor, coming back from foreign shores,
And he can bring to me a kerchief with a hundred florins.
And on the edge of the kerchief there is a message written,
– If you want, my girl, get married; if you want, become a nun.
And if you want, get dressed in black and wait for me.

their own ships. The song was often sung at weddings, again as the party proceeded to the groom's house.

Diamantoula

Down where the plane trees are thick by the cold water springs, my Diamantoula,
Were sitting two brave young men and a graceful young girl, my Diamantoula.
They were sitting, eating, drinking and talking there, my Diamantoula,
– Diamantoula, why are you such a sight; why so sallow?
Does the sun waste you away; does a ghost afflict you?
– The sun does not waste me away, nor does a ghost afflict me.
But love is wasting me away, my fine man, at midnight.

Της Λάμπρω

Κει πέρα βγαίνει ένας καπνός, σαν τι καπνός να είναι;
Οι βλάχοι κάνουν μια χαρά, παντρεύουνε τη Λάμπρω.
Κι έχουν αρνιά που ψένουνε, κριάρια σουβλισμένα.
Την παίρνει ένα κλεφτόπουλο και γιος του καπετάνου.
Κι οι βλάχοι το μετάνιωσαν και Λάμπρω δεν τη δίνουν.
– Εμείς θα την επάρουμε κι όλοι να σκοτωθούμε.
– Εμείς δεν θα τη δώσουμε κι όλοι ας σκοτωθούμε.

This song was composed by my mother's father for his marriage to Lamprini or Lampro Plevris in 1906. My grandfather was the son of one of the most prominent families in the village. She was the daughter of a Sarakatsan chief shepherd or *architselingas* and the wedding was a major social event of the time and of the area. She came to the wedding ceremony and celebration riding a white horse and escorted by scores of her father's family and friends.

The Sarakatsan were a Greek-speaking group of transhumant shepherds, who for centuries grazed their flocks in the summer on the upper reaches of the Pindus Range and elsewhere and descended to the plains in the winter. During the Turkish period they ranged throughout the mountainous regions of Epirus, Thessaly, Macedonia, Thrace and

Εδώ στου κυρ-γαμπρού τα σπίτια

Εδώ στου κυρ-γαμπρού τα σπίτια τι δασιά είν' τα κυπαρίσσια!
Μπάτε, αργέψτε τα καμπόσα, να διαβεί ο γαμπρός και η νύφη
και καμπόσοι συμπεθέροι.

A wedding song sung when the wedding party arrived at the bridegroom's house following the church ceremony. The cypress symbolized beauty and pride, and the fact that the trees are "thick" implies that the groom is well off. The reference to the in-laws refers to the old custom of not inviting the in-laws, except for a few, to the first day of the wedding feast.

Over there some smoke is rising

Over there some smoke is rising, what kind of smoke might it be?
The shepherds have a feast today, their daughter Lampro's wedding.
They have sheep which they are roasting and rams grilled on the skewer.
A young klepht is to marry her, and he is a captain's son.
But the shepherds have changed their minds and will not give up Lampro.
– We will take her away from you, though all of us may be killed.
– We will not give her up to you and let all of us be killed.

even Asia Minor. Some are still today found in Bulgaria. They were clannish, conservative and religious with a strict code of honor.
Traditionally they rarely married out of the group and when they did they would only marry other Greek-speaking Christians. After the liberation from Turkish rule of those areas where they lived and starting in the late 19th century, they began to settle down permanently in mountain villages, (often those near which they had traditionally summered like my mother's village), while still pursuing a transhumant mode of living. Acceptance by the villagers, who could also be stand-offish if not clannish, was achieved through godfathering and by marriage. My grandfather's marriage was one such successful example, in spite of the bellicose ending of the song.

Here at sir bridegroom's houses

Here at Sir Bridegroom's houses how thick are all the cypress.
Come in and thin them out so that the bride and groom may pass
As well as some of the in-laws.

Έβγα κυρά

Έβγα κυρά και πεθερά, για να δεχτεί την πέρδικα.
Ήλιος, φεγγαρί να φανεί, να δες τηνε π'ως περπατεί.
Σαν άγγελος με το σπαθί, αυτού στην πόρτα που θα μπεί,
κι αυτού στην πόρτα που θα μπεί, κόσα με κόσα θα πιαστεί.

This is sung as the bride is welcomed by the mother-in-law at the door of her hew home.
The reference to the angel with a sword is to the icon of the archangel Michael, who is
always depicted with a sword.
The last line is a humorous addition by my mother to indicate that the relationship between the bride and her mother-in-law was not always harmonious.

Καλωσόριστε

Καλωσόριστε στό σπίτι μας, καλωσόριστεί να είσαι,
χρόνια πολλά να έχεις κι πολλά παιδιά να κάνεις.

This and other verses like it were sung by the bridegroom's mother as she welcomed the
new bride.
The Greek word for children, *paidia*, in village parlance usually meant just boys. In other
versions of this welcome the mother-in-law says "may you have many *arsenika*," which
means "male ones." Girls meant dowries and dowries meant financial burdens.

Come out, O mistress

Come out, O mistress, mother of the groom, to bid a welcome to the partridge
May she appear like the sun and like the moon, look at her how she walks.
She is like an angel with its sword, there at the door where she will enter.
But there at the door where she will enter, she'll soon be caught pulling hair.

Welcome to our home

Welcome to our home and may you be blessed with good fortune,
May your years be many and may you have many children.

Σε τούτη τάβλα που ᾿μαστε

Σε τούτη τάβλα που ᾿μαστε, σε τούτο το τραπέζι,
τον Αγγελο φιλεύουμε και τον Χριστό κερνάμε.
Και την Παρθένο-Δέσποινα την διπλοπροσκυνάμε,
να μας χαρίσει τα κλειδιά, κλειδιά του Παραδείσου,
ν᾿ ανοίξω τον Παράδεισο, να δω τι έχει μέσα.
Δεξιά μεριά φτωχολογιά, κι αριστερά οι πλούσιοι.
Φτωχοί βαστάν στα χέρια τους λαμπάδες αναμμένες.
Πλούσιοι βαστάν στα χέρια τους σακούλες σφαλισμένες.
– Πάρτε φτωχοί τα γρόσια μας και δώστε μας λαμπάδες.
– Εδώ τα γρόσια δεν περνούν, τα γρόσια δεν διαβαίνουν.
εδώ περνάει λιβάνι και κερί και καθαρή ψυχούλα.

This is a table song to be sung and not danced, usually after a holiday meal, a wedding or baptism celebration. It is always the first song to be sung and is considered a prayer. I first heard it in July, 1956, on my first visit to my parent's village, after a mid-day meal of roasted lamb, pies, *pites*, filled with mountain greens or cheese, black olives, feta, homemade bread, cold watermelon and red wine. I was at a table in the courtyard of my mother's hillside family house. Gathered round was a host of newly-met relatives sitting under a cherry tree planted by her grandfather. Below was a panoramic view of the village and the encircling mountains. As we finished eating, the group fell silent for a mo-

At this round table

At this round table where we sit, at this our dining table,
We host and receive the Angel and Christ we treat and welcome.
And to our Lady Virgin, twice we bow our heads in rev'rence,
That she may grant to us the keys, keys to paradise bestow,
That I may open paradise to see what lies within there.
On the right stand all the poor, while on the left the wealthy.
In their hands all of the poor folk are holding lighted tapers.
In their hands all of the wealthy hold money bags well sealed.
– O you poor, take our coins of gold and give us lighted tapers.
– Here coins of gold have no value, gold coins find no acceptance,
Here incense and a candle count and a soul that's clean and pure.

ment and then began to sing this song softly at first but soon with fervor and seriousness.
At its conclusion, all turned to one another and gave the traditional Greek wish on such
an occasion "And Next Year Too," *kai tou chronou.*
Lady Virgin is one of the popular ways of addressing The Virgin Mary in prayer. Another
and more common term, both in prayer and in oaths, is the All-Holy one , *Panagia.* More
formally, however, in the liturgy and in the writings of the church, She is called the
Theotokos, meaning the "God-Bearer."

Κάτω στο δαφνοπόταμο

Κάτω στο δαφνοπόταμο που είν' οι δάφνες οι πολλές,
εκεί κάθεται ο κυρ-νονός και πελεκάει το μάρμαρο,
Να βγάλει αθάνατο νερό να πιούν τ' αναδιχτούδια του,
να πιούν να μην πεθάνουν.
Πολλά χρόνια να ζήσουν, ν' ασπρίσουν να γεράσουν,
να γίνουν σαν τον Όλυμπο, σαν τ' άσπρο περιστέρι.

This song is sung in honor of the best man or *koumparos* at the wedding dinner when they would cut the wedding cake or *kouloura* sent by the bride to the groom on the Friday before the marriage. It was sung to me as I was my uncle's best man at his wedding in 1956. *Koumparos* is the Greek form of the Italian *compare* or the Spanish *compadre* from the Latin *cum-pater*, meaning "like a father." Originally the word was used to mean godfather and over time came to mean best man as well. This relationship, whether as godfather or best man, was and still is among the Greeks a serious one.

Ecclesiastically, the godfather or godmother is considered as being the spiritual parent of the child responsible for assuring its moral development and in the old days expected to help the child whenever possible, especially if the real parents died. The relationship was considered so close that the child of a godfather could not marry his godchild. It was

The laurel river

Down by the laurel river where the laurels are so many,
The groom's best man is sitting there and hews a piece of marble,
To bring forth the water, the water of immortality,
So that the newlyweds may drink; may drink of it and never die.
May they live for many years; their hair grow white and they grow old,
May they be like Mount Olympos; may they be like the white dove.

a way, therefore, to bind together families otherwise not related. Traditionally the best man automatically became the godfather of the first child of the newlyweds. The godfather also had the right to choose the name of the child without seeking permission of the parents. He or she would usually consult but this was not required. The best man was in most cases the best friend or close relative of the groom but he could be his actual godfather. In fact, it was the custom to ask one's godfather first if he wanted to be the best man before asking someone else. The godfather could then propose his son, if he had one, and it was expected that the choice would be accepted. Thus, it was not unusual for the koumparos relationship to be renewed between the same families over generations; this was a desired and esteemed situation.

The last two lines are a formulaic couplet found in other songs as well.

Το παπάκι πάει την ποταμιά

Το παπάκι πάει την ποταμιά γυρεύοντας για συντροφιά.
– Πού πας, παπί μ', και δε μας λες, όλο διαβαίνεις κι όλο κλαις;
– Πάω να εύρω συντροφιά μες στην έρημη την ποταμιά.
– Πού πας παπάκι, καλό παπί, και συντροφιά σε καρτερεί;

A love song sung at the wedding feast.

Τώρα την αυγή

Τώρα την αυγή, τώρα σιμά να φέξει.
Τώρα τα πουλιά, τώρα τα χελιδόνια.
Τώρα οι πέρδικες συχνολαλούν και λένε,
– Ξύπνα, αγάπη μου, ξύπνα, γλυκό μου ταίρι.
Ξύπνα κι έφεξε, ξύπνα και πήρε μέρα.
Ξύπνα και φίλησε ματάκια λιγωμένα
κι άσπρονε λαιμό σαν το κρύο το νερό,
πόρχεται απ' τα χιόνια και από τα κρύσταλλα.

An old love song sung to a beautiful melody. It is usually the last song sung at the wedding celebration, as the best man takes leave of the newlyweds.

The duck

The duck goes by the riverside looking for companionship.
– Where are you going, little duck, and you don't tell us as you go weeping?
– I go to seek companionship by the lonely riverside.
– Where are you going, little duck, and companionship awaits you here?

Now the dawn has come

Now the dawn has come, now the dawn's about to break.
Now, all the many birds; now all the swallows, too.
Now, the partridges, as well, repeat and are saying,
– Wake up, my own dear love; wake up, my sweet companion.
Wake up, dawn has come; wake up, it's already day.
Wake up and give a kiss to those eyes that long with love
And to a neck so white like cold running water,
That flows out from among the snows and from the icy crystals.

Αγγέλω μ', κρένει η μάννα σου

Αγγέλω μ', κρένει η μάννα σου, δεν ξέρω τι σε θέλει.
Να πας, Αγγέλω μ', για νερό να πιούν τα παλικάρια.
– Τα παλικάρια, αν διψάν, στη βρύση να παν να πιούνε,
κι εγώ θα πάω στο κέντισμα με τ' άλλα τα κορίτσια.
Το κέντισμα είναι γλέντισμα και η ρόκα είναι σεργιάνι,
η παντρειά και ο αργαλειός είναι σκλαβιά μεγάλη.

This is a fun song and sung surprisingly enough at weddings. For many girls in the villages married life was, indeed, a hardship, particularly in the mountain villages where the conditions were harsh and the traditions confining. For example, a young bride was expected to do all of the heavier chores (going for water, cutting and carrying wood) in the house of the extended patriarchal family where she now lived. She was not to speak un-

Μην μας παρεξηγήσετε

Μην μας παρεξηγήσετε πόρθαμαν στο χωριό σας.
Εμείς τη νύφη παίρνουμε, και το χωριό δικό σας.

This was sung when they went to escort the bride back from a neighboring village.

Angela

Angela, your mother's calling you; I don't know what she wants.
Angela, she wants you to go for water, so that the young men can drink.
– If the young men are so thirsty, at the fountain let them drink,
But I'm going off to embroider with the rest of the young girls.
Embroidering is a pleasure and spinning, the time to stroll,
Marriage and sitting at the loom are such a great enslavement.

less spoken to for a year and when spoken to, she was to reply calling her father- and mother-in-law "master" and "mistress." These latter customs were falling into disuse by the time of my mother but the song reflects this earlier reality, which in terms of chores and hard work saw little change. Spinning was a time to stroll about. In the summer of 1956 in the village I saw women going to visit in the evening with distaffs in their hands.

Don't find fault

Don't find fault with us for coming to your village.
We're taking off the bride and the village is still yours.

Ξενιτικά και Μοιρολόγια
Songs of Absence and Lament

317. ΠΑΤΡΑΙ: Τὸ «Σατούρνια» εἰς
τὸν Λιμένα

ΒΙΟΜΗΧΑΝΙΑ
ΑΔΕΛΦΟΙ ΔΙΡΜΙΚΗ
ΑΘΗΝΑΙ

PATRAS: «Saturnia» dans le Port

The good ship Saturnia,
which brought Dimitrios and Vasiliki Scotes to America after their wedding.

Στην Αμερική

Όποιος θα πάει στην Αμερική
να κάτσει να συλλογισθεί.
Σαράντα μέρες θάλασσα,
και εξήνταδυο σκαλώματα.

This is a small poem my mother wrote when she was 14, long before she herself left for America, and which she had forgotten. She was reminded of it by the daughter of one of her lost friends, seventy-five years later.

Καλότυχα είναι τα βουνά

Καλότυχα είναι τα βουνά, καλόμοιροι οι κάμποι,
γιατί ποτέ δεν αρρωστάν και Χάρο δεν φοβάνται.
Το καλοκαίρι πράσινα και το χειμώνα άσπρα.

A variant on a well-known lament for the dead.

To America

Whoever wants to go to America
Best he sit down and think on it.
Forty days upon the sea,
Two and sixty ports of call.

How lucky are the mountains

How lucky are the mountains; how fortunate the rolling plains,
Because they never sicken and have no fear of Death.
Green during the summertime and throughout the winter white.

Με γέλασαν κάτι πουλιά

Με γέλασαν κάτι πουλιά, της άνοιξης τ' αηδόνια.
Με γέλασαν και μου 'πανε ποτέ δεν θ' αρρωστήσω,
ποτέ δεν θα πεθάνω.
Βάνω, φκιάνω τα σπίτια μου, ψηλότερα από τ' άλλα.
Φκιάνω και τα μπαλκόνια μου, καλύτερα από τ' άλλα.
Και στο μπαλκόνι κάθησα, τους κάμπους αγναντεύω.
Βλέπω τους κάμπους πράσινους και τα βουνά γαλάζια,
βλέπω κάποιον να 'ρχεται καβάλα στ' άλογό του.
Μαύρος κι αυτός και τ' άλογο, μαύρη και η φορεσιά του.
Καθόμουν και τον κοίταζα πού θα ξεπεζέψει.
Κι αυτός ήρθε και ξεπέζεψε μέσα στην αυλή μου.
Κι εγώ τον καλωσόρισα, να φάμε και να πιούμε.
Κι αυτός μ' απάντησε,
– Δεν ήρθα εδώ για φαΐ, για πιεί, ούτε για τραγούδια,
εμένα μ' έστειλε ο Θεός, μαζί μου να σε πάρω.
Εμένα με λένε Χάροντα, και μαζί μου θα σε πάρω.
Ούτε πλουσίους ντρέπομαι, ούτε φτωχούς λυπάμαι.

This is a lament or keening song, known as a *moirologi*. Such songs were sung at the wake before the dead person was taken to the church and at the graveside. Women usually sang them and some were specifically asked to come to the funeral because of their ability to compose and sing such songs.
Death is personified in Greek as Charos, a form of the ancient Charon, the ferryman of the dead in ancient Greek mythology. Despite being Christian for almost two thousand years,

Some birds once made a fool of me

Some birds once made a fool of me, the nightingales of spring.
They fooled me and they told me that I would never sicken,
That I would never die.
So, I went and built my houses higher than the others,
And I built my balconies better than the others.
On my balcony I sat and looked out far upon the plains.
I saw the plains were green, the mountains bluish in the distance,
Then I saw someone approaching and coming towards me on a horse.
He was black, as was his horse, and black was his attire.
I sat and watched him as he came, to see where he'd dismount.
He came and then dismounted in the middle of my courtyard.
So I got up to make him welcome, inviting him to eat, to drink.
But he answered me by saying,
– I've not come here to eat or drink, nor have I come for singing,
But almighty God has sent me to take you with me from here.
People call and name me Death and I shall take you with me.
I am not embarrassed by the rich nor have I pity for the poor.

the Greeks in their folklore still see death as a bitter and comfortless occurrence impos-
ing a reluctant departure from the beauty and pleasures of life on earth (as described in
the song) for the gloom and bleakness of the grave.
A good account of the beliefs of the Homeric Greeks concerning death and fate can be
found in Thomas Sefton's book, *The Gods Remain* (see bibliography).

Βγήκε η Χάρισσα

Βγήκε η Χάρισσα στη γειτονιά, στα μαύρα ήταν ντυμένη.
– Εμένα με λένε Χάρισσα κι είμαι του Χάρου η μάννα.
Συμμάστε, γυναίκες, τους άντρες σας και, μάννες, τα παιδιά σας.
Συμμάστε, μάννες, τα παιδιά και, αδερφές, τ' αδέρφια.
Εβγήκε ο Χάρος παγανιά και παίρνει όποιον θέλει.
Παίρνει τους νιους για το χωρό, τις νιες για τα τραγούδια.
Παίρνει και τα μικρά παιδιά για στολισμό της τάβλας.

The starkness of this lament needs no comment, other than to note that the death of young people and children was a common and bitter occurrence. Death preparing a party in the underworld hearkens back to the story of Hades trying to win over Persephone

Μάννα δεν θέλω κλάματα

Μάννα, δεν θέλω κλάματα, δεν θέλω μοιρολόγια.
Εμένα με κλαίνε τα βουνά, με κλαίνε και οι ψηλές ραχούλες.
Με κλαίει και μια κόρη όμορφη, στα μαύρα είναι ντυμένη.

A well-known lament from Epirus.

Τώρα είδα και κατάλαβα

Τώρα είδα και κατάλαβα τους ξένους πώς τους θάπτουν,
χωρίς λιβάνι και κερί, χωρίς παπά και διάκο.
Εδώ στη μαύρη ξενιτιά, εδώ στα μαύρα ξένα,
εδώ ο κούκος δεν λαλεί, η τρυγόνα δεν το λέει.
Το λέει ο πετροκότσυφας σαν μαύρο μοιρολόγι.

This is both a lament, *moirologi*, and a song of absence, *xenitiko*. It addresses one of the worst calamities a Greek family could imagine, the death of a loved one on foreign shores alone and without proper Orthodox burial.

Lady Death

Into the neighborhood came Lady Death and she was clad in black.
– People all call me Lady Death, the mother of Death am I.
Women, gather up your husbands and, mothers, your children, too.
Mothers, gather up your children and sisters, your dear brothers.
Death is out and on the prowl and whomever he wants he takes.
He takes young men off for the dance and takes young girls for the songs.
He takes the little children, too, as trimmings for his table.

with various diversions in order to get her to accept her role as his bride and queen of
his kingdom. When unmarried boys and girls died, they were often buried dressed as
brides and bridegrooms with wedding wreaths on their heads.

Mother, I don't want any weeping

Mother, I don't want any weeping, nor do I want you to mourn.
The mountains all weep for me, as well as the high ridges.
For me a pretty girl also weeps and she's dressed herself in black.

Now I have seen and understood

Now I have seen and understood how they bury foreigners,
Without incense and a candle without a priest or deacon.
Here in gloomy foreign places, here in gloomy foreign lands,
Here the cuckoo has no words; the turtledove does not speak.
The blackbird recounts and tells it like a dark song of keening.

Κλάψε με, μάννα

Κλάψε με, μάννα, κλάψε με την νύχτα με φεγγάρι,
και την αυγούλα με δροσιά ώσπου να πάρει ο ήλιος
Να 'ρθουν τα 'λάφια απ' τη βοσκή να σε παρηγορήσουν.
Όλα τα 'λάφια βγήκανε, κι όλα δροσολογιώνται,
και μια 'λαφίνα ταπεινή δεν πάει μαζί με τ' άλλα.
Όλο τ' απόσκια περπατεί και στα ζερβά κοιμάται,
όθ' εύρει γάργαρο νερό, θολώνει και το πίνει.
Ανάθεμά σε, κυνηγέ, πολύ πρωί που βγήκες.

This could be sung as either a lament for the dead, *moirologi*, or as a song for a loved one far from home, *xenitiko*. The doe has lost her fawn to a hunter, Death, and in her grief even clear spring water looks and tastes murky to her.

Θέλετε δέντρα ανθίσετε

Θέλετε δέντρα ανθίσετε, θέλετε ξεραθείτε.
Στον ίσκιο σας δεν κάθομαι, ούτε και στη δροσιά σας
Να καρτερώ την άνοιξη, τον Μάη με τα λουλούδια,
ν' ανθίσει ο γαύρος και η οξιά, να σκιώσουν τα λαγκάδια,
να βγούν οι βλάχοι στα βουνά, να βγούν οι βλαχοπούλες,
να βγούν τα λάγια πρόβατα με τα χρυσά κουδούνια.

This is a song of absence, *xenitiko*, based on an old klepht song. It was also sung as a lament or *moirologi*, emphasizing the beauties of the world to be left behind in death.

Weep for me, mother

Weep for me, mother, weep for me at night and by the moon,
But by dew time at early dawn when the sun is coming up
The deer may come from feeding to comfort and console you.
All the deer have ventured forth and all are playing in the dew,
But one doe is humble and is not going with the others.
She only walks among the shadows and sleeps in lonely places
And when she finds gurgling water it turns murky, yet she drinks it.
Damn you, hunter, for venturing out in the early morning.

If you want, O trees, you may bloom

If you want, O trees, you may bloom; if you want, you may wither.
I will not sit beneath your shade, nor sit beneath your coolness
To wait for the coming spring, for Maytime with its blossoms,
When the beech and hornbeam flower and shady are the hollows;
When the shepherds take to the hills and the shepherd girls go with them,
And flocks of black sheep follow wearing bells that are golden.

Περνάτε από τον Άγιο Θόδωρο

Περνάτε από τον Άγιο Θόδωρο κι από την Παρηγορίτσα,
ν' ακούσετε τα κλάματα, ανδρίκια μοιρολόγια.
Μοιρολογούν οι μάστοροι και κλαίν' οι μαθητάδες.
Το μαθητούδι έπεσε απ' το μεσιανό τον τρούλο.

This is an old song from Epirus. The two churches are in the town of Arta, which has several beautiful churches dating back to the time of the Despotate of Epirus (1204-1410). The Despotate was one of the Greek successor states to the East Roman Empire after the conquest of Constantinople, capital of the empire, by the Fourth Crusade in 1204. Most of its territories were finally absorbed by its major Greek rival, the empire of Nicaea. The latter reconquered Constantinople in 1261 and thereby reunited the contracted remnants of the Byzantine empire until the Turkish seizure of Constantinople in 1453.
The apprentice system was still prevalent in Greece until quite recently and young boys were given over by their usually poor parents to learn a trade like tailoring or whatever. For his room and board the boy was expected to do all the menial work until he learned

Της χήρας γιος ψυχορραγεί

Της χήρας γιος ψυχορραγεί στου καραβιού την πλώρη.
Δεν έχει μάννα να τον κλαίει, αδέρφια να τον κλάψουν.
Τον κλαίει ο καπετάνιος του μαζί με τόνε γιο του.
– Για σήκω απάνω, ναύτη μου, χρυσέ καραβοκύρη,
να κοπασάρεις το νερό, να βγούμε σε λιμάνι.

A keening song or lament, *moirologi*, composed by my mother.

Pass by the church of St. Theodore

Pass by the Church of St. Theodore and by the Church of the Virgin,
So you can hear all the crying and the keening of grown men.
Mourning are the master builders and the apprentices all weep.
The apprentice boy has fallen from the midmost of the domes.

the craft. If he was lucky, the master and his family treated him like a member of the
household; if not, like a servant or worse.
St. Theodore is one of the warrior saints of the Greek Church. These saints are usually depicted wearing fitted armor and carrying a sword. While some were martyred over the
centuries in battles fighting the Arab and later Turkish Muslims, others were martyred
earlier in pagan times. In any event, warrior saints like St. George, St. Dimitrios and St.
Theodore were often chosen as patron saints of churches during the Ottoman period, as
a way to show defiance of the Muslim oppressors. St. George was the patron of the church
in my mother's village.

The widow's son

The widow's son gives up his soul on the ship up at the prow.
No mother has he to weep for him, no sisters nor any brothers.
The captain is there to weep for him along with his only son,
– Get up, my sailor boy, get up beloved skipper,
And press the oars upon the waves that we may reach safe harbor.

Οι τέσσερις συμφορές

Η ξενιτιά, η αβανιά, θάνατος και η αγάπη,
τα τέσσερα ζυγίσθηκαν σ' ένα βαρύ στατέρι.
Ποιο είναι το βαρύτερο, βαρύτερο απ' όλα;
Ο ζωντανός ξεχωρισμός βαρύτερο απ' όλα.

Xenitia is a difficult word to render in English but the first six words in the translation of this song come close with an emphasis on the first word, "foreign" as in strange and alien coupled with a deep sense of loneliness and long separation. The theme of *xenitia* is common in songs from all over Greece but especially in the songs from Epirus, a poor mountain region whose children were often obliged to leave because of economic constraints. In later years my mother would often say that *xenitia* does not exist anymore, what with telephones and fast, relatively cheap transportation to anywhere in the world.
Love here refers not to the pleasures of love but rather to the difficulties which love faced in a traditional society where customs and taboos often made courtship a frustrating experience; it also refers to unrequited love. Greek makes a distinction between love as

Ποια δόλια μάννα το 'λεγε

Ποια δόλια μάννα το 'λεγε τ' αδέρφια δεν πονιώνται.
Τ' αδέρφια σχίζουν τα βουνά ώσπου ν' ανταμωθούνε.
Σαν βάισαν και ανταμώθηκαν σ' ένα χρυσό τραπέζι,
κι ένας τον άλλον έλεγε, ο ένας τον άλλον λέγει,
– Αδέρφια πώς περάσατε στα έρημα τα ξένα;
– Τα ξένα, θέλουν φρόνημα, θέλουν ταπεινοσύνη.
Στα ξένα ποιος θα σε χαρεί και ποιος θα σου γελάσει;
Πού είν' της μαννούλας τα φιλιά, τα χάδια του πατέρα;
Κι αν έρθει μέρα άπονη, στα ξένα ν' αρρωστήσεις,
Ποιος θα βρεθεί στο πλάι σου φάρμακα να σου δίνει;
Κι αν έρθει μέρα άχαρη στα ξένα να πεθάνεις,
ποιος θα βρεθεί στο πλάι σου, τα μάτια σου να κλείσει;
Και ποιος με πόνο με καημό για σένα θα θρηνήσει;

This well-known song expresses the anguish, which was felt by those who were obliged to leave family and home to seek their fortunes on unknown and often unforgiving foreign shores. Although it has the form of a folk song, it consists of excerpts from a longer poem by Kostas Krystallis (1868-1894), who is famous as "the poet of the mountains and

The weight of four afflictions

Foreign lands without kin or friend; next, misfortune. death and love,
These four were each put upon a scale, upon a heavy steelyard,
To see which was the heaviest. the heaviest of all.
To be living parted from kin and friend – heaviest of all.

agape and love as *eros*. *Agape* can have elements of *eros* in it but eros is more unthinking
passion. In Greek one can fall into or be caught by *eros*; one does not fall into *agape*.
In my mother's time, to have fallen into *eros* or to have married for *eros* was noted and
remarked upon, when it was expected that all marriages would be arranged and family-
approved ones. *Eros* could affect anyone but was often involved in canonically forbidden
relationships between first cousins, second cousins as well as between children of godparents. When this happened and it did from time to time, couples would elope or
threaten to. Strong efforts would be made to avoid such occurrences, making them rare.
The song employs a seldom used word for scale in the second line and I have tried to
convey this sense by using an equally rare but precise word in English.

What poor mother

What poor mother ever said brothers don't care for one another.
Brothers will cleave high mountains until they can meet up again.
Walking with weary steps, they met up at a golden table
And one was saying to the other and one to the other says,
– Brothers, how did you fare in those far-off and lonely places?
– Foreign lands require good sense and a humble manner.
In foreign lands who will delight in you and who will join you in laughter?
Where are your dear mother's kisses, the caresses of your father?
And should there come a cruel day and in foreign lands you sicken,
Who shall be by your bedside to give you medicine and care?
And should there come a luckless day and in foreign lands you die,
Who shall be found there by your side to shut and close your eyes?
And who with pain and sorrow will weep for you and mourn?

sheepfolds." He came from the village of Syrrako which is on the western slope of the
Tzoumerka and in his very brief life managed to write many poems and songs in the folk
idiom, which poems in time became part of the folk tradition of Epirus and of Greece.

Η παραπονιάρα καρδιά

Τι να την κάνω την καρδιά που 'ναι παραπονιάρα;
Βολές με κάνει να γελώ, βολές ν' αναστενάζω,
σε ανήφορο δεν περπατώ να μην την βαρυγκομήσω.
Κι αν καλοσυλλογισθώ, να κάθομαι να κλαίγω.
Ανάθεμά σε ξενιτιά, και συ και τα καλά σου,
παίρνεις της μάννας τα παιδιά και τα κρατάς κοντά σου.
Και μένει η μάννα μοναχή σαν έρημο πουλάκι.

The first four lines come from an old song, which my mother's paternal grandmother used to sing as a song of absence for her two sons who had emigrated to America. My mother composed the last three lines to give fuller expression to her grandmother's sorrow.

A heart of regrets

What to do with my heart, which is full of regrets?
Sometimes it makes me laugh; sometimes it makes me sigh,
So I don't take the uphill way to make it more embittered.
And if I start to really brood, I sit all alone and weep.
Damn you, foreign lands and shores, you and your fancy goods as well,
You take away a mother's children and you keep them there with you.
And the mother remains all alone, like a deserted bird.

Ανάθεμα τους μαραγκούς

Ανάθεμα τους μαραγκούς που κάνουν τα καράβια,
και ταξιδεύουν τα παιδιά πολύ μακριά στα ξένα.
Παίρνουν της μάννας τα παιδιά, της αδερφής τ' αδέρφια,
και πίσω οι μάννες καρτερούν καθώς και αδερφάδες.
Πήραν κι εμένα τ' αδέρφια μου, πολύ μακριά στα ξένα,
κι έχω χρόνια να τους δω, χρόνια να τους αντικρίσω.
Να 'μουν πουλί να πέταγα, την θάλασσα να σχίσω,
να τους φιλήσω μια φορά και πάλι να γυρίσω.

This song of absence, *xenitiko*, was composed by my mother's aunt, her father's sister, pining for her two brothers in America. This is a variant of songs with a similar theme.

Με γέλασε μια χαραυγή

Με γέλασε μια χαραυγή, τ' αστρί και το φεγγάρι.
Και βγήκα νύχτα στα βουνά ψηλά στα κορφοβούνια.
Κι έγειρα να κοιμηθώ, λίγο να ξανασάνω.
Κι ακούω τα πεύκα να βογκάν και τις οξιές να τρίζουν.
Κι ακούω την πετροπέρδικα πικρά να καταριέται,
να καταριέται τον αετό, τον πλουμιστό πετρίτη,
που γκρέμισε τα φύλλα της οξιάς και πήρε τα πουλιά της.

The first four lines of this song are found as a formulaic beginning in many klepht songs. My mother's father went on to compose his own version as a song of absence, *xenitiko*. The eagle in this song represents *xenitia*.

Curses be on the carpenters

Curses be on the carpenters, who can make and build the ships,
And the young men then travel off, far away to foreign shores.
They take away a mother's sons and take a sister's brothers
And behind them the mothers wait and their sisters wait as well.
They have taken my brothers, too, far away to foreign shores,
I've not seen them for many years, years since I have seen their faces.
Were I a bird and I could fly, I would cleave the open sea,
So I could kiss them only once and then come back home again.

An early dawn once deceived me

An early dawn once deceived me, the stars and the moon as well.
And by night I climbed the mountains, high among the mountain peaks.
Then I stopped and lay down awhile to refresh myself with sleep.
Soon I hear the pine trees moaning and the beeches creaking too
And I also hear the partridge, crying with bitter curses.
She was cursing at the eagle, the speckled rock-bound eagle,
Who tore away the beech tree leaves and carried off her fledglings.

Μαύρα μου χελιδόνια από την Αραπιά

Μαύρα μου χελιδόνια από την Αραπιά,
για χαμηλώστε λίγο τα φτερούγια σας,
να στείλω ένα γράμμα, μια ψιλή γραφή,
να στείλω στη μαννούλα μου να μην με καρτερεί.
Κι εδώ στα ξένα που ήρθα, εδώ παντρεύτηκα.
Μάγισσα γυναίκα πήρα, μάγισσα πεθερά.
Μαγεύουν τα ποτάμια και τις θάλασσες,
μαγεύουν τα καράβια και δεν έρχονται.
Με μάγεψαν κι εμένα και δεν έρχομαι.
Όταν βουλιέμαι να 'ρθω, ήλιος και ξαστεριά,
και όταν ξεκινάω, χιόνια και βροχές.

This is my mother's version of the theme found in many variants of this song of absence, *xenitiko*. The song describes the fate of many a young man, who went off to seek his fortune and thereby help his family back home, but never returned because of a foreign en-

Δυο πουλιά

Ένα πουλί θαλασσινό και ένα πουλί βουνίσιο,
τα δυο πουλιά μαλώνανε, τα δυο πουλιά μαλώνουν.
Γυρίζει το θαλασσινό και λέει στο βουνίσιο,
– Μη με μαλώνεις, βρε πουλί, και μη με παραπαίρης.
Εγώ, πουλί μ', δεν κάθομαι στον τόπο τον δικό σου.
Κι αν κάτσω Μάη και Θεριστή και όλον τον Αλωνάρη,
κι αν πάρω κι απ' τον Αύγουστο πέντ' έξι δέκα μέρες,
Θα φύγω, βρε πουλάκι μου, θα πάω μακριά στα ξένα.
Θα κάμεις χρόνια να με δεις, χρόνια να μου μιλήσεις,
θα κάμεις και πολύ καιρό να κρένεις τ' όνομά μου.

This song is a variant of a song, which is found in the collection of Fauriel, the Frenchman who published the first collection of Greek folk songs in 1823. It can be sung as a song of absence, *xenitiko*, as well as a keening song, *moirologi*, which is often the case with songs like this. My mother remembered a dear friend of her uncle (father's brother) singing it at the wake following the latter's untimely death as a young father in 1910 and the same friend singing it at her wedding in 1930 in anticipation of her ultimate departure for America.

Greek being a synthetic language, the names of the months are in the masculine gender and the months personified as a band of brothers. The reference in the song to reaping

Black swallows from Araby

O my swallows dark and black from the land of Araby,
Bring low your wings a bit,
So I can send a letter, a little written note,
To send it to my mother to wait for me no longer.
For, here on foreign shores I've gone and gotten married.
I've taken a sorceress as my wife; a sorceress is her mother.
They've put spells upon the rivers, they've put spells upon the seas,
They've put spells upon the ships and the ships do not arrive.
They've also put a spell on me and I cannot leave for home.
When I wish to leave for home, the sun appears with starlight,
And when I up and start to leave, snow appears with rain.

tanglement or marriage, much to the despair and often bitterness of his kin. *Arapia* in the
song means in modern Greek both Arabia and "the land of the black people." I have therefore, translated *Arapia* as Araby, to suggest this double meaning..

A seabird and a mountain bird

A seabird and a mountain bird fell out with one another,
The two birds both were quarreling, the two birds in a quarrel.
Then the seabird turns and says, and to the mountain bird it speaks,
– Don't quarrel with me, O mountain bird, don't go on with me in anger.
O bird, I will not remain and stay in this land you call your own.
And if I stay for May or June, June to reap, July to thresh,
And even if I take from August five or six or ten more days,
I am leaving, my little bird, for lands that are far away.
You will not see me for many years, nor speak to me for years to come,
Much time, indeed, will have to pass for you to call my name again.

in June and threshing in July derives from the Greek village custom of changing or punning on the names of most but not all of the months to reflect the main agrarian activity or characteristic of that month. Thus, January in formal Greek is *Ianouarios*. The
punning change in village or popular Greek is *Gennaris*, which sounds like the word meaning to give birth. Hence, *Gennaris* is the "Birther" of the year. February is *Phevrouarios*,
which is punned to *Phlevaris*, sounding like the word *phleva* or vein. Hence, *Phlevaris* is the
"Veiner" whose veins are swollen with the first spring rains. In this naming system June
is called *Theristes* or the "Reaper"; July is called *Alonares* or the "Thresher", while September is *Trygetes* or the "Grape-Harvester"

Πουλάκι ξένο ξενιτεμένο

Πουλάκι ξένο ξενιτεμένο, πουλί χαμένο,
πού να σταθώ;
Πού να φωλιάσω, να ξενυχτήσω,
να ξενυχτήσω, να μη χαθώ;
Κάθε κλαράκι βαστάει πουλάκι,
βαστάει πουλάκι ζευγαρωτό.
Βραδιάζει η μέρα, σκοτάδι φέρνει,
και δίχως ταίρι πού να σταθώ;
Πού να φωλιάσω, να ξενυχτήσω,
να ξενυχτήσω, να μη χαθώ;

This is a variant of a well-known poem written by Ioannis Velaras (1771-1823), a doctor from Ioannina, capital of Epirus and a major center of Greek learning and education in the 18th century during the dark period of the Turkish occupation. He was a writer of lyrical and satiric verse, and one of the first to use everyday speech in an effective, po-

Ξενιτεμένο μου πουλί

Ξενιτεμένο μου πουλί και παραπονεμένο,
η ξενιτιά σε χαίρεται κι εγώ 'χω τον καημό σου.
Τι να σου στείλω μάτια μου, αυτού στα ξένα που 'σαι;
Σου στέλνω μήλο σέπεται, κυδώνι μαραγκιάζει.
Σου στέλνω το δακράκι μου σ' ένα ψιλό μαντήλι,
κι εκείνο είναι καυτερό και καίει το μαντήλι.

The apple, quince and handkerchief were traditional tokens of love in Greek folklore.

Like a foreign bird

Like a foreign bird that's lost,
Where can I stay?
Where can I nest, where can I pass the night,
Where can I pass the night and not get lost?
Each small tree branch holds a little bird,
Holds a little bird, each one of a pair.
Day is turning into night, darkness falls
And without a mate where can I stay?
Where can I nest; where can I pass the night,
Where can I pass the night and not get lost?

etic manner. For this reason this poem has achieved folksong status like some of the
poems written by Robert Burns, for example. Its words and plaintive music are one of my
earliest memories of my mother.

My bird alone in foreign lands

O my bird alone in foreign lands with pain that's keen and deep,
Those foreign lands delight in you while I am left with yearning.
What can I send to you, my love, there among strangers where you are?
I send an apple but it rots; a quince dries up and shrivels.
I send you in a fine handkerchief a little tear of mine,
And that tear is burning hot and burns right through the handkerchief.

Μια λυγερή τραγούδαγε

Μια λυγερή τραγούδαγε σε μαρμαρένιο πύργο.
Της παίρνει ο αέρας τη φωνή, στα πέλαγα την πάει,
στα πέλαγα και στα νησιά που 'ρχονται τα καράβια.
Κι όσα καράβια τ' άκουσαν, κι όσοι καπεταναίοι
εις τα καράβια φώναξαν και στους καπεταναίους,
– Σταθείτε, καραβάκια μου, όλα με την αράδα
ν' ακούσετε μια λυγερή πως πικροτραγουδάει.
Έχει άνδρα στην ξενιτιά εδώ και πέντε χρόνια,
κι ακόμα δυο τον καρτερεί, τρία τον περιμένει.
Κι αν δεν έρθει κι αν δεν φανεί, καλόγρια θα γίνει.
Αυτόν να τρώει η ξενιτιά κι αυτή τα μαύρα ράσα.

This is a song of absence, *xenitiko*, which is known in other parts of Greece.

Τι έχεις καημένε σταυραετέ

– Τι έχεις, καημένε σταυραετέ, και σκούζεις και φωνάζεις;
Μην είν' τ' αυγά σου μελανά και τα πουλιά σου μαύρα;
– Ούτε τ' αυγά μου είναι μελανά, ούτε τα πουλιά μου μαύρα.
Έχω μια μάννα, μια κακιά, και μι' αδερφή γρουσούζα.
Μου λέν', – φεύγ' απ' το σπίτι μας, φεύγα και είν' δικό μας.
– Το 'χω προικιό απ' τη μάννα μου και χάρισμα τ' ανδρός μου.

This is a table song to be sung not danced. It might be described as a type of blues song, in Greek *paraponiariko*. Black is the color of death and grief, but what the singer, a male, is singing about in this song is not death but grief. He is bemoaning the injustice done him

Τρεις ξενιτεμένοι βολιούντανε

Τρεις ξενιτεμένοι βολιούντανε στον τόπο τους να πάνε.
Ο ένας θέλει τη Λαμπρή να πάει ν' ανάψει τη λαμπάδα, να πει «Χριστός Ανέστη.»
Ο άλλος θέλει τον Αύγουστο, που είναι το πανηγύρι.
Κι ο τρίτος τον Τρυγητή, που τρυγάν τ' αμπέλια.

A *xenitiko*, composed by my mother. September is the grape-picking month.

A graceful girl in a marble tower

A graceful girl was sitting once, high in a marble tower.
The wind comes up and takes her voice and carries it to the seas,
To the open seas and islands, where all the ships came and go.
And all those ships that heard her voice and all those many captains,
They called out to the other ships and to the other captains,
– Stand still, you ships so dear to me, all of you stand in a row
To hear how one graceful girl bitterly sings her song.
She has a husband in foreign lands, gone abroad for some five years,
She keeps watch for him for still two more and waits for another three.
And if he doesn't come and soon appear, she will go and become a nun.
Foreign lands can then torment him and her the nun's black habit.

Poor royal eagle

– What's the matter, poor royal eagle, that you shout and cry out so?
Are your eggs, perhaps, an inky black and your fledglings black as well?
– My eggs are not an inky black nor are my fledglings black as well.
I have a mother who is bad and a sister full of spite.
They tell me, – Go and leave our house, get out, because it's ours.
– It's my dowry from my mother, and my gift to my husband.

in the context of the dowry system, which drove many a son and brother into poverty and often into self-imposed exile to recoup. At the same time, it condemned many a girl to a bad marriage or no marriage at all in the event there was an insufficient or no dowry.

Three travelers

Three travelers are yearning greatly to seek again their homeland.
One wants to come back at Easter to light a taper and say, "Christ is risen."
The other wants to come in August when the festival takes place.
The third the month when grapes are picked and the vineyards harvested.

Ο Ρόβας εξεκίνησε

Ο Ρόβας εξεκίνησε, ο Ρόβας εξεκίνησε,
και στη Βλαχιά να πάει, γειά σου Ρόβα μου,
και στη Βλαχιά να πάει, πάπια χήνα μου.
[Να 'χεις το κρίμα μου, να 'χεις το κρίμα μου.]

Νύχτα σελώνει τ' άλογο, νύχτα σελώνει τ' άλογο,
νύχτα το καλιγώνει, γειά σου Ρόβα μου,
νύχτα το καλιγώνει, πάπια χήνα μου.
[Να 'χεις το κρίμα μου, να 'χεις το κρίμα μου.]

Βάζει τα πέταλα χρυσά, βάζει τα πέταλα χρυσά
και τα καρφιά 'σημένια, γειά σου Ρόβα μου,
και τα καρφιά 'σημένια πάπια χήνα μου.
[Να 'χεις το κρίμα μου, να 'χεις το κρίμα μου.]

Φλουριά κερνάει τα παιδιά, φλουριά κερνάει τα παιδιά
και γρόσια τις κουμπάρες, γειά σου Ρόβα μου,
και γρόσια τις κουμπάρες, πάπια χήνα μου.
[Να 'χεις το κρίμα μου, να 'χεις το κρίμα μου.]

– Ώρα καλή σου, Ρόβα μου, ώρα καλή σου Ρόβα μου,
καλά να πας και να 'ρθεις, γειά σου Ρόβα μου,
καλά να πας και να 'ρθεις, πάπια χήνα μου.
[Να 'χεις το κρίμα μου, να 'χεις το κρίμα μου.]

This is an old Epirote dance song of absence, *xenitiko*, dating from the time (early 18th century) when Greeks, especially from Epirus would go to Vlachia or Wallachia, present-day Romania, seeking their fortunes. Their dream was to succeed and then come back to

Rovas

Rovas was starting up to leave; Rovas was starting up to leave,
το leave and go to Vlachia, O Rovas farewell,
το go to Vlachia, O my duck, my goose.
[May you share my sorrow; may you share my sorrow.]

By night he saddles his good horse,
By night he also shoes it, O Rovas farewell,
By night he also shoes it, O my duck, my goose.
[May you share my sorrow; may you share my sorrow.]

He puts on horse-shoes made of gold; he puts on horse-shoes made of gold
And nails made out of silver, O Rovas farewell,
And nails made out of silver, O my duck, my goose.
[May you share my sorrow; may you share my sorrow.]

He gives gold coins to the children; he gives gold coins to the children
And silver to the godmothers, O Rovas, farewell,
And silver to the godmothers, O my duck, my goose.
[May you share my sorrow; may you share my sorrow.]

– Good luck to you, O Rovas dear; good luck to you, o Rovas dear,
Go and come back in good health, O Rovas farewell,
Go and come back in good health, O my duck, my goose.
[May you share my sorrow; may you share my sorrow.]

their families and villages to enjoy the fruit of their labors and the admiration of their relatives and fellows. Rovas apparently was one of the more successful, although the sorrow of his departure was obviously keenly felt and expressed.

Όλοι τον ήλιο κοίταζαν

Όλοι τον ήλιο κοίταζαν, πώς πάει να βασιλέψει,
και η κόρη που 'χε τον καημό τα πέλαγ' αγναντεύει,
τα πέλαγα και τα νησιά που 'ρχονται τα καράβια.
– Καράβια μου, βαρκούλες μου, που 'ρχεστε απ' τα ξένα,
μην είδατε τον άνδρα μου, τον αγαπητικό μου;
Σε τι τραπέζια κάθεται και σε τι ταβέρνες πίνει;
Σαν τι χεράκια τον κερνάν', και τα δικά μου τρέμουν;
Σαν τι ματάκια τον κοιτάν και τα δικά μου κλαίνε;

Many a woman was left behind in the village, as husbands went off to seek work down on the plains or farther off in Patras or Athens. In all cases these men would return after some months or at most a year. In my mother's time only unmarried young men and boys went off to America to help their families, usually to provide dowries for their sisters. Of course, the hope was not only to help with dowries but also to make it big while away and to come back for good. Sometimes this did not happen because of foreign entanglements, as related in this song, but sometimes, although rarely, leaving for foreign parts and staying abroad for so long was an escape from a bad marriage.

A poor, young, illiterate man in my mother's village left for America in the the early

The lonely wife

All were gazing at the sun as it set in royal spendor,
And a girl with grief and sorrow scans the distant open seas,
The open seas and islands where the ships come and go,
– Dear ships of mine, dear little boats, that come here from foreign shores,
Have any of you seen my man, have any seen my lover?
At what tables does he sit himself and in what taverns drink?
What hands are pouring him the wine, while mine can only tremble?
What eyes look and gaze upon him, while mine can only weep?

1900s, because of marital problems at home. Leaving his wife, he gave back to her the white fancy handkerchief traditionally exchanged as a sign of betrothal and told her that would be the last thing she'd ever get from him. By the 20s he had made it big in real estate and movie houses and decided to return to Greece to pass his final years. When he finally returned after an absence of more than 25 years, he was a stranger to her and she to him. They formally divorced. She with no children but a good settlement. He with no children but a new wife in Athens. During my mother's years, there was only one other such case of a man, who left his wife and family never to be seen again.

Στ' Αγρίνιο

Στ' Αγρίνιο βγαίν' ενά νερό, το λέν' ασημονέρο.
Το πίνουν οι Αγρινιώτισσες και παιδιά δεν κάνουν.
Να το είχε πιεί και η μάννα μου, πριν είχε κάμει εμένα.
Σαν μ' έκαμε, τι μ' ήθελε, σαν μ' έχει, τι με θέλει;
Εγώ στα ξένα περπατώ, στα ξένα γκιζεράω,
Και πιάνω ξένες για αδερφές, και ξένες για μαννάδες.

Agrinio is a small town in central Greece, famous for the cultivation of tobacco and olive oil.

Το είχε η τύχη μου

Το είχε η τύχη μου, το είχε το ριζικό μου
πάντα στα ξένα να γυρνώ, στα ξένα να πεθάνω.
Να πιάνω ξένες γι' αδερφές και ξένες για μαννάδες,
να είχα μάννα στη γειτονιά και αδερφή στη χώρα.

This is song of absence, *xenitiko*, composed by my mother, and a variant of the above.

In Agrinio

In Agrinio comes forth a stream, a stream of silver water.
The Agrinio women drink of it and then bear no children.
My mother, too, should have drunk of it before she went and bore me.
So she had me, what did she want with me? So she has me, what does she want?
I walk about in foreign lands, wander in foreign places,
And take as sisters foreigners and foreigners as mothers.

It was my luck

It was my luck, it was my fate, it was my destined fortune
That on foreign shores I should wander, on foreign shores to die;
To call foreign women, sisters, and foreign women, mothers,
That I might have a mother in the neighborhood and a sister in the town.

Σχολικά και Πατριωτικά
School and Patriotic Poems

Children outside the school in Theodoriana, 1950s.

Φεγγαράκι μου λαμπρό

Φεγγαράκι μου λαμπρό φέγγε μου να περπατώ.
Να πηγαίνω στο σχολειό, να μαθαίνω γράμματα,
γράμματα, διδάγματα, του Θεού τα πράγματα.

This is the first poem that I learned from my mother, along with the Lord's Prayer, the Greek national anthem and the alphabet in Greek. It is not a folk poem, having made its appearance in the mid-19th century as a popular children's poem. It has achieved folk status, however, and until recently all Greeks knew it. It refers to the days of the Turkish occupation when schooling was allegedly forbidden by the Turks and secret schools were operated at night. This has now been proven to be a myth. Certainly schools in the Turkish period were few and limited but never completely closed and usually operated by the church. As the 18th century went on, many important secular schools were established also in Constantinople and in places like Ioannina in Epirus and elsewhere. During this time in the villages, however, the priest was often the only literate person. Thus, he also acted as the teacher. My mother's paternal grandfather's grandfather was a priest and along with his uncle, a monk, established a monastery church school in the late 18th century. This poem had further resonance for me, growing up in the United States, and going to evening Greek school three times a week. After a two-and-half-hour session, we would often return home by the light of the moon. My first teacher was the

My little moon gleaming bright

My little moon gleaming bright, shine that I may walk tonight.
To go to school by your light, there to learn to read and write,
To read and write and to be taught about the things God has wrought.

parish priest, but later our community was fortunate to have among it a qualified and dedicated teacher, Mrs. Asimina Tsilimingra, a graduate of the Arsakeion, Greece's premier girls school at that time. For the first hour we had a reading lesson, and then on Monday, Greek grammar; Wednesday, Greek history; Friday, Bible and catechism. Following these formal studies, Mrs. Tsilimingra would also regale us with stories from Greek mythology. Her spellbinding accounts of the Iliad and the Odyssey were my introduction to that magical world and kept me going to Greek school even when I was tempted to skip to play with the "American" kids. Her spirited renditions of these tales are among my most treasured childhood memories.

Modern Greek calls the moon by the descriptive neuter word, *to phengari*, the shiner, while Ancient Greek identified it by the feminine word *selini* (*selene* in classical transliteration) meaning simply moon and paired with the masculine, *ilios* (*helios*) or sun. Both words are still employed, although *phengari* is now the most commonly used for moon with *selini* being confined to more formal literary or scientific discourse.

Ήρθε πάλι η άνοιξη

Ήρθε πάλι η άνοιξη, ήρθαν τα λουλούδια.
Και παντού χαράς χοροί και χαράς τραγούδια.
Έλιωσαν στις κορυφές των βουνών τα χιόνια.
Ήρθαν πάλι τα πουλιά και τα χελιδόνια.

Ο Μάιος μάς έφθασε

Ο Μάιος μάς έφθασε, εμπρός βήμα ταχύ,
να τον προϋπαντήσουμε, παιδιά, στην εξοχή.
Δώρα στα χέρια του πολλά και εύμορφα κρατεί
και τα μοιράζει γελαστός εις όποιον του ζητεί.
Πάμε και μεις να πάρουμε, μη χάνουμε καιρό.
Μας φθάνει ένα τριαντάφυλλο και ένα κλαρί χλωρό.

The months in Greek are grammatically in the masculine gender and therefore imagined as male figures.

Τριαντάφυλλο ανοιχτό

– Τριαντάφυλλο ανοιχτό, θα σε κόψω δεν βαστώ,
είπε το τρελό παιδάκι.
– Αν με κόψεις, σου κεντώ το μικρό χεράκι,
είπε το τριαντάφυλλο στο μικρό παιδάκι.

Many of the children's poems have a cautionary or hortatory tone. This is one verse of a larger children's poem written by A. Vlachos.

Once again spring has returned

Once again spring has returned; returned have all the flowers.
Dances of joy are everywhere; songs of joy fill the hours.
From the high peaks of the mountains has melted the fallen snow.
The birds and the nightingales have returned to us here below.

May has reached us at last

May has reached us at last; let's go forward with haste,
To the countryside, children, to welcome and greet him.
He holds in his hands many beautiful gifts
With a smile he bestows them on those who would ask.
Let us go and take some of them; let's not lose the time.
A rose is enough for us and a branch that is green.

O lovely rose open and red

– O lovely rose open and red, I cannot stop from cutting you,
A foolish little child up and said.
– If you cut me, your hand I'll sting
Said the rose to the dear little thing.

Ένας γέρος άνθρωπος

Ένας γέρος άνθρωπος στο χωράφι πήγαινε,
με την χονδρή την κάπα του.
Κι ο αέρας λάλησε με τον ήλιο μάλωσε,
– Όποιος έχει δύναμη παίρνει από τον γέροντα
τη χονδρή την κάπα του.
Φύσηξε, ξεφύσηξε, έσκασε στο φύσημα.
Άδικος ο κόπος του.
Και ο γέρος διπλά τυλίχτηκε στη χονδρή την κάπα του.
Έφεξεν ο ολόλαμπρος, καλοσύνη σκόρπισε.
Και ο γέρος έβγαλε τη χονδρή την κάπα του.
Και ο ήλιος λάλησε,
– Άκουσε και μάθε, σε περνώ στη δύναμη,
γιατί εσύ πας με το κακό και εγώ με το καλό.

This is one of the fables ascribed to Aesop.

Αρνάκι άσπρο και παχύ

Αρνάκι άσπρο και παχύ, της μάννας το καμάρι,
που εβγήκε στην εξοχή και στο χλωρό χορτάρι.
Απ' τη χαρά του την πολλή απρόσεκτα πηδούσε,
της μάννας του τη συμβουλή καθόλου δεν ψηφούσε.
– Καθώς, παιδί μου, προχωρείς και σαν ελάφι τρέχεις,
κακό θα πάθεις όσο μπορείς και πρέπει να προσέχεις.
Χαντάκι βρήκε και βαθύ, ορμά σαν παλικάρι,
να το πηδήσει προσπαθεί και σπάζει το ποδάρι.

A hortatory school poem.

The sun and the wind

An old man of many years was going out to his field,
Wearing his heavy cloak.
And the wind spoke out and said, while disputing with the sun,
– Whoever musters up the strength can seize and take from that old man
His cloak so big and heavy.
He blew and then he blew some more and burst with all his blowing.
Futile was his effort.
For the old man doubly wrapped himself in his cloak so big and heavy.
The bright orb of the sun began to shine, spreading its goodness everywhere.
And the old man of many years took off his cloak so big and heavy.
Then, the sun spoke out and said,
– Listen to me and learn why I surpass you in strength,
Because you try by force to have your way, but I take the course that's gentle.

A little lamb white and fat

A little lamb white and fat, its mother's pleasure and pride,
Went out to play in the fields 'mid the grass so green and wide.
Out of great happiness and joy rashly it did jump and leap,
Its mother's counsel good and wise it did not heed or keep.
– My child, as you go forward and like a deer run here and there,
Harm will befall you; so do your best, be watchful and take care.
He finds a ditch before him deep and like a hero brave and true,
Over it he tries to leap and breaks his leg in two!

Ένα αρνάκι το καημένο

Ένα αρνάκι, το καημένο, είχε πάει ξεχνιασμένο,
σ' ένα ποταμάκι για να πιει νεράκι.
Όμως η τύχη του κακή, ένας λύκος φτάν' εκεί.
– Σ' έπιασα του είπ' ευθύς, κλέπτη, θα τιμωρηθείς!
Ήρθες εις τον ποταμό μου και μου πίνεις το νερό μου.
– Όχι είπε το αρνάκι, έβλεπα το λιβαδάκι.
– Κι όμως πέρσι ένα βράδυ μ' έβριζες μες το κοπάδι.
– Μα πέρσι, είπε το καημένο, εγώ δεν ήμουν γεννημένο.
– Ω, ω, εγώ σφάλλω, το αδέλφι σου το άλλο.
– Κύριε λύκε, μα εγώ δεν έχω άλλο αδερφό.
– Άλλα ψέματα μου λές, όλα παραβολές.
– Μα της μάννας μου το γάλα, ούτε μια δεν ήπια στάλα.
– Κι αν δεν το 'πιες, το ποθούσες, με τα μάτια το ρουφούσες.
Σ' όλα δίνεις αποκρίσεις, τρέχα να δικηγορήσεις.
Και το στόμα του ανοίγει και το δύστυχο το πνίγει.

The moral here appears to be that if you fall into bad or dangerous company, you don't
have a chance, even if you appear to be as clever as a lawyer.

Νύχτα ο λαγός εβγήκε

Νύχτα ο λαγός εβγήκε, λαχανόκηπο ευρήκε.
Μπαίνει μέσα και αρχίζει την κοιλιά του να γεμίζει.
Δυστυχία του, παρέκει κυνηγός με το ντουφέκι,
τον φτωχόν παραμονεύει, πλησιάζει και σκοπεύει.
Μπαμ! Ηκούσθη στον αέρα, πλην τα βόλια πήγαν πέρα,
και το ζώο το καημένο ετινάχθη τρομαγμένο.
Τρέχει ο λαγός ακόμα με το λάχανο στο στόμα,
και εδιδάχθη να προσέχει πού εμβαίνει και πού τρέχει.

A poor unlucky little lamb

A poor unlucky little lamb, carefree and unsuspecting,
To the riverside it went to take a drink of water.
But to his great misfortune a wolf came upon him there.
– Caught you, he said straight away; you're a thief and you'll be punished
For coming to my river and drinking up my water.
– No, replied the little lamb, I was looking at the meadow.
– And yet one night a year ago you were cursing me to the flock.
– But last year I wasn't even born, said the poor little thing.
– Oh, oh, I must be mistaken, it was your other brother.
– But, mister wolf, I must tell you that I have no other brother.
– Other lies now you're telling me, all of them made-up tales.
– But I swear by my mother's milk I've not drunk a single drop.
– Even if you did not drink it, you lusted with your eyes and gulped it.
For everything you have answers; you should go and become a lawyer.
And then he opened wide his mouth and swallowed the unlucky lamb.

At night the rabbit ventured forth

At night the rabbit ventured forth and discovered a cabbage patch.
He went in and at once began to fill his stomach with a batch.
Great misfortune for him that night, a hunter with his gun was there,
Who watched the poor thing all the while then drew near and aimed with care.
Boom, in the wind a loud noise was heard, as the bullets sought out their prey,
And the poor little animal was startled in a frightening way.
The rabbit is still on the run with a cabbage in his mouth,
But now he has learnt to be more careful where he goes in and where he runs out.

Του σπιτιού ο φύλαξ

Του σπιτιού εδώ αυτός είναι ο φύλαξ ο πιστός.
Ποιος δεν τον γνωρίζει;
Υψηλά, τ' αφεντικά κοιμηθήκανε βαριά.
Πέρασε η ώρα.
Το γνωρίζει το σκυλί κι αγρυπνάει στην αυλή.
Γάβο, γάβο, τώρα,
για να ξέρουν οι κακοί που γυρνάν εδώ κι εκεί
κάτι να σουφρώσουνε.
Θα τους φάει το σκυλί, αν θα μπούνε στην αυλή,
δεν θα τη γλιτώσουνε.

Epirus was famous in ancient times for its dogs, especially the Molossian hound. The short-haired sheep dogs in present-day Epirus may not be directly related to those famous hounds but they are still reknowned for their size, intelligence, loyalty and ferocity.

On the day my mother was born, her father brought into the house a shepherd dog puppy, which over the years became her constant companion. As was the custom in the village, the dog was given a Turkish name, Choudouti. At some point, however, the dog grew too big to keep indoors and was relegated to a shelter in the courtyard. Apart from being my mother's pet, he also acted as the guard of the house and, when required, protector of the family's flock of sheep and goats. In the performance of his duties, he was most reliable. One night a family friend came to the house unannounced and was set upon by Choudouti, who might well have hurt him badly if not pulled off in time.

In 1918, during the Spanish Flu epidemic, my mother's family was wintering on the plains of Arta at a place called Romia. Fleeing the danger of the flu, the family took to the road to return to the village. In the hubbub of their departure as they passed through the town of Philippiada, Choudouti somehow became separated from the party and was lost.

The faithful guard

He is the ever faithful guard of the house that's standing here.

Who does not know of him?

High above in the house, his masters are fast asleep.

The hour is getting late.

The dog knows this and in the courtyard is alert and wakeful.

Now he barks, bow, wow, wow,

So the bad folks are aware, as roundabout they wander

Looking for something to grab.

The dog will bite all of them, if they get into the courtyard,

Not a one will escape him!

For several days, as the family wended its way back to the village, attempts were made to find the dog but to no avail. After the family had crosed the Arachthos river, which was in full spate at the time, the party stopped to rest. Suddenly Choudouti was seen on the other side of the river. Not realizing that the family was already across, he was sniffing about obviously trying to locate their tracks. At last he leapt into the river and swam across, while fighting a strong current which took him quite far down from where the family was. When he finally got across, he began running off in the direction of the village which was miles away, high up in the mountains. My mother's father and friends began chasing him on horseback, calling him to came back. Eventually they got him to understand and he was welcomed back, wet and hungry, as a long-lost child and hero. As he got older Choudouti could no longer perform his guard duties but he was cared for until the end with great love and affection by the family and especially by my mother. He died at the age of seventeen, deeply mourned. My mother's grandfather buried him at the edge of the family's large garden, so that he would always be close and could continue, as in life, to guard the house and those who lived there.

Στην θερμάστρα εμπρός

Στην θερμάστρα εμπρός ένας γάτος χονδρός
πάντ' απλώνεται.
Με τα μάτια κλειστά, αγαπά τα ζεστά,
να τεντώνεται
Και τα πόδια στιλπνά με τη γλώσσα συχνά
ξερολούεται.
Τεμπελιά, κανταργιά ροχαλίζει βαριά.
Τον ακούετε;
Κάτω χθες στην αυλή χύθηκε αίμα πολύ
απ' τα νύχια του.
Στα ποντίκια σφαγή, τον φθονούν στρατηγοί
για την τύχη του.

A portion of a larger poem by E. Tsantalidis, and one of my favourite childhood poems.

Το περιστεράκι

– Πετάς περιστεράκι στον κήπο, στην αυλή.
Δε βλέπεις το γεράκι, το άγριο πουλί;
– Πετάω και προσέχω πριν μ' εύρει το κακό
και φέρω στα παιδιά μου νερό και φαγητό.

By the fireplace

By the fireplace once more a fat cat lies before
And sprawls himself.
With his eyes tightly closed, he loves heat for repose
To stretch out himself.
He's got feet that are sleek and a tongue that can keep
Dry-bathing himself.
Laziness profound; he snores with much sound.
Do you hear him now?
Yesterday in the yard was much blood on the sward
Wrought by his claws.
Slaughter of mice occurred; envious generals stirred
By his good fortune.

The pigeon

– You fly, little pigeon, to the garden in the courtyard.
Don't you see the hawk nearby, that bird wild and savage?
– I fly and I am watchful before misfortune finds me
And I bring food and water to my children who await.

Η καλή νοικοκυρούλα

Πρωί πρωί θα σηκωθεί, αφού πλυθεί, αφού ντυθεί,
ευθύς θα πιάσει τη δουλειά της.
Νοικοκυρούλα χαρωπή, την τεμπελιά δεν τη γνωρίζει,
με την πολλή της προκοπή αυτή το σπίτι της στολίζει.
Ακούραστη και εργατική το βράδυ κάνει και νυχτέρι.
Στο έργο της προσεκτική και ό,τι δουλειά να πεις, την ξέρει.
Και μες στο σπίτι όλοι χαρά την αγαπούνε τη μικρούλα,
και της το λένε καθαρά, – Είσαι καλή νοικοκυρούλα.

The compliment of "the good housekeeper," the role hymned in this second or third grade school poem, was the highest a girl of the villages aspired to in my mother's day.

Σιγά, κοπέλα μου, σιγά

– Σιγά, κοπέλα μου, σιγά, μην τρέχεις έτσι, στάσου.
Κανείς, δα, δε σε κυνηγά και έχεις καιρό μπροστά σου.
– Πηγαίνω, μπάρμπα, στο γιατρό την κούκλα μου να γιάνει
Μου πούντιασε μες στο λουτρό, φοβάμαι μη πεθάνει.
– Βάλ' της ευθύς συναπισμό στο στήθος και στο πλάι.
Βαλ' της φανέλα στο λαιμό και πρόσεξε μη φάει.
– Της έκανα, η πικρή, πολλά, αλλά τα ίδια χάλια.
Τι ήθελα και στα καλά της έδινα στραγάλια;

Καλημερούδια σας πουλιά

Καλημερούδια σας, πουλιά, καλημερούδια, χήνα.
Την κούκλα λέν' Τριανταφυλλιά και το γατί Ψιψίνα.
Και αν με ρωτάτε και για πού, νωρίς τι τάχα βγήκα.
Πηγαίνω να προφθάσω τον παππού που με φιλεύει σύκα.

The little housekeeper

She's up early in the morning; once she's washed and she's dressed,
Straightaway she takes up her work.
A cheerful little housekeeper, of laziness she doesn't know a thing,
With her many useful talents she's an adornment to her home.
Tireless and hard working, at night she does evening chores as well.
At work, she is quite careful and knows whatever job you give her.
In the house everyone is happy; they all love her, the little girl,
And they tell her in words quite clear, – You are a good little housekeeper.

Slow down, my girl

– Slow down, my girl, slow down; don't run and wait up a bit.
Hey, no one is chasing you and you have much time before you.
– I'm going, uncle, to the doctor so he can cure my doll.
She caught a cold while in the bath and I'm afraid she'll die.
– Put a plaster on her quickly, on her chest and on her sides
And put a wool scarf on her neck and watch she doesn't eat.
– I'm so sad 'cause I've done even this, but still the same bad condition.
Why on earth was I feeding her all of those roasted chickpeas?

Top of the morning to you, birds

Top of the morning to you, birds; top of the morning, goose.
Rose is what my doll is called and my kitten is called Pussy.
And if you ask me where I'm going and why I'm out so early.
I'm going to catch up with my grandpapa, who treats me to his figs.

Δώσε μου την κούκλα

– Δώσε μου την κούκλα σου, δώσ' τη μου να παίξω.
– Δεν σου τη δίνω, δεν μπορώ, θα μου την χαλάσεις.
Το δικό μου το μωρό, εσύ θα μου το σπάσεις.

When she was three years old, my mother's father brought her a doll from Patras, the large seaport in the northern Peloponnese. She remembers it being as big as she was and very beautiful. She only had it a few months, however, as it was stolen while the family was spending the winter at the lowland pastures in Xeromero or Aitolo-Akarnania. She never had another one.

Ένας εγγονός μια μέρα

Ένας εγγονός μια μέρα έτρεχε δώθε πέρα,
να μην το πιάσει η μάμμη, η γριά με το καλάμι.
Μα της γρίας τα ποδάρια εβαστούσανε ακόμα,
και τον έπιασε η μάμμη, η γριά με το καλάμι.

The rod was often not spared in my mother's days in the village, but never in her family. Her grandfather used to say that animals should be hit, if needed, but never humans.

Με καράβια στα ταξίδια

Με καράβια στα ταξίδια το ναυτόπουλο γυρνά
μες στης θάλασσας το κύμα αυτό τα νιάτα του περνά.
Πεταχτό σαν το ξεφτέρι, ανεβαίνει στα πανιά
και με ρόζους εις το χέρι λύνει, δένει τα σχοινιά.

My mother's variant of a longer poem by N. Polemis.

Give me your little doll

– Give me your little doll; give it to me so I can play.
– I won't give her to you, I can't; you will ruin her for me.
You will take my baby doll and you are bound to break it.

A grandchild one day

A grandchild one day was running here and there and all about,
So the grandmother wouldn't catch him, the old woman with the switch.
But the old woman's legs were strong and still carried her quite well,
The grandmother soon caught him, that old woman with the switch.

The sailor boy

By ship the sailor boy roams about on far off journeys
'Mid the waves of the sea he passes his youthful days.
Quick like a crackerjack, he climbs high up on the sails
And with the knots in his hands he loosens and ties up the rigging.

Ήτανε μια κόρη

Ήτανε μια κόρη που κένταγε το μαντήλι
το βράδυ στο καντήλι.
Και πήγε ο ποντικός
και πήρε το φυτίλι,
που έφεγγε και κένταγε η κόρη το μαντήλι
το βράδυ στο καντήλι.
Και πήγε μία γάτα
και έφαγε τον ποντικό,
που πήρε το φυτίλι,
μέσα απ' το καντήλι,
που έφεγγε και κένταγε η κόρη το μαντήλι
το βράδυ στο καντήλι.
Και πήγε ένας σκύλος
και έπνιξε τη γάτα,
που έφαγε τον ποντικό,
που πήρε το φυτίλι,
μέσα απ' το καντήλι,
που έφεγγε και κένταγε η κόρη το μαντήλι
το βράδυ στο καντήλι.
Και έπεσε ένα ξύλο
και σκότωσε το σκύλο,
που έπνιξε τη γάτα,
που έφαγε τον ποντικό,
που πήρε το φυτίλι,
μέσα απ' το καντήλι,
που έφεγγε και κένταγε η κόρη το μαντήλι
το βράδυ στο καντήλι.
Κι άναψε ένας φούρνος
κι έκαψε το ξύλο,
που σκότωσε το σκύλο,
που έπνιξε τη γάτα,
που έφαγε τον ποντικό,
που πήρε το φυτίλι,
μέσα απ'το καντήλι,

Once, a young girl was embroidering

Once, a young girl was embroidering a kerchief
At night by the oil lamp.
And then a mouse up and went
And took away the lamp wick,
Which glowed while the girl was embroidering the kerchief
At night by the oil lamp.
And then a cat up and went
And ate up the little mouse,
Which took away the lamp wick,
Away from the oil lamp,
Which glowed while the girl was embroidering the kerchief
At night by the oil lamp.
And then a dog up and went
And strangled and choked the cat,
Which ate the little mouse,
Which took away the lamp wick,
Away from the oil lamp,
Which glowed while the girl was embroidering the kerchief
At night by the oil lamp.
And then a piece of wood fell down
And killed the poor old dog,
Which strangled and choked the cat,
Which ate the little mouse,
Which took away the lamp wick,
Away from the oil lamp,
Which glowed while the girl was embroidering the kerchief
At night by the oil lamp.
And then an oven fired up
And burnt the piece of wood,
Which killed the poor old dog,
Which strangled and choked the cat,
Which ate the little mouse,
Which took away the lamp wick,
Away from the oil lamp,

που έφεγγε και κένταγε η κόρη το μαντήλι
το βράδυ στο καντήλι.
Κι ήρθε ένα ποτάμι
και έσβησε το φούρνο,
που έκαψε το ξύλο,
που σκότωσε το σκύλο,
που έπνιξε τη γάτα,
που έφαγε τον ποντικό,
που πήρε το φυτίλι,
μέσα απ᾽ το καντήλι,
που έφεγγε και κένταγε η κόρη το μαντήλι
Το βράδυ στο καντήλι.
Και πήγε ένα βόδι
και ήπιε το ποτάμι,
που έσβησε το φούρνο,
που έκαψε το ξύλο,
που σκότωσε το σκύλο,
που έπνιξε τη γάτα,
που έφαγε τον ποντικό,
που πήρε το φυτίλι,
μέσα απ᾽ το καντήλι,
που έφεγγε και κένταγε η κόρη το μαντήλι
το βράδυ στο καντήλι.
Και πήγε ένας χασάπης
και έσφαξε το βόδι,
που ήπιε το ποτάμι,
που έσβησε το φούρνο,
που έκαψε το ξύλο,
που σκότωσε το σκύλο,
που έπνιξε τη γάτα,
που έφαγε τον ποντικό,
που πήρε το φυτίλι,
μέσα απ᾽ το καντήλι,
που έφεγγε και κένταγε η κόρη το μαντήλι
το βράδυ στο καντήλι.
Επήγε και ο Χάρος
και πήρε το χασάπη,

Which glowed while the girl was embroidering the kerchief
At night by the oil lamp.
And then a river came along
And put out the oven's fire,
Which burnt up the piece of wood,
Which killed off the poor old dog,
Which strangled and choked the cat,
Which ate the little mouse,
Which took away the lamp wick,
Away from the oil lamp,
Which glowed while the girl was embroidering the kerchief
At night by the oil lamp.
Then an ox came on by
And swallowed up the river,
Which put out the oven's fire,
Which burnt up the piece of wood,
Which killed off the poor old dog,
Which strangled and choked the cat,
Which ate the little mouse,
Which took away the lamp wick,
Away from the oil lamp,
Which glowed while the girls was embroidering the kerchief
At night by the oil lamp.
And then a butcher came along
And slaughtered well the ox,
Which swallowed up the river,
Which put out the oven's fire,
Which burnt up the piece of wood,
Which killed off the poor old dog,
Which strangled and choked the cat,
Which ate the little mouse,
Which took away the lamp wick,
Away from the oil lamp,
Which glowed while the girl was embroidering the kerchief
At night by the oil lamp.
And then Death came
And carried off the butcher man,

που έσφαξε το βόδι,
που ήπιε το ποτάμι,
που έσβησε το φούρνο,
που έκαψε το ξύλο,
που σκότωσε το σκύλο,
που έπνιξε τη γάτα,
που έφαγε τον ποντικό,
που πήρε το φυτίλι,
μέσα απ' το καντήλι,
που έφεγγε και κένταγε η κόρη το μαντήλι
το βράδυ στο καντήλι.
Ο Χάρος είναι εκείνος που ζει και βασιλεύει.

A rather grim memory test poem, that was often recited to pass the winter nights around the fireplace.

Who slaughtered well the ox,
Which swallowed up the river,
Which put out the oven's fire,
Which burnt up the piece of wood,
Which killed off the poor old dog,
Which strangled and choked the cat,
Which ate the little mouse,
Which took away the lamp wick,
Away from the oil lamp,
Which glowed while the girl was embroidering the kerchief
At night by the oil lamp.
For Death is the only one who lives and reigns over all.

Η εκκλησιά η ερημική

Εις το βουνό ψηλά εκεί είν' εκκλησιά ερημική.
Το σήμαντρό της δεν χτυπά, δεν έχει ψάλτη, ούτε παπά.
Ένα καντήλι θαμπερό κι ένα πέτρινο σταυρό
έχει στολίδι μοναχό το εκκλησάκι το φτωχό.
Αλλά, ο διαβάτης σαν περνά στέκεται και τον προσκυνά
και μ' ευλάβεια πολλή τον άσπρο το σταυρό φιλεί.
Επάνω στο σταυρό εκεί είναι εικόνα μυστική,
με αίμα την έγραψε ο Θεός και τη λατρεύει ο λαός.

A well-known poem by A. Vlachos, which I also learned in Greek school. The school was located in the parish hall of our local church, Holy Trinity. The church and the school were the center of the religious and social life of the Greek community in Harrisburg, as was the case in other Greek communities in the United States and elsewhere in the diaspora. Embellished with icons and frescoes in the Byzantine style before which vigil lamps hung, it complemented on a grander scale the small shrine of icons and vigil lamp which we and most Greeks had at home. Before this shrine with its flickering lamp, we would recite the Lord's prayer and cross ourselves before going to bed at night after also

The abandoned church

High up on the mountain there, stands an abandoned church.
It has no altar nor a priest and its bell no longer rings.
With one small flickering oil lamp, a simple cross of stone
Is the only decoration in that poor abandoned church.
But the traveler, as he passes by, stops a while and bows his head
And with deep and great devotion kisses the white cross of stone.
And there on that lonely cross is an icon of mystery,
God in blood has drawn and etched it and the people all revere it.

performing several *metanoies* or repentances, which took the form of prostrations in the Orthodox manner.

The icons were usually those of the patron saint of the head of the household as well as one of the Virgin and Child but there could be others as well. My mother had also brought with her an icon of St. George, the patron of her native village and given to her by her great uncle, the village priest. I spent many a wintry night lying in bed and watching the light from the vigil lamp play across the mounted image of the saint, making him appear to be actually slaying the dragon coiled around the feet of his white charger.

Επήραν την Αγια-Σοφιά

Επήραν την Αγια-Σοφιά, το μέγα μοναστήρι,
με τετρακόσια σήμαντρα και εκατό καμπάνες.
Κάθε καμπάνα και παπάς, κάθε παπάς και διάκος.
Και πριν να βγουν τα Άγια και ο Βασιλεύς του κόσμου,
φωνή εξήλθ' εξ ουρανού από αγγέλου στόμα,
– Μη κλαίτε, μην οδύρεσθε, την πήρανε την Πόλη.
Πάλι με χρόνια, με καιρούς, πάλι δικά μας θα 'ναι.

This is a portion of a well-known lament describing the fall of Constantinople to the Turks on May 29, 1453 after a heroic 8-week defense by 6000 men against an army of over 100,000. The memory of the beauty and splendor of St. Sophia, when it was the principal church of the Orthodox Christian world for almost a thousand years, lived on to sustain and console the Greeks during the four dark centuries of the Ottoman Turkish occupation. The gongs, *simantra*, are portable or hanging, rectangular, pieces of wood of a certain thickness which are struck by a wooden clapper; they are still used in monasteries to call the faithful to prayer.

During the Ottoman period it was forbidden to ring church bells but these gongs were tolerated. Legend has it that the liturgy of the Eucharist was being celebrated in the cathedral when the city fell. The lament refers to that solemn moment in the middle of the service when the Holy Gifts, the as yet unconsecrated bread and wine, are carried in procession through the church. Meanwhile, the congregation kneels and the choir chants the line in the Cherubic Hymn which says, "as the King of all we receive him."

The lament for Saint Sophia

They have taken Saint Sophia, that grand church and monastery,
With four hundred wooden gongs and bells numbering a hundred.
For every bell a single priest, for every priest a deacon.
And just before the Holy Gifts came forth to be hailed as King,
A voice called out from heav'n above, from an angel's mouth it came,
– Oh, do not weep, do not lament, the City has been taken.
Again in time and after years, again they will be ours.

Folk tales and more detailed versions of the lament are found in the ground-breaking N. Politis collection of folk songs and poems (see bibliography). These latter describe how the icons in the church began to weep, including that of the Virgin Mary, and go on to say that the voice addressed Her telling Her not to weep and that the church and the City would again be "Hers." The last line, however, as my mother remembered it, has "ours" and not "Hers" and is the way the lament is usually recited and quoted.

My mother's dream was always to make a pilgrimage to the church of St. Sophia. As a child I remember hearing her tell tales about Constantinople and the Empire of Byzantium. Her favorite book which she read and reread was the novel, Κασσιανή [Kassiani, which is a woman's name]. It told the story of the iconoclastic emperor, Theophilos (829-842), and his relations with Kassiani, a cultivated and beautiful woman. Having been spurned by Theophilos, she became a nun and eventually the writer of a famous hymn sung to this day during the Holy Tuesday services. My mother realized her dream of going on what in effect was a pilgrimage to the church of St. Sophia in 2000, her 93rd year.

Η σκλάβα πόλη

Η σκλάβα πόλη κάθεται στο Βόσπορο και κλαίει,
και ο φιδωτός ο Βόσπορος τη συμπονεί και λέει,
– Πες μου, κυρά μου ζηλευτή, πεντάμορφη κυρά μου,
γιατί ποτίζεις δάκρυα τα γαλανά νερά μου;
Σαν τι είναι που μου ζήτησες, κι εγώ να μη σ' το φέρω;
Μήπως με λύπησες φτωχόν και δίχως να το ξέρω;
Στα κάτασπρα τα πόδια σου δεν πέρασεν ημέρα
που να μη σου 'φερνα σκυφτός δώρα απ' τον κόσμο πέρα.
Τα μύρα της Ανατολής και τα μεταξωτά της
και τα χαλιά τ' ατίμητα, τα μυριοπλουμιστά της.
Και της Φραγκιάς τ' ασημικά και τα χρυσά στολίδια
και τ' άλλα της τα ξακουστά, τα τόσα της παιγνίδια.
Πες μου, λοιπόν, γιατί μου κλαις, πεντάμορφη κυρά μου;
Γιατί ποτίζεις δάκρυα τα γαλανά νερά μου;
– Μόνο ένα δώρο λαχταρώ και ακόμα το προσμένω
και ακόμα δεν μου το 'φερε το κύμα τ' αφρισμένο.
Μόνο ένα δώρο λαχταρούν τα μάτια μου και κλαίνε,
ατίμητο στ' ατίμητα, ελευθεριά το λένε.
Και ο Βόσπορος σαν τ' άκουσε κοιτάζει την κυρά του
και αναστενάζει θλιβερά στα γαλανά νερά του.

This poem describes the abiding influence the city of Constantine, Constantinople, had on the imagination and ethnic sentiments of the Greeks, particularly in the early days of the 20th century when there was hope that the City might be Christian and Greek once more.

The enslaved city

The enslaved city sits alone by the Bosporos and weeps
And the winding Bosporos shares her pain and says,
– Tell me, my lady so admired, most beautiful of ladies,
Why do you pour bitter tears into my blue waters?
What is it you have asked of me and I didn't bring it to you?
Perhaps, you pitied me as poor and I knew nothing of it?
A day never passed that I didn't lay at your feet
Gifts from far off places, which I brought on bended knee.
The myrrh and incense of the East and all its fine robes of silk
And its rare and priceless carpets, the ones of many patterns.
The silverware of the Franks and their ornaments of gold
And their other famous wares, their many toys and trinkets.
Tell me, then, why you do weep, most beautiful of ladies?
Why do you pour bitter tears into my blue waters?
– I long for one gift alone and I still await it
And the frothy wave has yet to bring it to me.
My eyes long for one gift alone and weep tears to see it,
Priceless among the priceless and freedom is its name.
Hearing this, the Bosporos gazes upon his lady
And gives a mournful sigh in the midst of his blue waters.

Θούριος του Ρήγα Φεραίου

Ως πότε, παληκάρια, να ζούμε στα στενά,
μονάχοι σαν λιοντάρια στις ράχες, στα βουνά;
Σπηλιές να κατοικούμε, να βλέπωμε κλαδιά,
να φεύγουμε απ' τον κόσμο για την πικρή σκλαβιά;
Να χάνωμε αδέλφια, Πατρίδα και γονείς,
τους φίλους, τα παιδιά μας κι ολούς τους συγγενείς;
Τι σ' ωφελεί να ζήσεις και να 'σαι στη σκλαβιά;
Στοχάσου πως σε ψήνουνε κάθ' ώρα στη φωτιά.
Σουλιώτοι και Μανιάτοι, λιοντάρια ξακουστά,
ως πότε στες σπηλιές σας κοιμάστε σφαλιστά;
Για 'λάτε μ' ένα ζήλο σε τούτο τον καιρό
να κάνομε τον όρκο επάνω στο Σταυρό.
Κι αν παραβώ τον όρκο να 'στράψει ο ουρανός
και να με κατακαύσει, να γίνω σαν καπνός,
Σ' ανατολή και δύση και νότο και βορρά
να λάμψει αστροπελέκι για την ελευθεριά.

Καλύτερα μια ώρα ελεύθερη ζωή
παρά σαράντα χρόνια σκλαβιά και φυλακή!

This is a small portion of a long and passionate poem, calling for revolt and freedom, written by Rhigas Pheraios or Velestinlis, who was born in 1757 in the village of Velestino in Thessaly. A prolific writer and journalist, he was an ardent advocate of independence not only for the Greeks but for all the subject peoples in the Ottoman Empire. His battle

The battle song of Rhigas Pheraios

How long, O brave young men, must we live in narrow passes,
Like lions, alone on ridges and high upon the mountains?
To make a dwelling place of caves with wilderness before us,
Because of bitter slavery compelled to forsake the world?
To leave our brothers and our sisters, our parents and our homeland,
To leave behind our kin and children, our friends and our companions?
What good is it to be alive when you live in slavery?
Just think how they torment you, in fire you pass each hour.
O men of Souli, O men of Mani, O lions of renown,
'Til when will you stay sleeping, confined and closed up in caves?
Come, now, with single-minded zeal at this time and season
And let us all take an oath upon the holy cross.
And if this oath I transgress, may heaven fill with lightning
To strike me and consume me so I become like smoke,
In the east and in the west and in the north and south
To glow like a thunderbolt for the sake of freedom.

O better one hour of a life that is free
Than forty years of prison and of slavery!

song, inspired by the Marseillaise, was translated into Serbian, Bulgarian and Romanian
and the last two lines became the rallying cry of all those in revolt against the Turks.
Every Greek knew and still knows them. Rhigas was handed over to the Turks by the Aus-
trians, who executed him, in 1798 in Belgrade.

Ο γερο-Δήμος και η πόλη

Παιδιά, γι' ακούστε με και με, τον γέρο καπετάνο,
που τα μαλλιά μ' ασπρίσανε στον πόλεμο επάνω.
Α, παραγέρασα, παιδιά, το άπιαστο λιοντάρι
δεν είναι εκείνο που 'ξευρα, με θέλημα και χάρη.
Στον πόλεμο γεννήθηκα, μαθήτεψα παιδάκι
στου Γεροζήδρα το σχολειό και στου Καραϊσκάκη.
Από τα χρόνια του Αλή τους Τούρκους πολεμούσα.
Είδαν πολλά τα μάτια μου εκεί που περπατούσα.
Παιδιά ωσάν τα έλατα στον πόλεμο θρεμμένα,
με μάτι μαύρο σαν ελιά, με στήθια δασωμένα,
μ' ένα σταυρό στο χέρι τους και μια καλή μαχαίρα
επελεκούσαν την Τουρκιά, τους λύκους, νύχτα μέρα.
Ημείς απάνω στα ψηλά κι αυτοί στα κάτω μέρη,
τη χώρα μας μοιράζαμε μ' αυτούς με το μαχαίρι.
Αχ, δεν πρόφθασε να ιδεί και το δικό σας μάτι
τον Τούρκο όταν άφριζε και χόρευε το άτι.
Χίλιοι μετρούσαν μοναχά και Φράγκοι ξεψυχούσαν,
και μόνο τα κλεφτόπουλα τον δρόμο τους κρατούσαν.
Παίδια, εχάθηκε η Τουρκιά, δεν είναι γενιτσάροι.
Εκείνους τους σκοτόσαμε, τους πήρε το φεγγάρι.
Ποιοι είναι αυτοί που σήκωσαν επάνω το κεφάλι;
Ποιοι είν' αυτοί που κάνουνε τώρα το παλικάρι;
Ποιοι Σέρβοι, ποιοι Βούλγαροι και ποιοι οι Ζεργοβίνοι;
Χωρίς τη φουστανέλα μας μπορεί φωτιά να γίνει;
Για σηκωθείτε μιά αυγή με τα σωστά σας όλοι
και το σταυρό σας κάνετε να πάρουμε την Πόλη.
Την Πόλη, την Αγια-Σοφιά, δικά μας θα 'ναι πάλι.
Εμείς θα την επάρουμε, εμείς και όχι άλλοι.
Εκεί θα προσκυνήσουμε, γιατί, γιατί παιδιά μου,
με τ' όνομά της μοναχά ευφραίνεται η καρδιά μου.
Κι ένα κερί ανάψετε ακόμα και για μένα,
μες στην Αγία Τράπεζα, παιδιά ευτυχισμένα.
Κι ας κράξει ένας από σας, όταν θα μπείτε όλοι,
Ο γερο-Δήμος μοναχά δεν μπήκε μες την Πόλη.

Old man Dimos and the city

Boys, hear me, too, a little while, this captain old and tired
With hair which now has all turned white, fighting in many battles.
Oh, I have grown old, my boys; this lion, who couldn't be captured
Is not the one I used to know, blest with a will and talent.
In battle was I born and bred and, as a boy, learned the trade
At the school of old man Zidras and of Karaiskakis.
From the years of Ali Pasha I waged war upon the Turks.
Many sights have my eyes beheld, there where I walked and wandered.
The boys were tall like fir trees then, nurtured in war and battle
With eyes dark and black as olives and with chests thick and matted.
Holding a cross in one hand and in the other a good sword,
They hacked away at Turks, those wolves, first by day and then by night.
We were up upon the highlands and they on the plains below.
With the blade we were dividing our dearest homeland with them.
Oh, your eyes never had the chance to look upon and to see
The Turk when his horse was frothing and was leaping all about.
Only a thousand of us counted, while Franks gave up the ghost.
Only the brave, young klephts held fast to the road they had taken.
Boys, Turkey has been swept away; the janissaries are no more.
We have slain the whole lot of them; the moon knows well their passing.
Who are they who've now raised their heads and fill themselves with boldness?
Who are they who now dare to think that they can play the hero?
Who among the Serbs, the Bulgars; who among the Montenegrins?
Can fire of battle start to blaze without our foustanella?
So, all of you wake up at dawn with your wits quick about you
And cross yourselves, each one of you, and pray we take the City.
The City and Saint Sophia will once again be ours.
We alone shall take and have Her, we alone and no one else.
We again will bow our heads there and kneel in holy worship
Because Her very name fills my heart with joy and bliss.
And one candle please light for me, please light one for me as well
And place it on the high altar there, you lucky boys of mine.
And when you all get in at last, let one of you stand and shout
That only old man Dimos did not get into the City.

Τα δυο ντουφέκια

Εκεί που η μάχη έγινε σε δυο βουνά 'πό κάτω
περνά διαβάτης, σέρνοντα βαριά τα βήματά του.
Και βλέπει εκεί παράπερα ριγμένο ένα ντουφέκι,
'ματοβαμμένο κι έρημο, και βλέπει εκεί παρέκει
άλλο ντουφέκι σε πυκνά χαμόκλαδα κρυμμένο.
Μέσα σε όνειρα πικρά κοιμάται αποσταμένο.
Σκύβει ο διαβάτης και ρωτά το πρώτο το ντουφέκι,
– Πες μου, ντουφέκι που φορείς το βάτο για στεφάνι,
το παλικάρι που σφιχτά στα χέρια του σ' εκράτη.
Και το ντουφέκι τ' απαντά, – Διαβάτη, σκύψε ακόμα,
προσκύνα με γονατιστός και φίλησε το χώμα.
Το παλικάρι που σφιχτά στα χέρια του μ' ευράτη.
Και μες στα νέφη του καπνού στου Χάρου τα τραπέζια,
ένα βόλι τούρκικο τον έβρηκε μες στα στήθη,
και τον εξάπλωσε βαριά, χωρίς μιλιά να βγάλει.
Θαρρώ και βλέπω την πληγή, θαρρώ και βλέπω αίμα.
Εκείνον τον εθάψανε σαν τίμιο παλικάρι,
και μένα μ' απαράτησαν σαν άταφο κουφάρι.
Σκύβει ο διαβάτης και ρωτά το δεύτερο ντουφέκι.
Και το ντουφέκι τ' απαντά, – Μη με ρωτάς, διαβάτη,
κάλλιο να μην είχα γεννηθεί, παρά που μ' είχε φέρει
άδικη μοίρα κι άπονη σ' ενός δειλού το χέρι.
Μόλις η μάχη άρχισε, και γύρω βροντολόγα,
κι έπεσε η πρώτη κανονιά κι έπεσε η πρώτη φλόγα,
εκείνος στρέφεται με μιας, με ρίχνει στα χορτάρια,
και φεύγει, φεύγει αγύριστα και τρέχει, τρέχει ακόμα.
Κατάρα να 'ναι ο δρόμος του και το στερνό το χώμα.

[Note for Old man Dimos and the city, page 280-81.]
This poem dates to the period in modern Greek history, late nineteenth and early twentieth centuries, when the Greek people still hoped for the reconquest and liberation of Constantinople, or "The City" as it was known, from the Turks, who had seized it in 1453. This hope was finally shattered by the defeat of the Greek armies in Asia Minor in 1922. Dimos is a form of Dimitrios, Old Man Dimos, Zidras and Karaiskakis were famous klephts, who fought against the Turks during the war for independence (1821-28). The Serbs, Bulgarians and Montenegrins were allies of the Greeks during the first Balkan War in 1912.

The two muskets

There where the battle took place, over there and beneath two mountains
A traveler passes, dragging his feet with steps slow and heavy.
And there farther off he sees a musket, thrown down and cast aside,
Abandoned and covered with blood; yet still farther off he sees
Another musket, hidden deep in thick, low-lying branches.
Alone and at a distance it sleeps a sleep of bitter dreams.
The traveler then bends down and asks of the first musket,
– Tell me, musket, you who wear that thorny bush for a crown,
About that brave man who held you tightly and clasped you in his hands.
And the musket answered saying, – Bend still lower, traveler,
Honor me on your knees and kiss the earth before you.
A brave man once held me tightly and clasped me in his hands.
Amid clouds and haze from smoke, where Death lays out his tables,
He was struck by a Turkish bullet, which found its way to his heart,
And cut him down and laid him low; yet not a word he uttered.
I can still see the wound it made, I can still see the blood.
They took him and they buried him like a worthy hero,
They left me and abandoned me like a corpse without a grave.
The traveler then bent and asked the same of the second musket.
And the musket answered him and said, – Do not ask me, O traveler,
Far better, had I not been made, to be taken and given over
By unjust and cruel fate into a coward's hand.
For, just as the battle started and all about was thunder,
When the first cannonade began and the first round of fire,
That man at once turned his back and threw me among the weeds,
And flees, flees without looking back and runs and is running still.
Curses be on the road he takes and on his final resting place.

The foustanella was the white kilt worn by the klephts, the mountain villagers of mainland Greece and in military khaki color by the Evzones who fought as light infantry, bravely and successfully, as late as in WWII.

[Note for the poem above.]
A patriotic poem, typical of the war-filled years which modern Greece experienced for most of its first century of freedom.

Στης Ηπείρου τα βουνά

Στης Ηπείρου τα βουνά, τα βαριοχιονισμένα,
που πολεμάν οι Έλληνες, παιδιά ανδρειωμένα.
Πιάνουν χιλιάδες Ιταλούς, τυράννους και βαρβάρους,
που παν να πολεμήσουνε χωρίς να έχουν θάρρος.

This poem was written my mother in the winter of 1940 after the Italians had invaded Greece on October 28th of that year. A longer version was later published by the Greek-language newspaper in New York, *Atlantis*, but this portion was all she could remember in her hundredth year. This was a time of pride and exultation for Greeks everywhere as "the fighting Evzones from hell," the wartime description of the khaki-kilted Greek soldiers, inflicted the first major defeat on the forces of the Axis and gave hope to the beleagured British.

Ελλάδα μου γλυκιά

Για σένα Ελλάδα μου γλυκιά, που τόσο σ' αγαπώ,
τα χείλη μου θα ψάλλουν τραγούδι με καημό.
Και η γη του παραδείσου, που είναι ερημιά,
τη χάρη τη δική σου δεν την έχ' ούτ' αυτή καμιά.

On the mountains of Epirus

Up on the mountains of Epirus, all covered heavily with snow,
There the Greeks are fighting, young boys, brave and manly.
They're capturing thousands of Italians, oppressors and barbarians,
Who've gone off to war and battle, lacking bravery and boldness.

Although soon overrun by the merciless Nazi war machine, Greece's rout of the Italians
and its heroic stand against the Germans with the support of British and Australian/New
Zealand contingents delayed Hitler's invasion of the Soviet Union in June, 1941 by several weeks. This meant that the onset of the Russian winter took place before the German
war objectives could be achieved and, thereby, gave the demoralized Russians time to re-
group, dig in and begin the slow, bloody, eventual expulsion of the invader.

Sweet Greece of mine

To you, sweet Greece of mine, to you whom I love so much,
My lips will sing a song of yearning.
Even the land of Paradise, which is empty and forlorn,
Even it does not possess your charm and your beauty.

Ύμνος εις την ελευθερίαν

Σε γνωρίζω από την κόψη
του σπαθιού την τρομερή.
Σε γνωρίζω από την όψη,
που με βία μετράει την γη.

Απ' τα κόκκαλα βγαλμένη
των Ελλήνων τα ιερά,
και σαν πρώτα ανδρειωμένη
χαίρε, ω χαίρε, Ελευθεριά!

Εκεί μέσα εκατοικούσες,
πικραμένη, εντροπαλή.
Κι ένα στόμα ακαρτερούσες,
έλα πάλι, να σου πει.

Άργειε να 'λθει εκείνη ημέρα,
και ήταν όλα σιωπηλά,
γιατί τα 'σκιαζε η φοβέρα
και τα πλάκωνε η σκλαβιά.

Δυστυχής παρηγορία
μόνη σου έμενε, να λες
περασμένα μεγαλεία
και διηγώντας τα να κλαις.

These are the opening quatrains of a long poem completed in 1824 by Dionysios Solomos, the national poet of Greece. He was a native of the island of Zakynthos (also known as Zante and at that time controlled by the British). He wrote the poem during the first three years of the Greek uprising against the Turks when the Greek cause was enjoying initial success.

The poem consists of 158 quatrains and is as much dedicated to Greece as it is to liberty.

Hymn to liberty

Oh, I know thee by the keen edge
Of the sword, so fraught with fear.
Oh, I know thee by the swift look
That scans the land both far and near.

From the sacred bones arisen
Of the Greeks who died for thee,
And as of yore, brave and valiant,
Hail, oh, hail, O liberty.

'Mid the bones there, thou wert dwelling,
Embittered and shame-faced too.
Waiting for a voice to tell thee,
Come again the hour is due.

Yet, the day was late in coming
And all was hushed in silence,
Because terror cast a shadow
And slavery crushed with violence.

Oh, how unfortunate thou wert!
Thine only consolation
Was to tell of thy past glories
And weep in isolation.

Describing the plight of enslaved Greece, it goes on to recount the victories of the Greeks over the Turks as well as the horrors of the struggle, while calling for support against the Muslim oppressors from fellow European Christians and from "the land of Washington." The first two quatrains were adopted as the national anthem of Greece. As all Greeks do, my mother knew the first two quatrains and taught them to her children. She remembered most of the third and fourth quatrains and all of the fifth.

Τα Τελευταία της Μητέρας
Mother's Last Poems

Vasiliki Scotes in her 99th year, photographed at home in Pennsylvania.

Είμαι ξένος στην ξενιτιά

Είμαι ξένος στην ξενιτιά κι έχω πόνο στην καρδιά.
Δεν έχω μητέρα κι αδερφό τα ντέρτια μου να πω.
Έχω τα δέντρα συντροφιά και τα πουλιά κουβέντα.

A song of absence, *xenitiko*, composed by my mother.

Δε μπορώ να περπατήσω

Δε μπορώ να περπατήσω, τα βουνά να τριγυρίσω,
τα βουνά και τις ραχούλες κι όλες τις κρύες βρυσούλες.
Τα γερατειά τριγυρίσαν και τα νιάτα ξαφανίσαν.
Άλλο τίποτα δεν μένει, η καρδιά η πονεμένη,
μόνο μέρες να μετράει και φίλους ν' αποχαιρετάει.

My mother wrote this poem in September, 2005, her ninety-seventh year.

Θα βγω ψηλά

Θα βγω ψηλά κατάραχα στης Κωστηλάτας τις ραχούλες
που μέρα νύχτα εκεί γλεντάν όμορφες Θοδωριανιτοπούλες.
Με τις κεντητές ποδιές τους και τ' άσπρα τα μαντήλια,
με τ' ασημοζώναρα και τα χρυσά στολίδια.
Να δω την Περδικόβρυση, να πιω το κρυονέρι.

My mother composed this poem in her 98th year as she reminisced about the village.

A stranger on foreign shores

I'm a stranger on foreign shores and have in my heart much pain.
I've no mother, nor a brother to tell them of my sorrows.
Only the trees for company, the birds for conversation.

I can no longer rise to walk

I can no longer rise to walk, walk and wander about the mountains,
About the mountains and high ridges, by all the springs of ice cold water.
Now, old age wanders about me, vanished is the time of youth.
And nothing else remains to do for a heart of pain and sorrow,
But only to be counting days and say a last farewell to friends.

I'll go up high on the crests

I'll go up high on the crests, on the dear peaks of Kostilata
Where day and night pretty girls of Theodoriana feast and dance.
Wearing their embroidered aprons and their kerchiefs of white,
With their belts all of silver and their ornaments of gold.
There again to see the Partridge spring and drink from it cold water.

Ψηλά στα διάσελα

Βγήκα ψηλά στα διάσελα
[Θανάση, Θανάση, μωρέ Βλαχοθανάση.]
και γναύτεψα τριγύρω.
[Θανάση, Θανάση.]
Τριγύρω, γύρω θάλασσα.
[Θανάση, Θανάση, μωρέ Βλαχοθανάση.]
Στη μεσή πλέει καράβι.
[Θανάση, Θανάση.]
Καθόμουν και το κοίταζα
[Θανάση, Θανάση, μωρέ Βλαχοθανάση.]
σε τι λιμάνι παει.
[Θανάση, Θανάση.]
Λιμάνι εκέι δεν ήτανε,
[Θανάση, Θανάση, μωρέ Βλαχοθανάση.]
ούτε ακρογιάλι.
[Θανάση, Θανάση.]
Χωρίς κατάρτια και πανιά,
[Θανάση, Θανάση, μωρέ Βλαχοθανάση.]
και διχώς καπετάνιο
[Θανάση, Θανάση.]
Το κύμα ήταν ναύκληρος
[Θανάση, Θανάση, μωρέ Βλαχοθανάση.]
Το παει όπου θέλει.
[Θανάση, Θανάση.]

My mother remembered this song being sung by her mother as she worked in the fields while she, then around age five, took care of her baby brother who was named Thanasis, as in the song. My mother could only remember the first four lines of the song, so in her ninety-ninth year (August 2007) and in the manner of the traditional oral poets of her youth she proceeded to compose her own closing version consisting of the last eight lines. She based her version on the recollection that her mother's song was about a ship that had been captured by pirates.

The Vlachothanasis addressed in the interjections to the song could refer to the father of the ship's captain who has gone up to the lookout point scanning the seas for the ship's return.

Thanasis is a shortened form of Athanasios, a name very popular in Epirus. The mean-

The lookout point

I climbed high to the lookout point
[Thanasis, O Vlachothanasis.]
And gazed all around me.
[Thanasis, Thanasis.]
All around was open sea.
[Thanasis, O Vlachothanasis.]
In the midst floated a ship.
[Thanasis, Thanasis.]
I sat and watched it to make out
[Thanasis, O Vlachothanasis.]
Which harbor it was seeking.
[Thanasis, Thanasis.]
Yet, no harbor could be found there,
[Thanasis, O Vlachothanasis.]
Nor even the seashore's edge.
[Thanasis, Thanasis.]
Without its masts, without its sails,
[Thanasis, O Vlachothanasis.]
And without its captain, too,
[Thanasis, Thanasis.]
The swelling wave was the boatswain now,
[Thanasis, O Vlachothanasis.]
Taking the ship where it willed.
[Thanasis, Thanasis.]

ing of the name is 'immortal'. This also happens to be my baptismal name as it was that of my grandfather, his grandfather before him and of numerous uncles and cousins on both sides of the family. In America the name was rendered by the early Greek immigrants as Tom or Arthur, neither of which is a correct equivalent. The *vlacho-* prefix to the name can mean 'shepherd', that is, Shepherd Thanasis. *Vlacho-* can also refer to a transhumant people called Vlachs found in Greece and elsewhere in the Balkans whose language is descended from Latin and is similar to Romanian. In fact, a region of present-day Romania was known as Wallachia, or land of the Vlachs, during the Ottoman period. *Vlachos* can also mean 'hick' or 'country bumpkin'. That is not the meaning intended in this song.

Όταν ήμουνα μικρή

Όταν ήμουνα μικρή είχα φαντασίες
πως ήμουνα πριγκίπισσα μέσα σε δυο παλάτια,
Φορούσα στο κεφάλι μου και μια χρυσή κορώνα.
Τότε κοιτάζω και τα πόδια μου, αλλά ήταν χωρίς παπούτσια.
Και γύρω μου εκοίταξα αν άλλος με κοιτάζει.
Κανείς δεν ήταν πλάι μου, μονάχα η σκιά μου.
Μελαγχολία μ' έπιασε, τα μάτια μου δακρύσαν,
και ένα απ' τα παλάτια μου με ρώτησε, τι κλαίω.
Κι εγώ του απάντησα: – Μόνον η καρδιά μου ξέρει.
Και σε αποχαιρετώ και στην ξενιτιά πηγαίνω,
και ό,τι με εδίδαξες μαζί μου θα τα πάρω.
Περάσανε τα χρόνια ωραία και καλά, καλά κι ευτυχισμένα.
Κι έμεινα στη μέση από τα δυο, δεν ξέρω ποιο να 'κλέξω.
Το ένα που με γέννησε, τ' όνομά του είν' Ελλάδα.
Και το δεύτερο Αμερική, πολύ μακριά στα ξένα.
Η Ελλάδα μου 'πε – ώρα καλή και να μην με ξεχάσεις.
Η Αμερική με καλωσόρισε με ανοιχτές τις πόρτες.
Σ' ευχαριστώ πατρίδα πρώτη και 'συ δεύτερη πατρίδα,
που μ' αγκάλιασες σφιχτά, σαν δική σου θυγατέρα.
Σας ευχαριστώ εξίσου και τους δυό, σαν αληθινές μαννάδες.
Ο Θεός να σας ευλογεί και πάντα να σας φυλάει,
Ελλάδα και Αμερική.

My mother composed this poem in March, 2006, her 98th year, while lying sick in the hospital.

When I was a little girl

When I was a little girl, I had many dreams and fancies
That I was a princess in the midst of two palaces,
And I was wearing on my head a crown made of gold.
Then, I looked down at my feet but they both were without shoes.
And I looked all around me to see if someone else was watching.
At my side no one was standing, only my shadow by me.
Sadness then overcame me; my eyes filled up with tears,
And one of my palaces asked me to learn why I was crying.
And I answered it and said, – My heart alone knows the reason.
And I bid farewell to you; I am leaving for foreign lands,
And I shall take away with me whatever you have taught me.
The years went by and passed, they were beautiful and good, good and happy.
And I remained caught between the two, not knowing which one to choose.
The first one gave me birth and Greece is its name.
The second is America far off on distant shores.
Greece wished me all the best and said, – Don't go away and forget me.
America welcomed me with all its doors wide-open.
I thank you, my first homeland, and you, my second homeland,
You, who embraced me, oh, so tightly as if I were your daughter.
Equally I thank the two of you, you have been true mothers to me.
May God bless the both of you and watch over you forever,
Greece and America!

Bibliography

All of the songs and poems in this collection (with the exception of the additional verses to the Christmas and New Year's Carols and the National Anthem) were dictated to me by my mother from memory. I have not attempted to "correct" or modify them in any way in light of other versions or renditions, which during my research I located in previously published collections. The latter I consulted only for the purposes of dating, of comparison and of regional distribution, whenever that was possible.

My mother provided all of the information relating to the customs and traditions of the village as well a some of the historical material. For the latter I have also relied on several books in Greek on the history of Epirus, as given below. Above all, however, I have read and consulted, *Theodoriana*, by my distant cousin and dear friend, Rigas-George S. Skoutelas. This definitive and scholarly work is also in Greek and I strongly recommend it for its thorough account of the history and customs of that beautiful village. In addition, there are several books in English, which I read for background purposes and which I list here for those who might wish to pursue the matter further.

Beaton, Roderick. *Folk Poetry of Modern Greece*. Cambridge: Cambridge University Press, 1980.

Blum, Richard and Eva. *The Dangerous Hour The Lore and Culture of Crisis and Mystery In Rural Greece*. New York: Charles Scribner's Sons, 1970.

Crane, David. *Lord Byron's Jackal A life of Edward John Trelawny*. London: Harper Collins Publishers, 1998.

Campbell, J. K. *Honour, Family and Patronage A Study of Institutional and Moral Values in a Greek Mountain Community*. Oxford: Oxford University Press, 1968.

Fauriel, Claude. *Ελληνικά Δημοτικά Τραγούδια*. Επιμέλεια Α. Πολίτης. 2η έκδοση. Τόμος Α-Β. Ηράκλειο: Πανεπιστημιακές Εκδόσεις, 2000.

Fermor, Patrick L. *Roumeli: Travels in Northern Greece*. London: Penguin, 1983

Fleming, K. E. *The Muslim Bonaparte: Diplomacy and Orientalism in Ali Pasha's Greece*. Princeton: Princeton University Press, 1999.

Foss, Arthur. *Epirus*. London and Boston: Faber and Faber, 1978.

Kostandaras, Dean J. *Infamy and Revolt The Rise of the National Problem In Early Modern Greek Thought*. East European Monographs. New York: Columbia University Press, 2006.

Plomer, William. *The Diamond of Jannina: Ali Pasha 1741-1822*. New York: Taplinger, 1970.

Sakellariou, M. B., General Editor. *Epirus: 4000 Years of Greek History*. Athens: Ekdotike Athenon, 1997.

Saunier, G. *Ξενητιάς: Το Δημοτικό Τραγούδι*. Αθήνα: Ερμής, 1990.

Sefton, Thomas *The Gods Remain: Old European Religion as Found in Greece, in Germanic Countries and Elsewhere*. Brooklyn: Kolonos Press, 2001.

Spencer, Terence. *Fair Greece Sad Relic*. Bath: Cedric Chivers Portway, 1974.

St. Clair, William. *That Greece Might Still Be Free: The Philhellenes in The War of Independence*. London: Oxford University Press, 1972.

Sugar, Peter F. *Southeastern Europe under Ottoman Rule (1354-1804): A History of East Central Europe*. Vol. V. Seattle: University of Washington Press, 1977.

Trypanis, C. A. *Greek Poetry from Homer to Seferis*. London and Boston: Faber and Faber, 1981.

Watts, Niki. *The Greek Folk Songs*. Studies in Modern Greek. New Rochelle, New York: Aristide D. Caratzas, Publisher, 1988.

Αραβαντινός, Π. *Δημοτικά Τραγούδια της Ηπείρου: Συλλογή Δημώδων Ασμάτων*. Athens: Π. Πέρρη 1880 (reprinted: Εκδόσεις Δαμιανός-Δωδώνη, 1996).

—. *Ιστορία Αλή Πασά του Τεπελένη*. Athens: Εκδόσεις Δωδώνη, 2004.

Βρανούσης, Λ. Ι. *Ρήγας*. Αθήνα: Αετός, 1970.

Δημητρακόπουλος, Σ. *Ιστορία και Δημοτικό Τραγούδι*. 3η Έκδοση. Αθήνα: Βιβλιοπωλεία Παρουσία, 1998.

Δροσίνης, Γ. *Δημοτικά Τραγούδια της Αγάπης*. Αθήνα: Σιδέρη, 1908.

Ιωάννου, Γεώργος. *Παραλογές*. Αθήνα: Ερμής, 1983.

—. *Τα Δημοτικά μας Τραγούδια*. Αθήναι: Έκδοση Ταχυδρόμου, 1966.

Μπαμπινιώτης, Γ. *Λεξικό της Νέας Ελληνικής Γλώσσας*. Αθήνα: ΕΠΕ, 1998.

Παππάς, Ν. *Ελληνικά Δημοτικά Τραγούδια*. Αθήνα: Παππαδημητρίου, 1953.

Παππακώστας, Ν. Χ. *Ηπειρώτικα-Αθαμάνικα*. Αθήνα, 1967.

Παχτικός, Γ. Δ. *260 Δημώδη Ελληνικά Άσματα*. Αθήνα: Π. Δ.Σακκελαρίου, 1905 (reprinted, Αθήνα: Δ. Ν. Καραβία, 1982).

Περραιβός, Χ. *Ιστορία του Σουλλίου και Πάργας*. Αθήνα: Φ. Καραμπίνης–Κ. Βέφας, 1857 (reprinted, Αθήνα: Δ. Ν. Καραβία, 1980).

Πολίτης, Αλέξης. *Το Δημοτικό Τραγούδι: Κλέφτικα*. Αθήνα: Εστία, 2001.

Πολίτης, Ν. *Εκλογαί απο τα Τραγούδια*. Αθήναι: Βιβλιοπωλείον Του Ελληνικού Λαού Βαγιόνακη-Γρηγοροπούλου, 1958.

—. *Κλέφτικα Τραγούδια*. Αθήναι: Εκδόσεις Ιστορική Έρευνα [ND].

Σκουτέλας, Ρήγας-Γιώργος Σ. *Θεοδώριανα - Άρτας*. Αθήνα: Έκδοση Κοινότητας Θεοδωριάνων, 2006.

Σπυριδάκης, Γ. Κ., Γ. Α. Μέγας, και Δ. Α. Πετρόπουλος, *Ελληνικά Δημοτικά Τραγούδια (Εκλογή)*. Τομ. Α. Αθήνα: Ακαδημία Αθηνών, 1962.

—. και Σ. Δ. Περιστέρης, *Ελληνικά Δημοτικά Τραγούδια*. Τομ. Γ. Αθήνα: Ακαδημία Αθηνών, 1968.

Τομαδάκης, Ν. Β. *Διονύσιος Σολωμός*. Αθήνα: Αετός, 1954.

Χαλατσάς, Δημ. *Ληστρικά Τραγούδια*. 2η έκδοση. Αθήνα: Εστία, 2003.

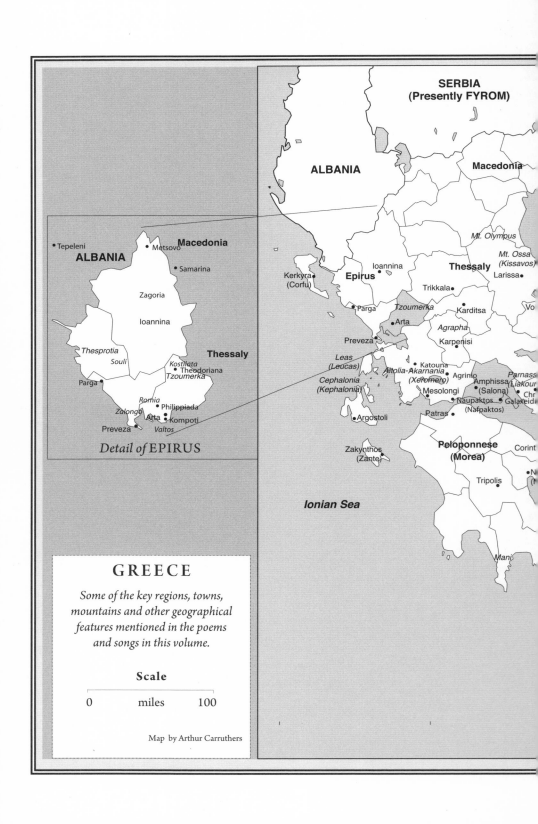

SERBIA
(Presently FYROM)

ALBANIA

Macedonia

Mt. Olympus

Mt. Ossa
(Kissavos)

Ioannina

Epirus

Thessaly

Larissa

Kerkyra
(Corfu)

Trikkala

Parga

Tzoumerka

Karditsa

Vo

Arta

Agrapha

Preveza

Karpenisi

Leas
(Leucas)

Katouna

Aitolia-Akarnania
(Xeromero)

Agrinio

Parnass

Cephalonia
(Kephalonia)

Amphissa
(Salona)

Liakour

Mesolongi

Naupaktos
(Nafpaktos)

Chr

Galaxeidi

Argostoli

Patras

Peloponnese
(Morea)

Corint

Zakynthos
(Zante)

Tripolis

N
(

Ionian Sea

Mani

Detail of EPIRUS

Tepeleni

Macedonia

Metsovo

ALBANIA

Samarina

Zagoria

Ioannina

Thesprotia

Souli

Thessaly

Kostilata

Theodoriana

Tzoumerka

Parga

Romia

Philippiada

Zalongo

Arta

Kompoti

Preveza

Valtos

GREECE

*Some of the key regions, towns,
mountains and other geographical
features mentioned in the poems
and songs in this volume.*

Scale

0   miles   100

Map by Arthur Carruthers